The Practice of Theory

College Section Committee

The Practice of Theory

Teacher Research in Composition

Ruth E. Ray
Wayne State University

National Council of Teachers of English
1111 W. Kenyon Road, Urbana, Illinois 61801-1096

Library of Congress Cataloging-in-Publication Data

Ray, Ruth E., 1954–
  The practice of theory : teacher research in composition / Ruth E. Ray.
    p. cm.
  Includes bibliographical references and index.
  ISBN 0-8141-3660-5
  1. English language—Composition and exercises—Study and teaching—Research—United States. 2. English language—Rhetoric—Study and teaching—Research—United States. 3. Action research in education—United States. I. Title
  LB 1576.R39 1993
  808'.042'07—dc20   92-41456
                                            CIP

Contents

Acknowledgments

I would like to express my gratitude to the following people for their assistance in the completion of this manuscript:

Ellen Barton, academic confidante and friend, who read every chapter carefully and "talked up" the book with students and colleagues whenever she got the chance. Everyone should have such an advocate.

Anonymous Reviewer #2 from NCTE who gave the early draft a good, stiff critique and forced me to consider more carefully how the feminist perspective described in Chapter 2 might inform a revision of graduate education in composition.

The National Writing Project teachers of metro Detroit who opened up their world to me through interviews and meetings during the summer of 1990.

The students in my 1991 English 702 seminar who had enough faith to conduct interpretive research in their own classrooms and then let me write about it.

Tina Pawlak and Diane Kasunic, my Mastermind partners, who resolutely spoke of this book as a "done deal" every time I expressed any doubts about finishing it.

Michael Spooner, senior editor for publications, whose positivity, coupled with his intelligence and accessibility, made working with NCTE a pleasure.

Introduction:
The Search for a Perspective

This book began as a personal search, motivated by my own need to know how I as a composition specialist fit into a university English department in which the teaching of literature and the practice of literary criticism are the primary activities. An ongoing issue for me has been to understand and articulate my relationship to my literary colleagues: What interests and concerns do we share? How might the connections I see between their inquiries and mine enhance my own teaching and research in composition? In the process of researching and writing this book, I came to realize that my personal issue was more largely representative of the issues facing composition faculty everywhere. Thus, by way of introducing this book and its motives, I offer in these first few pages an autobiographical statement. I hope that readers will see in my background elements of their own professional lives which will help them understand the theoretical connections I have made, the conclusions I have drawn, and my reasons for looking to feminist studies and teacher research for a broader perspective on composition.

A teacher at heart, from my first day as assistant professor I felt at odds with many of my colleagues who were literary critics and theoreticians. My educational and professional experiences were not the credentials of a literary theorist: I had an undergraduate degree in journalism and experience as a newspaper reporter and feature writer; I had worked in public relations; spent two years as a technical writer; worked as a tutor and part-time teacher of remedial writing; earned a master's degree in linguistics and composition; spent seven years as a nontenure-track lecturer while directing a tutoring lab, served as assistant director of composition, coordinated placement and proficiency testing, and taught all forms of undergraduate writing; and earned a doctor of arts degree with an emphasis in composition theory and applied linguistics.

By the time my dissertation was completed, I had already spent nearly ten years as an adjunct faculty member and lecturer in composition. Still, I was not fully prepared for life on the tenure track, where my previous experience did not really "count" for much in terms of a scholarly record. What mattered now was what I thought and wrote. However, my research, which I saw as a natural outgrowth of teaching and tutoring, was anomalous to many of my colleagues: they asked me to justify my tacit belief that composition was "intellectually respectable"; challenged me to support the "empirical bias" of my work; critiqued it for being "too pedagogical," "atheoretical," and even "anti-theoretical"; and accused me of meandering across disciplines. I remember distinctly the question a full professor asked me after I had presented a chapter of my dissertation to the assembled English faculty in 1987: "So what exactly do you call your kind of research?" he asked, genuinely puzzled. "What *field* are you in?" And I remember fumbling for a response, suddenly ambivalent and defensive about my work. This defensiveness, I think, represents the current stance of composition studies as a field.

My first and second years on the tenure track were periods of great frustration and self-analysis. I began to internalize the negative critique that seemed always just under the surface of conversations with literary colleagues. I seriously questioned what I was doing and where I fit (indeed, *whether* I fit) into the intellectual scheme of things. Even though my teaching evaluations were outstanding and I had experienced feelings of great accomplishment in my writing and research, I began to wonder if I should look for another kind of career—one as far away from the university as possible. At one particularly low point, I picked up a library book called *Working It Out* (Ruddick and Daniels 1977), in which women from various disciplines talk about their work in academe, the problems they have had as women scholars, and the importance of relating one's work to one's life. One of the essays, told from the perspective of a woman in another discipline (philosophy) whose work did not "fit" with the expectations of her department, seemed to be telling my story. In "A Work of One's Own," Sara Ruddick talks about coming to terms with the divisions that had burdened her life and caused her to lose confidence in herself—"divisions between work and pleasure, male and female, professional and amateur, political and personal, all aspects of the damaging separation of work from love" (144). I began to think that my own frustrations might be a result of the separations that had been forged between the things I cared most about: literature and composition, theory and practice, teaching and research.

Starting with Ruddick, I followed a circuitous route through the research on women in academe (Aisenberg and Harrington, Simeone, Komarovsky, Bateson) and American feminist criticism, beginning with Virginia Woolf. From this new perspective, I saw my personal dilemma in larger terms, realizing that I was experiencing the typical dilemmas facing thinkers in all new areas of inquiry, especially those which are multidisciplinary. Feminist criticism is particularly relevant to a better understanding of composition studies because the majority of practitioners in the field are women, and a majority of these women hold marginalized, nontenured positions in universities. Yet the gendered politics and "feminization" of composition as a field have only recently been acknowledged (Miller, Flynn), let alone openly discussed or fully explored.

In feminist criticism I have found an empowering response to the divisive and destructive split between theory and practice. Rather than accept the traditional dichotomy between theory and practice, why not revise and redefine theory? Why not put practice at the center of a new kind of theorizing? Why not openly admit the politics of our theorizing? These responses, of course, are not unique to feminist criticism. Revisionist concepts of the theory-practice relationship are at the center of many other discourses—Marxist theory and hermeneutics to name only two—but I took my tutelage from feminist studies. I therefore offer this learning to my readers, filtered as it is through my own experiences as a college composition teacher and a researcher of writing trying to come to terms with "theory," as I have come to define it, and its relationship to teaching.

The issues raised in this book are not merely the outcomes of a personal odyssey. In fact, they are the issues of an entire field struggling at the edge of a new discourse—one that values both teaching and research and that speaks to theorists and practitioners alike. It is my contention that the development of such a discourse is crucial to the maturation of composition studies as a field. Rather than defining composition in terms of traditional oppositions (theory versus practice, research versus teaching, literature versus composition) and signifying the quality of our work and the relevance of our findings in terms of these divisions, composition scholars need to better explore connections and interrelationships. I see teacher research as a means by which to do so because it is based on the premise that theory comes from many places, including the classroom, and that theory is generated by many people, including teachers in collaboration with students and other teachers.

Because the teacher-research movement is still in its early stages, and because it is most influential among K–12 teachers who do not always publish their findings, its epistemology and methodology have not been fully articulated. Indeed, most teacher-researchers themselves are unaware of the full purpose or potential of practitioner inquiry within the field of composition studies. This book, then, is written for practicing teacher-researchers as well as for those who are new to teacher research. It describes practitioner inquiry from the perspective of a teacher-researcher herself who is looking for the bigger picture, searching for connections between this form of inquiry and others in composition and literary studies. My role in writing this book could be described as "theorist-practitioner," the name that Dixie Goswami and Peter Stillman give to university researchers who see themselves as teachers as well as theory makers. In their seminal book *Reclaiming the Classroom* (1987), Goswami and Stillman distinguish between theorist-practitioners who promote teacher research, such as James Berlin, James Britton, Ann Berthoff, Shirley Brice Heath, Ken Macrorie, and Janet Emig, and teacher-practitioners who promote teacher research, such as the K–12 teachers involved in the classroom inquiry program at the Breadloaf School of English. Although Goswami and Stillman gloss over the distinctions between these two groups, I invoke them as a point of discussion. A major difference is that, where teacher-practitioners search primarily within the classroom for insights about learning, theorist-practitioners search the larger field as well, generalizing about the significance of practitioner inquiry to knowledge making in composition.

My intention in this book is to offer a critical perspective on the teacher-research movement as a whole and to argue that graduate programs, informed by the teacher-research perspective, must train the next generation of composition scholars to work as both theorist-practitioners and teacher-practitioners. Toward this end, the book is presented in three parts: section I, "Challenging the Theory-Practice Relationship," discusses the move toward theory and away from practice as the basis for inquiry in composition over the last twenty-five years. It also proposes an alternative to this division based on revised definitions of *theorizing* and *teaching* and stronger connections between personal knowing and academic knowledge making, as drawn from recent composition research and feminist studies. Section II, "Articulating the Teacher-Research Perspective, K–12," argues that practitioner inquiry offers a different way of thinking about research and an alternative means of drawing the connections between theory and practice. The work of practicing teacher-researchers illustrates that a realignment of theory and practice *can* be successfully generated at the individual level by teachers trying to understand their own classrooms. Section III, "Toward Theory-Based Practice and Practice-Based Theory," describes my own teacher research with graduate students and outlines a teacher-research approach to graduate studies in composition.

I Challenging the Theory-Practice Relationship

1 The Move toward Theory in Composition

One of the primary issues in composition studies today is the role of theory and its relationship to practice. For some, teachers in particular, the field has reached a critical point in terms of this relationship. This perspective is apparent in Jane Peterson's impassioned address to the 1990 Conference on College Composition and Communication in which she claimed, to a standing ovation, that the field must now reclaim the importance of teaching. Peterson's primary point was that a hierarchy has been established in composition studies which privileges research over teaching and which fails to see teaching itself as a form of inquiry and knowledge making. Following Peterson, Howard Tinberg makes an even stronger argument that we must buck "the trend—I would almost call it a mad rush—toward theory within the discipline," which he asserts "might just as well be described as a rush to get out of the classroom" because it is accompanied by a "ghettoization of 'practitioners' and a discrediting of what they do" (1991, 37).

How have composition teachers come to this defensive position in regards to teaching? How have the members of the Conference on College Composition and Communication (an organization whose original concern, as Peterson notes, was the pedagogical issue of what to do with freshman English) come to feel that they must justify the importance of teaching? And, in a larger sense, how will this current stance affect the future development of composition studies?

I raise these questions in an effort to understand the nature of composition and how it came to be what it is today. My discussion in this chapter is concerned, essentially, with epistemological issues— with the basis and purpose of knowledge making in the field. More specifically, I chronicle the development of a perceived dichotomy between theory and practice as these have come to be defined and argue that the future strength of composition as a research field lies in our understanding and making full use of both, each always in relationship to the other. I begin by following a trail of definitions and redefinitions of *research* and *theory* in the composition literature over the past thirty years, thereby providing a historical explanation for how I came to define the terms in this book.

3

Research in Composition

As a "serious research field," Composition (spelled with a capital *C*, as Stephen North suggests [1987]) is generally considered to have begun in 1963 with the publication of Richard Braddock, Richard Lloyd-Jones, and Lowell Schoer's *Research in Written Composition*. In reviewing composition research up to that date, the authors found the body of work (504 studies) seriously lacking in intellectual rigor and called for an empirical revision of composition studies. Research up to that time had been largely concerned with pedagogical issues, and many studies had relied on evidence from the classroom. The authors believed that the key to legitimacy in composition was to dissociate from that which was anecdotal and teacherly and to adopt that which was scientific and scholarly; at the time, these two perspectives seemed mutually exclusive. The privileging of science is evident in both the written request which led to the publication of *Research in Written Composition* and in the conclusions of the study itself. An ad hoc committee of the NCTE Executive Committee, in order to determine the "state of knowledge in composition," initiated an effort "to review what is known and what is not known about the teaching and learning of composition and the conditions under which it is taught, for the purpose of preparing for publication a special scientifically based report on what is known in this area" (quoted in North 1987, 16). The resulting document by Braddock, Lloyd-Jones, and Schoer concludes that "today's research in Composition, taken as a whole, may be compared to chemical research as it emerged from the period of alchemy" (1963, 5). These excerpts clearly illustrate that the call for research from Braddock and colleagues was meant to move composition out of the dark ages of uninformed speculation and into the light of modern science.

After the publication of *Research in Written Composition*, historical, rhetorical, and other forms of composition research continued to develop, but many researchers in the field increased their efforts to conduct empirical studies, modeling writing research after clinical psychology, which emphasized controlled data gathering and attempted a rigorous "objectivity." In her review of empirical research in composition, Anne Ruggles Gere explains that the "standard view of science" underlying this type of research

> assumes a closed system (such as that of the laboratory) where all variables can be controlled or at least accounted for. . . . Another aspect of the standard view of science is the assumption that theories are tested against "facts," that it is possible to assume a

set of givens against which hypotheses can be measured. . . .
Implicit in such studies is another standard-view assumption,
that causal relations are regular and contingent, that explanation
and prediction are exactly symmetrical. (1985, 118)

Further characteristics of research conducted under the standard
view of science include the following: it aims at description, explanation, and prediction; it is marked by a naturalist metaphysics and
an empiricist methodology; it produces hypotheses which are
falsifiable; it relies on decontextualized experimentation which can
be replicated; and it defines success as cumulative progress toward
"demarcating soluble puzzles within the discipline from mere problems" (Connors 1983, 6–7). In summary, composition researchers
working under the scientific model construct hypotheses about
writing and writing behavior; collect data, such as written texts and
protocols, in as controlled a manner as possible; analyze and describe
these data; attempt to verify their findings through similarly controlled studies; and work to generalize from these studies in order to
create profiles or models of teaching and writing. Many composition
studies of this kind, too, have examined teaching approaches and
have described their effects on student learning, defining *teaching* as
narrowly as possible so as to control or at least account for other
factors that may also be affecting learning. A classic example of this
latter type of study is Donald Daiker, Andrew Kerek, and Max
Morenberg's research on sentence combining (1978).

Following the scientific model, all well-formed composition research, by definition, must meet certain methodological criteria.
Thus one effect of the scientific model on composition studies has
been an increased interest in methodology. Robert Connors likens the
situation in empirical composition studies to that in cognitive psychology, where the problems encountered during research are typically treated as methodological rather than epistemological. For
example, a theory or model claiming to explain some element of
cognitive activity is suggested, and experiments are designed to test
the theory. When the results are inconclusive or conflicting, the
experimental design is revised and more experiments are conducted.
If the new experimental design still does not yield conclusive results,
empiricist researchers tend to move on to other "more researchable"
questions and issues on the basis that, if the problem cannot be solved
methodologically, it cannot be solved (Connors 1983, 13). Because of
the complexity of the phenomena under study, composition researchers, like cognitive psychologists, have been unable to build the formal
models of composing they had hoped for or to predict the outcomes

of their experimental studies on writing. As a result of this situation, Connors concludes that there is little chance of cumulation or certainty of knowledge in composition research rooted exclusively in scientific research:

> Methodologically rigorous, carefully controlled, and technically advanced though some aspects of psychologically based research into composition may be, they do not make composition studies a mature scientific field with a paradigm of its own, and they do not even show conclusively that it is a preparidigmatic field—at least not one whose first paradigm is anywhere in sight. (17)

This is not to say that the field should completely reject the scientific model of research, for it is still useful to conduct statistical and quantifiable studies in our search for verifiable knowledge, just as long as we

> stop fooling ourselves about the nature of the field. We are not a science and will not be one in the foreseeable future, and we must beware lest our understandable desire to share in the cachet of science lead us to a barren enactment of imitation science. . . . The universe of discourse is larger than the universe of science, and seductive though the puzzle-solving of normal science may be, it has always been the task of rhetoricians to try to solve problems and not puzzles. It is the old burden of humanistic learning, and every day we must shoulder it anew. (1983, 19–20)

In the past ten years in particular, researchers have acknowledged the limitations of the scientific method for composition and, in response, have moved in two directions: the first is toward what Gere calls a "new empiricism," and the second is toward a more humanistic inquiry.

The New Empiricism

The standard view of science has undergone a major shift in the past several years. In *The Structure of Scientific Revolutions* (1970), one of the works which has helped bring about this shift, Thomas Kuhn argues that science, like any other area of scholarly inquiry, is a socially constructed field and not the "objective" search for existing truths it is assumed to be. Instead of working as neutral observers and recorders of "reality," scientists, both individually and collectively, select what to see and construct their seeing in terms of preconceived theories and expectations. In other words, individual interpretation affects all observation, even that which is conducted scientifically. Gere claims that, influenced by Kuhn and others, "composition research [has] openly acknowledged the theories inherent in 'objective' observation" (1985, 121) and has moved toward a new kind of empiricism. She sees this new form of data-based research in Cooper and Odell's 1978 update of the Braddock, Lloyd-Jones, and Sahoer collection, which foregrounds the content of research over the methodology, raises questions that challenge previously unexamined uses of key terms such as *composition,* and calls for an exploration of new methodologies for the study of writing, including qualitative studies such as ethnographies and case studies. The Cooper and Odell collection asks "fundamental questions about writing and about the intellectual demands posed by various types of writing. Where they are concerned with methodology, it is not a methodology consonant with the standard view of science. Rather, they urge studies that consider the significant as well as the measurable" (Gere, 122). Cooper and Odell question a priori categories of composition research, such as the meaning of the terms *writing* and *research.* A further difference in this "new" empiricism is that it focuses more on the learning process itself, rather than on the effects that certain pedagogies have on learning. Cooper and Odell's approach is still empirical because it is based on observation of writing and writing situations and because it depends on the collection of this evidence to support beliefs and conclusions. What distinguishes it from the "old" empiricism is its tendency to "put questions about composition first and methodology second"; to encourage a more eclectic approach to knowledge building in which a variety of methods and research paradigms are followed; and to problematize previously accepted concepts and terminology (Gere, 121–22).

Many teacher-research studies, especially those which are influenced by social science models of inquiry, would fall into the category of new empiricism. These studies adopt specific observational procedures from sociology and anthropology, as represented in the work of Odell (1987), Doheny-Farina and Odell (1985), and Kantor, Kirby, and Goetz (1981). Classroom-based inquiry is described in socioogical terms that distinguish it from the natural sciences: it is qualitative rather than quantitative; hypothesis-generating rather than hypothesis-testing; inductive rather than deductive; contextualized and naturalistic rather than controlled and scientific. Teacher research which looks to social science is concerned with the reliability of data and the validity of findings, considering these methodological issues: Was the research conducted unobtrusively in the school or classroom by a participant-observer who was accepted and trusted? If questionnaires were used, were they clearly written and nondirective? Were fieldnotes and tapes meticulously inscribed, transcribed, coded, and cross-coded? Such studies also carefully note the researchers' role in the study and relationship to participants, as well as their interpretive perspective. Examples of classroom-based research that is particularly influenced by the social science model of inquiry include Pamela Grossman's *The Making of a Teacher* (1990); Ann Haas Dyson's "Learning to Write/Learning to Do School: Emergent Writers' Interpretations of School Literacy Tasks" (1984); and Carol Berkenkotter, Thomas Huckin, and John Ackerman's "Conventions, Conversations, and the Writer: Case Study of a Student in a Rhetoric Ph.D. Program" (1988). These studies were done by a university researcher or group of researchers who collaborated with teachers and students on the projects. When teachers themselves initiate classroom-based research, they tend to conduct their inquiry more informally, which is why their work has been challenged by university empiricists such as Sandra Stotsky, who claims that "the rigor of classroom research leaves much to be desired" (1989, 756).

The shift to a new empiricism, overall, has been beneficial for both teacher-researchers and the field of composition, for it has opened up new possibilities for research and thinking. The new empirical approach is of some concern to more traditional empiricists, however, because it challenges "the distinction, implicit in the practices of the well-established natural sciences, between the development of theories representing the structures of nature . . . and the application of these theories to explain, diagnose, and predict those particulars and events of interest to us" (Manicas and Secord 1983, 403; quoted in Gere 1985, 123). Gere, for example, claims that "because composition research has for so many years been primarily practical (and therefore concerned with application), it is particularly vulnerable to this *confusion* of theory and application" (emphasis mine). Thus Gere sees "the emergence of teacher researchers [as] a concrete illustration of how far this confusion may extend. . . . They pose an epistemological problem because they conflate theory and application" and because, as practitioners, they cannot "look at issues of composition in purely theoretical terms" (123). Gere suggests that new empiricism needs to construct an alternative to this "epistemological problem," but she does not offer a viable one, nor does she explain how the alternative would solve the "problem" of teacher-researchers "conflating" theory and practice.

One of the ongoing issues in empirical research—new or old—is the relationship between theory and practice, research and teaching in composition. Traditional empiricism would have us separate them, while new empiricism would have us question and challenge this division. The fact that Gere praises the new empiricism for questioning a priori terms such as *writing* but criticizes it for questioning the a priori status of theory as separate from practice shows how deeply rooted this distinction really is.

The problem for composition research has been that many empiricists still follow what Connors calls "the romance of science" in seeking legitimacy by privileging research over practice. This separatist view assumes that knowledge is advanced in a field through a first stage of "purely theoretical" exploration, which is then followed by a second stage of practical application. North describes how this view underlies much composition research by

> establish[ing] what amounts to a science/technology relationship, with the Practitioners cast pretty much as technicians: the inquirers find out how the world works, and then tell the technicians, who behave accordingly. . . . Indigenous Practitioner knowledge and method are a concern only insofar as they may obstruct the introduction and application of the new, imported knowledge. If [teacher] lore and its production can be said to have a positive function at all, it is only as a starting point—a foil, almost—for investigations seeking real knowledge. (1987, 331)

The trouble with this view is that it places teachers and researchers in a hierarchy, with researchers holding the top position as knowledge makers and teachers holding the lower position as knowledge receivers (or even more negatively, obstructors of knowledge making). It also makes clear distinctions between methods for developing knowledge (empirical research) and the practice of disseminating that knowledge (teaching). In so doing, this view actively works against the development of a productive interrelationship between teaching and researching in the field of composition.

Humanistic Inquiry

Another approach to addressing the limitations of empirical research in composition is to embrace a more humanistic inquiry. William Irmscher argues for this approach in his attempts at "finding a comfortable identity" for composition as a research field. He asserts that the field has been "plagued by the scientific nemesis" too long and that it has suffered in "defer[ring] to the world view of English-Educationists," including Braddock, Lloyd-Jones, and Schoer, and George Hillocks, whose 1986 *Research on Written Composition* further updates the Braddock report. From the humanist perspective, instead of looking to science, compositionists can find better methods in English studies, where they "share common ground . . . with critics, textualists, historiographers, bibliographers, linguists, novelists, and poets, each of whom differs in approach, but all of whom represent the tradition of humane letters" (Irmscher 1987, 85). A humanistic methodology, as Irmscher sees it, would encourage introspection and hypothesizing by recognizing the interpretive nature of all research, the importance of personal variables and idiosyncrasies in knowledge making, the relevance of doubt as a source of knowledge and further investigation, and the insight gained from particularities as well as generalizations (86). Humanistic approaches to research "represent the same kinds of inquiry and attitudes that an author might adopt in 'researching' a novel, not less thorough than scholarly inquiry, not less demanding, not less true to experience. The task would be to present the fullness of experience" (87). Such research could take a variety of forms, including personal narrative, biography, case study, and ethnography.

Many teacher-researchers, especially those working in K–12 classrooms, have for some time conducted the type of humanistic inquiry that Irmscher describes. They have often thought of their research in terms of narrative, rather than extended case study, as practiced in psychology, or formal ethnography, as practiced in the social sciences. Thomas Newkirk is one proponent of the narrative approach to case-study research in composition. He asserts that writing classroom-based stories is a more honest and interesting endeavor than writing case studies informed by the social sciences, because the latter tend to be "schizophrenic" in their denial of the narrative impulse in order to adhere to rules of methodological rigor (1992). He goes so far as to assert that "attempts to accommodate the traditional experimental paradigm [replicability, validity, and generalizability] stunt the growth of the case-study method" (1991, 129). Newkirk calls instead for research which re-creates the full, rich experience of the teacher in the classroom, described in all its particularity. Evoking anthropologist Clifford Geertz's term "local knowledge," Newkirk argues that teacher "lore"—customs, common sense, lived experience—is an essential reminder that all research studies are in fact "stories": "Narratives are embedded in all academic discourse—even the most austere; each has conventions for telling that indicate to the writer what should be attended to and what should be ignored" (1991, 132). One of Newkirk's major claims for classroom-based inquiry is that the source of authority in educational research is teachers' "intimate knowledge of the classroom and students, from intuitions honed by making thousands of judgments and observations of student work. It does not come through deference to expert opinion or through suppressing intuitive resources in favor of more distanced—and more academically respectable—means of observation" (1991, 133). The very titles of teacher-research studies which follow the humanistic model of inquiry openly celebrate their narrative impulse: consider, for example, Nancie Atwell's *In the Middle* (1987b), Julie Jensen's *Stories to Grow On* (1989), David Schaafsma's *Eating on the Street* (in press), and Jerome Harste, Virginia Woodward, and Carolyn Burke's *Language Stories and Literacy Lessons* (1984).

Irmscher's urging that composition needs to look to the humanities rather than the sciences or the social sciences for its model of inquiry is neither new nor surprising. Composition researchers in general have tended to align themselves with the humanities, particularly literary studies. This is largely because most composition programs are located in departments of English and because most compositionists (at least the first generation of composition scholars) were initially trained as literary scholars. It is therefore not surprising that compositionists would look to the humanities for a method of inquiry. It is also understandable, then, that compositionists have begun to talk about *theory* (an English studies term) rather than *research* (a term from the sciences) as the basis for knowledge making in the field. *Theory* has become the prominent term in English studies over the past twenty years, ever since the field began to substitute theory for criticism as its primary pursuit.

Theory in Composition

Just as compositionists previously looked to science as a legitimizing and unifying force in the field, they are now looking increasingly to literary theory. Although it is true that the scientific model is also informed by theory—typically a foundationalist theory which assumes the existence of invariant truths that hold across cultural and political contexts—what it foregrounds is observation and method rather than epistemology. In fact, the theory underlying the scientific paradigm is often assumed and left unarticulated. The contemporary approach to literary studies, however, is in direct opposition to this foundationalist view, as Stanley Fish's term "anti-foundationalism" implies. Anti-foundationalism (also known very generally as "social constructionism" or "poststructuralism") denies the existence of universal truths, claiming that all inquiry, all findings, all "truths" are inseparable from the historical, political, and cultural contingencies that produce them. In short, all knowledge is "socially constructed," and the inquiring self is always "situated" within a belief system, whether one realizes it or not. The anti-foundationalist argument against foundationalism is that the latter theory "fails, lies in ruins, because it is from the very first implicated in everything it claims to transcend" (Fish 1989, 345). As Fish notes, anti-foundationalist theory underlies much current work in literary studies as well as in several other disciplines. For example, anti-foundationalist theories are promoted

> in philosophy by Richard Rorty, Hilary Putnam, W. V. Quine; in anthropology by Clifford Geertz and Victor Turner; in history by Hayden White; in sociology by the entire tradition of the sociology of knowledge and more recently by the ethnomethodologists; in hermeneutics by Heidegger, Gadamer, and Derrida; in the general sciences of man by Foucault; in the history of science by Thomas Kuhn; in the history of art by Michael Fried; in legal theory by Philip Bobbit and Sanford Levinson; in literary theory by Barbara Herrnstein Smith, Walter Michaels, Steven Knapp, John Fekete, Jonathan Culler, Terry Eagleton, Frank Lentricchia, Jane Tompkins, Stanley Fish, and on and on. Obviously it is not an isolated argument; in fact, today one could say that it is the *going* argument. (Fish 199, 345; emphasis his)

Compositionists, too, have moved toward anti-foundationalism, as indicated in the work of Patricia Bizzell, James Berlin, Linda Brodkey, David Bartholomae, Marilyn Cooper and Michael Holzman, Elizabeth Flynn, Susan Miller, and Louise Wetherbee Phelps, to name just a few. Increasingly, teacher-researchers have also been influenced by anti-foundationalism, especially that which is informed by the work of Clifford Geertz and James Clifford in anthropology, Martin Heidegger and Hans-Georg Gadamer in hermeneutics, Ira Shor and Paulo Freire in education, and Kenneth Bruffee in composition.

The influence of anti-foundationalism is so strong in literary studies that when literary scholars talk about "theory" in the 1990s, they are generally referring to the "going" theory of anti-foundationalism. This talk, as Fish notes, tends to engender either fear or hope: fear from the foundationalists, who resist and feel beleaguered by the anti-foundationalists, and hope from those who see in anti-foundationalism new possibilities for innovation and growth in English studies.

Early calls for "theory" in composition studies were not so influenced by anti-foundationalism. In fact, they relied on several foundationalist assumptions, including the importance of a single "composition theory" and the need to develop models that describe "the writing process," as if distinct from culture or context. These early attempts at defining theory often were cast in terms of research-ers versus teachers, with teachers cast as antitheorists.

One of the first published calls for theory in composition—John Warnock's 1976 article entitled "Who's Afraid of Theory?"—refers to the fear of composition teachers who are "anti-theory" because they believe that generalized theories of writing are inadequate and some-times even harmful to the teaching of composition. Warnock defines theory etymologically in an effort to remove negative connotations from the term:

> The word *theory* comes from the Greek *thea,* meaning "a view-ing." Theater has the same root. Etymologically, then, the word implies a frame, a text and a context, a completed act of relating parts to parts and parts to wholes. . . . By *theory,* I mean something like "structure of meaningful relationships" or "that abstract conception of the whole by which the relations of part to part and part to whole may be well understood." (17)

Warnock goes on to explain that all teaching, indeed all human activity, is informed by theory, whether acknowledged or not. Hence, "in a composition classroom, the question cannot be theory *or* practice; it must be theory *of* practice" (17; emphasis his). Making this theory explicit and then holding it up for examination and critique, Warnock argues, will promote both knowledge making *and* more responsible teaching. Warnock argues that composition is in need of "a unified theory of discourse" which would provide a strong conceptual base for the field and eliminate fragmentation in research, as well as uninformed pedagogy.

Three years later, Nancy Sommers reasserted "The Need for Theory in Composition Research" (1979), claiming that composition research "is dominated by studies with methodological or pedagogical inten-tions" which "lack a clearly articulated theoretical base" and which have not only "yielded very little to the development of a theory of the composing process, but also . . . have restricted our thinking about composition to classroom problems" (46). In this article, Sommers claims that the research focus on teaching methodologies, such as journal writing and role-playing, "is like a concern for a technology before there is a science to support it" (46). She uses the pejorative term "anti-theory" to describe composition teachers and researchers who focus their attention on finding or developing new teaching methods. Although she does not explicitly define the term "theory," Sommers refers to it in contrast to current research and teaching practices that do not challenge a priori beliefs or question underlying assumptions. As examples of "atheoretical" research, she offers various studies of revision which focus on teaching methodology without ever questioning the overly simplified stage model of writing (prewriting, writing, rewriting) or challenging the conventional views of revision which associate it with a final act of tidiness and polish, rather than an ongoing generation and exploration of meaning.

Another aspect of theory, as Sommers conceives it, is an emphasis on writing and learning processes as opposed to "methodological questions and classroom problems." In her call for more intellectual inquiry, she places theory in direct opposition to teaching, saying that "theoretical research on the composing process is embryonic in comparison with the senectitude of instructional studies" (1979, 49). She also associates "solid theoretical research" with the future development of "alternative models of the composing process that will allow us to generate important researchable questions about the operations and sub-processes of the composing process" (49). For her, good composition research has a theoretical rather than a pedagogical impetus and looks to create knowledge for the larger field, not for the individual classroom. Nowhere does she consider the possibility that these two ends—general field knowledge as well as specific class-room knowledge—could be compatible or mutually supportive. In other words, the foundationalist belief in a fundamental separation of theory and practice underlies Sommers's call for theory.

In "Toward a Theory of Composition," Lil Brannon also relies on some foundationalist criteria for establishing the field, including the belief in the possibility of an all-encompassing theory of composition and an interest in model building as the basis for that theory. She defines theory as "an attempt to derive the general principles that underlie composing and to formulate an inclusive description of the nature and value of composing and the nature of learning to write" (1985, 8). Her goal for composition studies is to establish a single dominant theory based on a "philosophy of composition" that under-lies all research and thereby unifies the field. In this view, theory both guides observation and develops in response to it, while research tests theory and provides an intellectual environment conducive to its further development. One of the best forms of research for this purpose is model building. Examples of models that composition researchers have created include Flower and Hayes's cognitive pro-cess model; James Moffett's model of writing development; and the tripartite model (poetic, expressive, and transactional) of Britton et al. Other models that have been influential in establishing composition theory, according to Brannon's definition, include Piaget's and Vygotsky's models of language learning and Perry's model of intellectual and ethical development in the liberal arts. In calling for a unified theory and relying on model building as the basis on which to create the general principles underlying composition, Brannon is clearly taking a social science perspective on development of the field. She does, however, acknowledge other perspectives, and she encourages the involvement of teachers in constructing the field, especially since one of the questions underlying the theory of composition she envisions is, "How can schools, particularly teachers of writing, assist the development of writers?"

The most recent definitions of theory in composition reflect the profound influence that anti-foundationalism has had in departments of English. Peter Elbow describes this influence in *What Is English?* (1990). The overriding purpose of the book, commissioned by the Executive Council of the Modern Language Association, is to discuss the issues which arose at the English Coalition Conference in the summer of 1987. A central theme of that conference was the nature and purpose of theory in English studies. Elbow draws heavily on definitions provided by literary scholars Gerald Graff and Kathleen McCormick, both of whom attended the conference and are informed by the anti-foundationalist belief in multiple theories rather than one all-encompassing Theory. Graff, for example, sees "literary theory not as a set of systematic principles, necessarily, or as a founding philosophy, but simply as an enquiry into assumptions, premises, and legitimating principles and concepts" (Elbow, 52). McCormick sees theory as a form of self-consciousness or awareness of "the situated nature of our positions and interpretations" and an ability "to acknowledge that [these positions and interpretations] come about as a result of certain beliefs, principles, and broader ideologies—to see that they are not universally true but rather historically situated" (Elbow, 63).

Graff's and McCormick's definitions represent two different positions on what it means to be "theoretically aware," though both assert that theories are ever present, implicitly if not explicitly, and that no one is ever without theory. The difference between Graff's and McCormick's positions is primarily political. The first position (Graff's) makes a claim about epistemology in saying that theory involves looking at premises and assumptions, but it does not promote any particular theory or epistemological position. Proponents of this position refer to theory variously as a "lens" through which to view writing and writers, an "interpretive guide" for reading and responding, or a "stance" from which to speak, such as a Marxist, feminist, or psychoanalytic stance. The argument for this perspective on theory is that it motivates a field to undergo perpetual change. In the words of Louise Wetherbee Phelps, it has the potential to "galvanize" or "disrupt" a community, "changing its very questions, undermining long-held beliefs, introducing ambiguities, revealing complexities, setting new tasks, forcing risks" (1991, 36–37). The second position (McCormick's) makes a stronger epistemological claim in asserting that, not only does theory involve looking at our premises and assumptions, but it also requires that we *necessarily* see these premises as situated and therefore never universally true. Thus there can be no "right" interpretation and no "true" knowledge. "[T]here's a momentous political and professional choice that people must make here: whether or not to fuse one's epistemological position with one's commitment to a theoretical stance; whether or not to say, 'If you want to be theoretically aware, you must agree with me about epistemology'" (Elbow 1990, 55–56).

Elbow argues for the first position on the grounds that it is more open and allows for healthy disagreement within composition studies. The second position, though it has potential to promote unity within the field, can be exclusionary: "We are saying to many [foundationalist] colleagues in the profession, '[anti-foundationalist] theory, in itself, shows that you are wrong—by definition,' thus ensuring that those colleagues will treat theory as the enemy" (1990, 57). He sees in the second position a self-righteousness and an elitism that in the end can only fragment composition studies further. What the field needs, instead, is "theoretical humility," whereby all members of the profession are included under an umbrella of theory that allows for active, if not peaceful, coexistence of diverse theoretical positions:

> Theory, defined largely, could help the profession have a better conversation and figure out what it needs to figure out. If defined more narrowly—as in the second epistemological position (and especially if done covertly while pretending to be open)—"theory" just becomes one more party in the tiresome fights that go round and round in the profession of English. Will we welcome full difference or just those kinds of difference that feel comfortable? (57)

The second position on theory, in claiming superiority over the first position, has paradoxically attempted to claim "foundational status" as central truth. Thus English studies, as McCormick acknowledges, is in danger of promoting anti-foundationalist theory itself as the new canon. This canonical perspective on theory is not surprising, according to Elbow, given that English is a profession "with a tradition of making people feel excluded" (1990, 80). Indeed, a problem at the conference and in the field of English studies at large is slippage between the first and second positions, which inevitably leads to fear of, resistance to, and even hostility toward theory, especially among teachers, who are among the first to be excluded.

The two positions are quite different in scope and intention. We might call the first position "theory with a little *t*" and the second "theory with a capital *T*," the latter to signify what ethnographer John Van Maanen, drawing on Geertz, calls "grand theory" or "acclaimed theory." From the second position in anthropology, Theory is an analytical framework which allows the "humble fieldworker to stand on the shoulders of giants (and see farther) by using well-received constructs as receptacles" for his or her own observations and findings. From the first position, theory is "an advance if it is more incisive—whatever that may mean—than those that preceded it; but it stands less on their shoulders than, challenged and challenging, runs by their side" (Van Maanen 1988, 25). We might see teachers as theorists with a little *t* and university researchers such as McCormick as theorists with a capital *T*. Both groups conduct intellectual inquiry and construct new knowledge, be it in small settings (the classroom) or large (the field of English studies).

Defining the Theory-Practice Relationship in Composition

Just as there are differing positions on the meaning and purpose of theory in composition studies, there are differing positions on the meaning and purpose of practice and its relationship to theory. As has already been shown, foundationalists traditionally assume the separation of theory and practice, while anti-foundationalists are more likely to challenge this and other atomistic tendencies in English studies. From the anti-foundationalist perspective, if one assumes that theory is implicated in every practice, it is, technically speaking, impossible to separate theory from practice. But this does not mean that all anti-foundationalists are interested in discussing the implications of theory for practice or vice versa. The issue for most anti-foundationalists is one of focus, of deciding which aspect of the theory-practice relationship to foreground. Thus Elbow distinguishes between a *generalized* anti-foundationalist theory, which examines situatedness in the abstract and an *active theory*, which treats "analyzing and theory making as active questioning and real leverage" (1990, 84). The first case is theory-with-a-capital-*T*; it is an intellectual engagement done for the sake of extending and promoting theory itself. The second case is theory-with-a-little-*t*; it is both an intellectual and a practical engagement done for the sake of developing self-understanding and promoting change in schools and classrooms. Other terms for "active theory," which explicitly focuses on the dialectical relationship between theory and practice, are "grounded theory" and "practical theory." Elbow obviously prefers this latter type of theory, as do many other composition scholars, including Patricia Bizzell, Louise Wetherbee Phelps, James Berlin, and nearly all teacher-researchers. Phelps, for example, argues that "theory doesn't exist for its own sake, or shouldn't. However formidably abstract, it is a form of intelligibility that the theorist tries to give to personal dilemmas, deeply felt. Like all writing, theory is a way to make sense of life" (1988, viii). Obviously influenced by feminist theory, Phelps describes the tensions and conflicts between theory and practice in terms of "the dialectical relation between yin and yang, feminine and masculine principles" (xii).

Not all composition theorists share the view that active theory is necessary to the development of composition as a field, however. Gary Olson (1991) considers Phelps's perspective "reasonable and productive," but challenges the tacit assumption that composition always is and should be practice oriented. He claims that this assumption does a "great disservice" to the field because it discourages broader conceptualization of composition as a more abstract study of language, meaning, and interpretation in written discourse. Olson's argument is that composition studies must encourage both practice-oriented theorizing and "purely theoretical" work that has no apparent application to teaching. From his perspective, theory and practice in composition *can* be profitably separated, much as the mind can be separated from the body: while "teaching may be the lifeblood of the field, theory is its heart and mind." Olson's argument reflects the more traditional (and, I would claim, the more patriarchal) stance on theory as a strictly intellectual enterprise, and it is this view which prevails in contemporary literary studies, Graff and McCormick aside. (American feminist criticism is a notable exception, as will be illustrated in the next chapter.)

The literary perspective on the separation of theory and practice is particularly evident in Stanley Fish's "Anti-Foundationalism, Theory Hope, and the Teaching of Composition." Himself an anti-foundationalist literary critic, Fish argues in this chapter of *Doing What Comes Naturally* that there is no "methodological payoff for composition in the arguments of anti-foundationalism" (1989, 346). His claim is that composition specialists are mistaken in assuming that (1) anti-foundationalism as a model of epistemology provides directions for *achieving* that epistemology; (2) learning the lesson of anti-foundationalism (that we are always and already situated) necessarily means that "we will thereby become more self-consciously situated and inhabit our situatedness in a more effective way"; and (3) the teaching of anti-foundationalism to ourselves and our students will facilitate the teaching and learning of writing (347–48).

In regard to the first and second assumptions, Fish, taking the strong view of Theory promoted by McCormick, argues that "if all knowledge is situational and we are always and already in a situation, then we can never be at any distance from the knowledge we need. Anti-foundationalism cannot give us the knowledge we seek because its lesson is that we already have it" (1989, 353). As to the third assumption, Fish's point is that it is impossible to teach situatedness because "a situation is not an entity, but a bundle of tacit or unspoken assumptions that is simultaneously organizing the world and changing in response to its own organizing work. A situation is always on the wing, and any attempt to capture it will only succeed in fixing it in a shape it no longer has" (352); therefore, "to make the notion of tacit knowledge either into a recipe for learning or into a set of requirements for a 'good' pedagogy is to exempt it from its own insight" and to turn an anti-foundationalist argument into a foundationalist one. Fish offers a pithy summary of his argument that there are no practical (teaching) implications of anti-foundationalist theory:

> [T]he knowledge that one is in a situation has no particular payoff for any situation you happen to be in, because the constraints of that situation will not be relaxed by that knowledge. It follows, then, that teaching our students the lesson of anti-foundationalism, while it will put them in possession of a new philosophical perspective, will not give them a tool for operating in the world they already inhabit. Being told that you are in a situation will help you neither to dwell in it more perfectly nor to *write* within it more successfully. When Bizzell urges that we "teach students that there are such things as discourse conventions," that is, teach anti-foundationalism . . . she believes that a description of how we come to know what we know can be turned into a set of directions for knowing. As a searching critique of method, anti-foundationalism cannot itself be made the basis of a method without losing its anti-foundationalist character. (351)

The only logical conclusion for Fish, then, is that "practice has nothing to do with [anti-foundationalist] theory, at least in the sense of being enabled and justified by theory" (355).

Fish's argument at first seems convincing because it hinges on a shift in conceptualizing that is so commonly practiced and so rarely questioned that it makes perfect sense: he defines theory from an anti-foundationalist position and practice from a foundationalist position. In other words, theory is an epistemology—a perspective on the world and a way of understanding and making knowledge, while teaching is the transmission of knowledge ready-made. This shift allows Fish to talk about teaching in terms of a given *content,* and his argument against any theory-practice relationship seems a foregone conclusion: because teaching is the transmission of fixed knowledge and because anti-foundationalism argues against the existence of fixed knowledge, there cannot be a fixed content for the teaching of writing (because in fixing it, we are altering it). In other words, without a fixed content, theory obviously holds no implications for teaching.

However, we can also define teaching from an anti-foundationalist position, which would require that we consider it, too, as a way of seeing and knowing that is deeply implicated in social, cultural, and historical contexts. From this perspective, there is a strong relationship between anti-foundationalist theory and practice, for theory informs not so much *what* we teach (the content of our teaching), but *how* we teach (the process of our teaching). Anti-foundationalism, then, makes us aware that teaching and learning, as well as the knowledge that is taught and learned, are always situated and that, just as knowledge is fluid within contexts, so is teaching. Elbow best articulates this anti-foundationalist view of teaching in his comments about the teaching and learning of theory:

> There are certain important questions one must ask about the practice of emphasizing theory. Is the study of theory an invitation to students and teachers to make their own hypotheses or to study those of others? Is theory a practice or a content? Is the pursuit of theory participatory and experiential and process-oriented—helping students to do their own reflecting back on premises and assumptions about reading and writing—or is it content-oriented in the sense of asking students merely to learn and absorb the theories of others? Does the pursuit of theory invite everyday language—with teachers using everyday, nonjargon language and students invited to put their investigations into their own language—or does it invite mostly sanctioned or canonical language and jargon? (1990, 81)

For Elbow, theory enables new ways of seeing and understanding, as well as alternative ways of articulating that understanding. But theory is not primary in the sense that it precedes practice and "justifies" it, as it is for Fish. In fact, when we conceive of teaching as an epistemology, we must grant that practice is sometimes prior to theory, since our practical or tacit knowledge implies far more than we can know or articulate theoretically, as Michael Polanyi has pointed out. This is why Elbow argues that

> our success in pursuing and increasing theoretical knowledge usually depends on respecting and trusting practice for a while and afterward interrogating it as a rich source for new theory. . . . [I]t is shrewd and sophisticated for teachers to proceed using practical wisdom and even intuition and then to stop and say, "Now what were we doing? What are the premises and consequences of our practices?" (1990, 87–88)

Anti-foundationalist scholars who see teaching and theory in a hierarchical relationship, with theory as primary and teaching as the transmission of theory through course content, will obviously take issue with Elbow's emphasis. However, scholars who see teaching and theory in a more interactive relationship will accept the view that theorizing often begins with an actual person—even a teacher—working in a specific environment that has forced him or her to examine and reflect upon that situation, and later to generalize and hypothesize about it in regard to other situations. One of the strong subthemes of *What Is English?* is Elbow's belief that "our thinking about professional and scholarly and theoretical matters is improved when the participants are committed teachers—are particularly teachers from all levels," kindergarten through college (1990, 218). Thus teaching does not just inform theory from a distance; teaching *is* theorizing, and teachers are theorists in the sense that they create new knowledge by examining and reflecting on the assumptions and principles that underlie the construction of their own particular classrooms.

Integrating Theory and Practice in Composition Studies

Given these shifting definitions of research and theory, as well as the relationship between theory and practice, we can now better understand the defensive stances of Jane Peterson (1991) and Howard Tinberg (1991). As community college faculty members who are deeply committed to the teaching of writing, they are reacting to developments in English studies which have created a hierarchical relationship between teaching and research, where teaching represents the low end of the hierarchy and theory the high point. They are reacting not to theory per se, but to the politics of theory—to a situation which promotes Theory at the expense of practice, as seen in the experiential evidence they bring to bear. Peterson notes, for example, that professionals in the field are always qualified in terms of their scholarship (what have they published lately?) and never in terms of their pedagogy (what teaching awards have they won?); that "classroom mentality" is a pejorative term in a way that "research mentality" could never be; and that teachers have internalized the profession's negative attitude toward pedagogy and therefore refer to themselves as "just teachers" (in the same way that many women, also the victims of a demeaning social hierarchy which devalues their work, refer to themselves as "just housewives"). Tinberg refers to the fact that teachers' narratives of their own classrooms are barely acknowledged at professional meetings and rarely printed in journals; that composition scholars such as Stephen North acknowledge the importance of teacher knowledge, yet reinforce its lack of credibility within the profession; and that "the tilt toward critical theory is nearly complete" in prestigious graduate programs in composition which eschew the pedagogical aspects of the field by discouraging students from taking jobs with heavy teaching loads so that they may devote more time to research. Both Peterson and Tinberg call for a better balance between theory and practice and name classroom-based inquiry as a means toward this end.

Composition teachers' current defensiveness in regard to theory and research need not be a problem within the field. In fact, it could be a healthy and productive sign of continued growth toward knowledge, according to scholars Louise Wetherbee Phelps and Patricia Harkin. Phelps urges us to consider that "the resistance of a wise practice to theory redeems us from the danger of claiming to predict or dictate human life rather than trying to explain or understand it. Practical wisdom reminds us that theoretical systems are never exhaustive or adequate to phenomena, and thus undercuts their totalizing tendencies" (1991, 884). And Harkin argues that, because practice blurs relations of cause and effect, it deals more effectively with "overdetermined" situations in which established disciplines have projected single cause-effect relationships, failed to admit contradictions, and have looked only "at what they recognize or, more precisely, see[n] only what they recognize no matter where they look" (1991, 130). Free of disciplinary constraints, practice (what Harkin calls "lore," following North) constructs knowledge much less narrowly: [U]nlike the linear, cause-and-effect relations that are represented by disciplinary techniques, lore arranges its data serially, spatially, paratactically, like a rhizome, however they work." As a result of this arrangement, lore can help us "avoid the unfortunate aspects of disciplinarity, particularly its tendency to simplify to the point of occulting its ideological implications and making us think that its narrowness is normal" (134–35).

I believe, along with Peterson and Tinberg, that teachers need to "reclaim the classroom" through careful observation of and reflection on their own teaching in order to have the counterbalancing influence on disciplinary knowledge making that Harkin describes. When teachers begin to engage in principled practice that recognizes their roles as knowledge makers, they will inevitably contribute to the making of composition theory by forcing other scholars to question their assumptions and conclusions.

There is also a pragmatic argument for seeing practitioners as knowledge makers in composition. If we accept Richard Fulkerson's recent definition of composition theory (1990), we cannot escape the fact that such theory can only be constructed with the full participation of teachers. He asserts that a theory of composition should consider what good writing is, how texts are created, how writing should be taught, and, more broadly, what constitutes knowledge in the field of composition studies. Because these questions must be addressed in a variety of contexts, both academic and nonacademic, it is not possible for composition scholars in universities to construct this knowledge independently. Compositionists in the 1990s will have to broaden their concept of "research" and "researchers," opening up the field to practitioners in a multitude of settings, listening to what they say, learning from their observations, and acknowledging the importance and credibility of what they know. In order for composition scholars and practitioners to establish this knowledge base together, they need to begin by acknowledging and respecting their differences, as well as their similarities:

> [T]he health of composition, and the reintegration of its two communities, depends on their ability to independently develop different strengths, in view of one another but without the domination of either. We must understand better what those different contributions are in order to achieve a just and productive partnership of equals. While thinking won't make it so, until we can *conceive* such an equality philosophically, we have no hope of making it politically viable. (Phelps 1991, 883)

The defensive stance of teachers, then, has the potential to force theorists to examine their assumptions, acknowledge the limitations of their research, and look to expert practitioners for help in constructing the field. In the next few chapters, I lay out some of the implications of taking a stance which integrates theory and practice. In Chapter 2, for example, I illustrate how American feminist critics have integrated theory and practice by drawing on women's experience and the personal knowledge born thereof. In Chapter 3, I provide a more detailed argument that the theory-practice relationship can be further developed in composition through teacher research by describing the intellectual and political forces underlying the K–12 movement in Great Britain, Australia, and the United States. In Chapters 4 and 5, I describe the specific knowledge created by two different groups of teachers—experienced K–12 teachers in the National Writing Project and students in a graduate seminar on teacher research. Chapter 6 argues for an alternative approach to teaching composition at the graduate level which encourages students to challenge and extend disciplinary techniques for creating knowledge. These latter chapters, which exemplify my own teacher research, enact my argument that teaching *can be* a form of theorizing and that teacher research is a valuable form of knowledge making.

2 Theory and Practice from a Feminist Perspective

[F]eminism is the site where the theory/practice nexus is being most creatively interrogated. . . . [Feminism's] long-standing tendencies toward self-reflexivity provide some experience of both rendering problematic and provisional our most firmly held assumptions and, nevertheless, acting in the world, taking a stand.

—Patti Lather, 1991

The tension between theory and practice is of course not unique to composition studies. It is prevalent in many other disciplines, especially those which have strong "service" or pragmatic roles inside or outside the university. There are, for example, longstanding intellectual and political debates between theoretical linguists and applied linguists, research psychologists and clinical practitioners, architects and drafters, sociologists and ethnographers. In this chapter, I consider one particular area of inquiry within English studies—feminist literary criticism—to show how feminists have challenged the assumptions underlying the theory-practice split and have proposed a reorientation toward theory that grows out of practice. My claim is that teacher-researchers can gain a perspective on the theory-practice relationship from feminist criticism, a perspective which, to use Patti Lather's phrase (1991), will make them a serious "contender for legitimacy" within the institutions they seek to change. Although feminist criticism is certainly not the only perspective from which teacher-researchers could articulate their purpose and politics, it is, I will argue, one that is most consistent with the teacher-research agenda. Feminist studies is particularly relevant, given the "feminization of composition" (Miller 1991a) and the fact that a majority of teachers and prospective teacher-researchers are women. Further, composition teachers have been a marginalized group, particularly within the university, just as women have been a politically and intellectually marginalized group within society. The teacher-researcher movement, then, can find in feminist studies an empowering argument and rationale for the importance of this work within universities.

I begin this discussion with a caveat: in these next pages, I focus exclusively on Anglo-American feminist criticism, with only passing reference to French feminist theory. The difference between the two, as Toril Moi notes in her *Sexual/Textual Politics* (1985), is one of intellectual tradition rather than national demarcation. Many scholars in American universities contribute to French feminist theory, although the reverse is not often true—French feminists, as a rule, do not practice Anglo-American feminist criticism. Why French feminism travels well and Anglo-American criticism does not is a subject for another book. The point here is that the two groups have very different agendas. They do not generally agree on the nature and purpose of feminist literary studies, on the uses of theory, or on the relationships between theory and practice.

Because I am here more interested in experience than textuality and in actively changing the perceived relationships between theory and practice, Anglo-American feminist criticism is more directly related to my purpose, for it "aims less to deconstruct than to construct" (Todd 1988, 41). Anglo-American feminist criticism is in large part "a mode of praxis. The point is not merely to interpret literature in various ways; the point is to *change the world* . . . [understanding that] literature acts on the world by acting on its readers" (Schweickart 1986, 39). The Anglo-American feminist perspective, given its origins in the women's movement, its focus on women's experience, and its emphasis on "grounded" or active theory, speaks directly to my interest in reorienting theory and practice in composition. French feminist criticism, with its basis in poststructuralist, deconstructive, and psychoanalytic theory, is more abstract; that is, it puts "the *idea* of woman before the *experience* of women" (Todd 1988, 14; emphasis mine). The problem with French feminism as a perspective from which to understand the relationship between theory and practice is "its ultimate antagonism to any political statement and any reformist activity: if everything is deconstructible, so are the very words that contain the notion, and there is nowhere a position from which to act" (Todd, 44). My discussion of *feminist criticism,* then, and my subsequent use of that term refer exclusively to the work of Anglo-American critics. Readers interested in the French feminist perspective are invited to examine the work of its exemplars, Helene Cixous, Luce Irigaray, and Julia Kristeva, as well as the many introductions to and commentaries on these works, including those by Moi, Janet Todd, and Elaine Marks and Isabelle de Courtivron.

Also by way of initial definition, I wish to delimit as clearly as possible what I mean by a "feminist" perspective and the practice of "feminist criticism." Acknowledging the different intellectual traditions, research paradigms, and conflicting political positions inherent in the term *feminist* as it is currently used by Anglo-American critics, I follow Rita Felski in adopting Alison Jaggar's broad definition as "all those forms of theory and practice that seek, no matter on what grounds and by what means, to end the subordination of women" (quoted in Felski 1989, 13). I follow Todd in adopting Patricia Spacks's definition of feminist criticism as "any mode that approaches a text with primary concern for the nature of the female experience in it—the fictional experience of characters, the deducible or imaginable experience of an author, the experience implicit in language or structure" (quoted in Todd 1988, 5), as well as the experience of the female reader and critic. I would add to these formulations another distinguishing feature of both feminism and feminist criticism: both insist that we acknowledge differences, not only of gender, but also of race, class, and sexual orientation. These definitions resonate for me as a teacher-researcher working in a field which has been attempting to dissociate itself, through theory and research, from the daily practices of teaching. For me, the feminist agenda directly parallels the teacher-research agenda: teacher research approaches composition with a primary concern for the nature of teachers' and students' experiences; it seeks to end the subordination of teachers to researchers; and it attempts to end the domination of theory over practice. In the process, teacher research, too, focuses on particularities and differences in the ways that teaching and learning transpire.

It should be noted, too, that these definitions are working constructs—negotiated meanings that are not meant to suggest general agreement among feminists. Diversity and change are primary traits of feminist criticism. Thus current theorists acknowledge that the category of "woman" must become plural rather than singular so as to account for differences within feminist discourse, as well as between feminist and other critical discourses. That is to say, there is not one feminism but many feminisms. Flynn and Schweickart describe the problem of generalizing about feminism while trying to account for differences:

> The play of difference presupposes and induces a play of identity. Every feminist theorist is faced with the challenge of devising a rhetoric that avoids the repressive exclusions that could ensue from theoretical constructs, a rhetoric of equivocal generalizations, if you will, that incorporates gestures pointing to the provisional and heuristic status of the categories in which her work is phrased. (1986, xiv)

I see the meanings of *feminist* and *feminist criticism* to be in a healthy state of flux, and I ask the reader to accept with me the provisional status of these terms for the purposes of the discussion to follow.

Why Feminist Criticism?

Feminist criticism is rich in insights for composition studies. Indeed, composition scholars are showing a heightened interest in feminist studies these days. At the 1990 Conference on College Composition and Communication, twenty-one papers were presented on gender and writing, a category which did not exist in the program three years previously. Major publications such as *College Composition and Communication* and the *Journal of Advanced Composition* have called for articles on the relationships between gender and writing, feminist theory and composition theory. And collections are beginning to appear on gender and pedagogy (Gabriel and Smithson 1990; Caywood and Overing 1987). The appeal of feminist studies is understandable, as Elizabeth Flynn (1988) has pointed out, given that composition studies has been shaped in large part by women (among them Janet Emig, Mina Shaughnessy, Ann Berthoff, Winifred Horner, Maxine Hairston, Shirley Brice Heath, Linda Flower, and Andrea Lunsford) and given that "the marginality of the field of composition studies is linked in important ways to the political marginality of its constituents, many of whom are women who teach part-time" (Flynn 1988, 424). Since feminists have worked to better understand the struggles of oppressed groups through knowledge of the social and political systems which oppress them, it is understandable that compositionists, who see themselves as an oppressed group in academe, would look to feminist discourse. Many compositionists have assumed the position of cultural and institutional marginality, thereby making a political and rhetorical decision to "exaggerat[e] [their] difficulties 'in order to develop in one another a sense of heroic solidarity in the face of overwhelming odds'" (Ruthven quoted in Todd 1988, 8).

Specifically, composition researchers have looked to feminist work in literature (primarily that of Adrienne Rich and Elaine Showalter) and to feminist studies in the social sciences (primarily those of Carol Gilligan, Nancy Chodorow, and Mary Field Belenky et al.) for a language and perspective from which to articulate their experience and thinking about "gendered" writing, teaching, and learning. As a result of these research connections, teachers and scholars in the field are working toward developing a "feminist theory of composition" (Lamb 1991). The merging of feminist literary theory and composition involves identifying androcentrism in composition research and pedagogy—evidenced by an emphasis on individualism, hierarchical thinking, strong boundaries, and an adversarial stance—and recuperating "feminine" modes of thinking—evidenced by an emphasis on relatedness, mutuality, flexible boundaries, and a nonoppositional stance (Flynn 1991, 6). The merging of these two areas, as well as the theoretical implications of this merger for knowledge making in the field, will undoubtedly be one of the richest subjects of inquiry for compositionists in the next few years.

Feminist studies has much to offer teacher research in particular, as well as composition studies in general. There are many instructive parallels between feminist literary criticism and teacher research, not the least of which is their shared goal of addressing inaccuracies and inequities in research and teaching. Both are redemptive and revisionary in nature and purpose. Teacher-researchers have sought to reveal and challenge the "false hierarchy of knowledge" (Knoblauch and Brannon 1988), which privileges and valorizes the role of theory and university theorists, while ignoring and trivializing the role of teaching and teachers in the making of knowledge. Their method has been to reevaluate the meaning of teaching, reconsider the purposes of research, challenge the processes by which research is conducted, and broaden the community within which research is generated and shared. Feminist critics, similarly, have sought to reveal and challenge the power relations inscribed in texts through which divisive assumptions and practices are perpetuated. Their method has been to recover the works of women writers, reread the canon, reevaluate aesthetic criteria, challenge the epistemological assumptions underlying traditional theory and criticism, and revise the curriculum to include feminist thinking and writing. Both teacher research and feminist criticism have been motivated by a desire to bring the marginal to the center, and both attempt to give voice and status to diverse groups in minority positions.

Further, both feminist criticism and teacher research have been called "revolutionary" in the challenges they pose to established lines of authority and in the changes they seek. (Teacher research, though, is a "quiet revolution," as Richard Bullock [1987] indicates, while feminist criticism most assuredly is not.) Both groups have questioned the assumptions underlying traditional research and theory, including the "killer dichotomies" (Berthoff 1987) of reason versus feeling, general versus particular, public versus private, objectivity versus subjectivity, and theory versus practice. Speaking for feminist critics, Sandra Gilbert notes that "feminist connections between the personal and the political, the theoretical and the practical, renew those bonds of feeling and thought that T. S. Eliot, that paradigmatic patriarchal critic, regarded as irrevocably severed" (1985, 40). Similarly, teacher-researchers, as Knoblauch and Brannon indicate, rely on a phenomenological model of inquiry which asserts "the inseparableness of observer and object observed, the inevitable reflexivity of human research" (1988, 19). Glenda Bissex (1987) has adopted the term "dynamic objectivity" from the work of feminist scientist Evelyn Fox Keller, who defines the term in the following words:

> Dynamic objectivity aims at a form of knowledge that grants to the world around us its independent integrity but does so in a way that remains cognizant of, indeed relies on, our connectivity with that world. In this, dynamic objectivity is not unlike empathy, a form of knowledge of other persons that draws explicitly on the commonality of feelings and experiences in order to enrich one's understanding of another in his or her own right. (Fox Keller 1985, 117)

Researchers who work from the perspective of dynamic objectivity feel a "kinship" with their subjects and thus seek to understand and learn from them, not to control or dominate them, as researchers following the traditional scientific paradigm have done.

Perhaps the most significant parallel between feminist research and teacher research is the fact that both challenge and extend established epistemologies or theories of knowledge. They raise new questions about who can know, what can be known, what constitutes evidence for knowledge, and what kind of knowledge is valued:

> Feminists have argued that traditional epistemologies, whether intentionally or unintentionally, systematically exclude the possibility that women could be "knowers" or *agents of knowledge;* they claim that the voice of science is a masculine one; that history is written from only the point of view of men (of the dominant class and race); that the subject of a traditional sociological sentence is always assumed to be a man. They have proposed alternative theories of knowledge that legitimate women as knowers. (Malson et al. 1986, 3; emphasis theirs)

Similarly, teacher-researchers have asserted—more often implicitly than explicitly—that traditional epistemologies systematically exclude the possibility that *teachers* can be knowers or agents of knowledge. They claim that the voice of most research and theory is not the teacher's voice and that the history of education has been written predominantly from the researcher's point of view, with little or no acknowledgment of the teacher's perspective. Teacher-researchers have begun to question what ethnographer James Clifford calls the "specification of discourses," asking "who speaks, who writes? when and where? with or to whom? under what institutional and historical constraints?" (1988, 13). Given these parallels, teacher-researchers can take from feminist studies ways to address these questions, specify their own discourse, and legitimate themselves as knowledge makers within the field of composition studies.

The parallels between the feminist movement and the teacher-research movement clearly exist, but very little has been made of this connection in composition studies (although Sandra Hollingsworth [1990b] has drawn the parallels in her research on teacher training in education). Yet feminist literary criticism can provide directions for developing a practice of theory as well as a theory of practice in the field of composition. One of the most significant contributions of feminist criticism is its response to the "race for theory" in literary studies. Amidst the movement in English departments toward increasingly theoretical scholarship, many feminist critics have insisted on the equal importance of personal experience and the *practice* of feminism to theoretical knowledge making in English studies. The strength of Anglo-American feminism has been "its political implications, its refusal to separate the project of feminist criticism from the project of feminism, however defined" (Todd 1988, 135).

The Race for Theory in Feminist Criticism

The place of theory has been at the center of much debate in feminist studies. The primary issue, as articulated by feminists, has been what the connections are, if any, between feminist "empirical" studies, which claim gender differences on the basis of textual evidence, and modern critical theory, which takes a more philosophical approach. The problem is that, "while feminist criticism was one of the daughters of the women's movement, its other parent was the old patriarchal institution of literary criticism and theory; and it has had to come to terms with the meaning of its mixed origins" (Showalter 1985b, 8). In addition, since the mid-1970s, the highly theoretical writing of British and French feminists has circulated widely in the United States. This work, and that of other contemporary literary theorists, directly challenges many of the assumptions underlying Anglo-American feminist writing, most notably the humanist belief in a unified self, the possibility of an "authentic" representation of that self in writing, the question of essential differences between men and women, and the existence of a "reality" that women experience uniquely and convey directly in their writing. Given these theoretical issues and the fact that feminist criticism, in order to be taken seriously within academe, must "satisfy the very criteria it is trying to challenge and subvert," "[t]he aspiring feminist critic . . . has apparently only two options: to work to reform those criteria from within the academic institution, producing a judicious critical discourse that strives to maintain its feminism without grossly upsetting the academic establishment, or to write off the academic criteria of evaluation as reactionary and of no importance to her work" (Moi 1985, 23).

Many early feminist critics took the second option. They addressed the issue of theory defensively, asking not so much "what can theory do for us?" but "what might theory do *to* us?" In other words, will the adoption or revision of Marxist, structuralist, and poststructuralist theories enlighten or diminish the feminist enterprise? (Showalter 1985b). Sandra Gilbert and Susan Gubar frame the question this way: "By placing feminist criticism in the context of the predominantly patriarchal history of ideas, are we implying that such criticism can or should be aligned with traditions that have almost always been oppressive to women? How, after all, can feminist theory be continuous with the modes of thought it seeks to disrupt?" (1989, 165). In their introduction to *Feminist Theory in Practice and Process,* Micheline Malson et al. (1986) raise the same issue, arguing that, if theory is an endeavor of generalizing and abstracting and if feminist studies is by definition a "critique of totalizing systems in the male tradition," then how and why would feminists want to embrace theory, much less try to articulate a single feminist Theory?

This same issue, I would argue, underlies teacher research. The parallel questions here are: Why would teachers want to embrace theory and what is the place, if any, of theory in the conceptualization and articulation of teacher research? Possible answers to these questions can be found in American feminist critics' response to the call for theory.

One response is that of Barbara Christian (1989), who suggests that feminists resist "the race for theory," which she believes leads toward overgeneralizations, restrictive definitions of feminism, alienating language and style, exclusivity, elitism, and hegemony. Also taking this position is Nina Baym, who argues in "Why I Don't Do Feminist Theory" that by valorizing theory, feminists are merely trying to appease an audience of prestigious male critics in order to win its respect. She finds that feminist criticism succeeds in academe only when it dismisses earlier feminist criticism as "naïve" and grounds its analysis in the theories "currently in vogue with the men who make theory" (1987, 45). For her, current literary theory is totalizing and prescriptive, as well as judgmental and constraining; as such, it defeats the feminist agenda. The main suspicion about theory is perhaps best explained by Mia Campioni and Elizabeth Gross in their article on Marxism and feminism: "Why is it necessary to unify/ solidify what may be fluid, diverse and changing, if not in order to block and control it? Diverse, changeable, strategic knowledges pose a potential threat that must be minimized—that of the incapacity of theory, of *any* theory to capture reality in its entirety or in its essence" (1983, 127; quoted in Lather 1991, 24).

These arguments are a reaction to the epistemological position on theory described in Chapter 1 as theory-with-a-capital-*T*. From this position, theory is a privileged method of analysis upon a prescribed body of texts which gains status by excluding and negating other methods. The early feminist response to it perfectly illustrates Elbow's prediction that those who practice the excluded methods will react defensively and "treat theory as the enemy" (1990, 57).

Another response to the call for theory, a far more convincing one, is for feminists to accept the importance of theory, but to see it in terms of the alternative epistemological position described in Chapter 1 as theory-with-a-small-*t*. This position grants much less status to theory, considering it a lens or perspective from which to examine beliefs and assumptions. From this position, there are many valuable theories and many perspectives from which to analyze texts.

Feminist critics Showalter and Malson et al. argue from this second position on theory. In "Feminist Criticism in the Wilderness," Showalter, citing Geertz, proposes that feminists practice the close analysis and "thick description" that characterize cultural anthropology. She asserts that

> no theory, however suggestive, can be a substitute for the close and extensive knowledge of women's texts which constitutes our essential subject. Cultural anthropology and social history can perhaps offer us a terminology and a diagram of women's cultural situation. But feminist critics must use this concept in relation to what women actually write, not in relation to a theoretical, political, metaphorical, or visionary ideal of what women ought to write. (1985a, 266)

Malson et al., in their characterization of Anglo-American feminist theory, also emphasize the importance of "envision[ing] theories that encompass . . . lived realities and concrete practices," thereby hoping to "escape creating overly deterministic constructs and instead to encourage notions of subjectivity that recognize a mutable historical position" (1986, 6–7).

These feminists realize that a criticism with women's experience at its base appears naïvely empirical and essentialist in an age of psychoanalytic criticism and poststructuralism, where the play of language and an all-encompassing "textuality" problematize many assumptions underlying Anglo-American criticism. Yet Todd persuasively challenges the French-inspired critiques of Anglo-American criticism. She argues that, in its substitution of an intellectual construct—the "women effect"—for a material and political reality—"woman"—feminism

> inevitably dies in the exchange, since, if there is no woman in the representations of history, only representation itself, then there is no one to liberate. Feminism as simply the complex play of humanist ideology is obviously no feminism at all and it can easily be dematerialized into an anachronism. And yet there are women still; they do not get jobs because they are women, they raise children alone because they are women, and they write out of the same indestructible fact. (1988, 80)[1]

Showalter makes a slightly different argument, claiming that Anglo-American criticism is "as theoretically sophisticated as its continental sister" (1987, 36) in its interrogation of all texts and its attempts to characterize and ascribe value to the female imagination. While Todd sees French and Anglo-American criticism as conflicting perspectives which are mutually exclusive, Showalter sees them as two different directions within the history of one feminist criticism. While the French critics have moved toward what Alice Jardine (1985) calls gynesis (an exploration of textual representations of sexual difference), Anglo-American critics have moved toward what Showalter calls gynocritics (a sociohistorical exploration of women's writing which accounts for variables such as race, class, and culture). These two perspectives need not be in opposition, but can instead inform each other, "enriched by dialectical possibilities" in ways that allow feminist criticism to proceed on both fronts (Showalter 1987, 37). The dialectic relationship between French and Anglo-American feminist criticism, then, works in this way: "If literary theory can be used to illuminate contemporary feminist writing, it is also the case that aspects of women's current literary practices can be drawn upon to problematize the more abstract and speculative claims of feminist theory" (Felski 1989, 1).

To accommodate both Anglo-American feminist criticism and French feminist criticism under the rubric of "feminist theory,"

Showalter must conceive of "theory" in broader terms than is popular in current literary studies. The two, after all, have very different origins and agendas. Anglo-American feminist criticism has its roots in the women's movement; consequently, its interests are social and political, as well as textual. American feminist critics have focused on reevaluating women's writing and developing a feminist canon, while also supporting the publication of more women's writing and the increase of women's representation and power in English studies. French feminist criticism, with its roots in the theories of Lacan and Derrida, is a more philosophical exploration of the production of sexual difference in language. French feminist critics have shown comparatively little interest in challenging the literary canon or establishing a feminist one. To see the two criticisms as part of the same feminist theory, Showalter must conceive of "theory" in the way that Gerald Graff proposes—as "a discourse that is generated when assumptions and concepts which once went without saying have become objects of discussion and dispute," including concepts such as text, author, reader, meaning, and interpretation (Graff 1989, 254). Such analysis requires a critical perspective and a willingness to reflect on one's own thinking. In other words, "when intellectual critique is reflexive and self-critical, that is, when it both questions *and* questions how its questions have been and are being posed, then intellectual critique is truly philosophical" and therefore theoretical (Young-Bruehl 1986, 37; emphasis hers). These broader constructs open up the province of theorizing, ascribing as much value to interpretive, provisional theories as to grand, all-encompassing ones.

The Relationship between Feminist Theory and Feminist Practice

In adopting the alternative position on theory, how have Anglo-American feminists such as Showalter sought to integrate this theory with feminist practice? And to what effect, politically and intellectually? One answer to these questions is that, by situating feminist theory within the broader social context of the feminist movement, feminist critics have worked to integrate more fully personal experience, political activism, and intellectualizing.

A characteristic feature of Anglo-American feminist criticism is its emphasis on the personal—on the lived experiences of author, reader, and critic. Proponents consider this creative and imaginative personalizing to be responsible in large part for the enduring political influence of feminist criticism. Indeed, Todd asserts that "one of the strengths of feminist criticism has been its welcoming of the personal, however crude, naïve and untheorized it may sometimes appear and however problematic and constructed the self can be assumed to be. It still remains a refreshing emphasis that the reader is a subject herself and that she does not spend all her time reading" (1988, 7). Much early feminist criticism in particular relied heavily on the expression of personal experience, including the critic's thoughts and feelings as a woman reading men's texts in patriarchal institutions. The appeal of books such as Judith Fetterley's *The Resisting Reader* (1978) attests to the role these personal narratives played in the consciousness raising of women readers. As Fetterley recalls, "It took feminism to enable me finally to see and understand the extraordinary gap between theory and practice in the teaching of literature as I experienced it. . . . Regardless of the theory offered in justification, as it is currently practiced within the academy, reading functions primarily to rein-force the identity and perspective which the male teacher/reader brings to the text" (1986, 150). Fetterley proposes that women resist the established readings and develop their own meanings based on personal experiences and perspectives, thus challenging the pre-mises of traditionally sanctioned interpretations (153).

Feminist critics have also revealed academic and intellectual backgrounds as part of their critical discourse. For example, in her "Women's Time: Women's Space," Showalter discusses in some detail her position in the late 1960s as "a faculty wife with a small child trying to write what seemed to be a hopeless dissertation on the double critical standard applied to Victorian women novelists" (1987, 34). At the time, there were few precedents for Showalter's scholarship, and the prospects for publication and a professional future built on women's writing seemed slim. Not until she joined the women's movement did she come to see her work and her struggles to articulate its importance as both a personal and a political issue. She came to see that "passionate" interest in women's writing was related to her own situation as a writer working on the margins of a patriarchal academy. Thus criticism, for Showalter, provided a means of connecting with other women writers, understanding herself as a writer, and situating her work within a larger sociohistorical context that gave it broader meaning and purpose. Showalter's experiences as a writer, which she suggests represent those of most early feminist critics, provide the impetus for her later formulation of gynocritics: "The interest in women's writing . . . that is crucial to gynocritics preceded theoretical formulations and came initially from the femi-nist critic's own experiences as a writer and from her identification with the anxieties and conflicts women writers faced in patriarchal culture" (39). For this reason, Showalter believes that a history of feminist criticism, if she were to write one, would include the personal stories of pioneers in the field: "It would explain how Gilbert met Gubar, how Catharine Stimpson and Domna Stanton came to edit *Signs,* how the Bunting Institute became a critical community. It would include the voices of black and lesbian and Marxist feminist critics discussing the factors of race, sexuality, and class" (34).

The personal voice of feminist writing sends several powerful messages, both implicit and explicit. It is effective, in part, because it seems daring; the critic appears to be taking great personal risks in eschewing the authoritative voice of academe, addressing her own questions and exposing her insecurities. Personal writing seems decidedly "nonacademic," which makes it especially persuasive to feminist readers who equate "academic" with that which is totalizing, patriarchal, hegemonic. Further, personal writing is accessible to nonacademics, for it invites all readers to enter the discourse on their own experiential terms; a feminist discourse with such a wide appeal is appropriate, given that academics make up only a small percentage of the feminist readership. In contrast, much academic discourse excludes readers who do not share the highly specialized philosophical language and theoretical knowledge of the author.

The use of the personal by feminists is both a rhetorical and a political stance. Elisabeth Young-Bruehl discusses the appeal of first-person feminist texts in which critics "start their inquiries on the ground of their subjectivities" (1991, 15). She supports the feminist-inspired "autobiographical turn" of recent academic writing, claiming that

> those scholars, who, writing from multicultural or suppressed cultural perspectives, construct their work around the scrupulous observation of their "I's" are creating the most compelling texts in academia today. These texts place directly and continually before all of us questions about how anyone can understand present forms of sexism or racism or cultural imperialism who has not experienced them. And they remind scholars that the mystery of identity and its relationship to culture can never be banished from scholarship—no matter how supposedly objective are its procedures and products. (18)

Young-Bruehl also points out that scholarship in the first-person can be compelling and empowering for the scholar who is writing it. When done well, such writing is insightful and exploratory; it pushes the writer into new territory, both personal and intellectual. The "I's" of the best autobiographical scholarship "feel as though they have

gotten onto the page only after a long journey, a long private appren-
ticeship in self-knowledge" (18).

The personal voice in feminist writing has, in addition, served as
a means of political activism. It is, in effect, a form of consciousness
raising, where consciousness refers to "a collective process that both
comprehends social structures and acts upon them" and consciousness raising refers to "the process that mediates between our inner and
outer worlds" (Malson et al. 1986, 6). The phrase "to mediate between
our inner and outer worlds" resonates for most feminist critics, whose
academic training has taught them that they must separate the
intellectual from the personal and purge their writing of the influences of an inner life. The effect of this dichotomizing is, as many
critics have discovered, self-negating and stultifying. In "Me and My
Shadow" (1989), Jane Tompkins exposes this conflict in what the
editors of *Lingua franca* have called "a kind of manifesto for personal
writing":

> These beings [the Duke University critic and the person Jane
> Tompkins] exist separately but not apart. One writes for profes-
> sional journals, the other in diaries, late at night. One uses words
> like "context" and "intelligibility," likes to win arguments, see
> her name in print, and give graduate students hardheaded advice.
> The other has hardly ever been heard from. She had a short story
> published once in a university literary magazine, but her works
> exist chiefly in notebooks and manila folders labelled "Journal"
> and "Private." This person talks on the telephone a lot to her
> friends, has seen psychiatrists, likes cappuccino, worries about
> the state of her soul. Her father is ill right now, and one of her
> friends recently committed suicide. (quoted in *Lingua franca*
> 1991, 1[3]:19)

What Tompkins is doing, to use another resounding phrase, is an act
of power, and she is asking all women writers to join her in it: "The
public-private dichotomy, which is to say, the public-private hierarchy is a founding condition of female oppression. I say to hell with it"
(quoted in *Lingua franca*, 19).[2] Tompkins is also asserting the need to
write about the dichotomy, for, in the words of Sandra Harding, "until
our dualistic practices are changed (divisions of social experience
into mental versus manual, into abstract versus concrete, into emotional versus emotion denying), we are forced to think and exist
within the very dichotomizing we criticize. . . . We cannot afford to
dismiss them as irrelevant as long as they structure our lives and our
consciousness" (1987, 32).

Feminists are not, however, saying that the personal voice is
inherently "good" or "right" or "true." Rather, they are saying that it

cannot and should not be denied or resisted. From the feminist perspective, the integration of the public and the private make both discourses better—more accountable to their various constituencies. The private speaks for the multiple voices within; the public speaks for the multiple voices without. In its grounding in the writer's personal experience, as well as other women's experiences, feminist writing claims that "there is no such thing as a problem without a person (or groups of them) who have this problem; a problem is always a problem *for* someone or other" (Harding 1987, 6). Further, such writing, in generating its problematics from the perspective of women's experiences "also uses these experiences as a significant indicator of the 'reality' against which hypotheses are tested . . . the goal of this inquiry is to provide for women explanations of social phenomena that they want and need" (7–8).

What effect has this feminist perspective had on criticism and theory making in academe? It has had an enormous effect on women writers and feminist critics. It has had less effect on changing the (still largely male-inspired) institution of literary criticism. Those writing histories of literary criticism, with the exception of pro-feminist versions such as Terry Eagleton's *Literary Theory* (1983), still "miss the accounts of real confrontations between critical positions" because their abstractions are "too coarse to accommodate the false starts, the lucky breaks, the material pressures, the intellectual slog, or, least of all, the human drama that make up a living critical movement" (Showalter 1987, 33). However, there is growing evidence that modern critical theory is coming to respect and embrace feminist criticism. For example, Showalter sees promise in the trend among male literary theorists such as Eagleton "to acknowledge that feminist criticism offers a paradigm for the kind of criticism they really want to do, that it seems to offer a way out of the labyrinth of indeterminacy, non-interference and self-referentiality post-structuralism has built for itself" (42). And she is hopeful that modern criticism in general, taking its cue from feminist criticism, will "begin to question the myths of its own immaculate conception in the realms of pure and universal thought" (42).

Teacher Research from a Feminist Perspective

What might teacher-researchers learn from the ways feminist critics have articulated the relationships between theory and practice? To begin with, teacher research that is informed by feminist studies would assert the importance of diversity in knowledge making; it would claim that the methods of teacher research are as essential to the making of composition theory as any other research methods. Taking their cue from feminist studies, teacher-researchers would insist on their status as theory makers. Further, they would turn their analyses onto themselves, as well as their classrooms, to discuss and dispute the assumptions underlying teacher research and the research paradigms it challenges. In so doing, they would recognize the rhetorical and political power inherent in the personal voice, affirming the importance of their experiential knowledge as teachers. Finally, teacher-researchers, viewing their work from a feminist perspective, would find confirmation in the fact that their challenge to current perspectives on research and theory has the dynamic potential to create a rethinking and a reevaluation of composition studies as it is now constructed.

Just as no totalizing literary theory can account for the differences in race, class, and gender that feminist criticism acknowledges, no totalizing composition theory can account for the differences across classrooms and educational contexts that teacher research conveys. Teachers are in the unique position of being able to speak from within the classroom and represent the voices of their students—voices that are seldom heard in the formal conversations of academic research. The questions that teachers pose from within the worlds of their classrooms are indeed close to the heart of education. They are questions like the ones that motivated Shirley Brice Heath's ten-year ethnographic study of literacy, *Ways with Words*. The guiding question for Heath, which grew out of concerns raised by teachers in her training course, was this: "What [are] the effects of preschool home and community environments on the learning of those language structures and uses which [are] needed in classrooms and job settings?" (1983, 2). Significant questions such as this underlie other teacher inquiry, such as Sondra Perl and Nancy Wilson's study of six teachers in the Shoreham-Wading River School District. In his foreword to Perl and Wilson's *Through Teachers' Eyes*, James Moffett says that the classroom-generated issues underlying this teacher-research project include questions "about what a process approach to writing actually is, whether it always succeeds, and whether teachers are attracted to it for personal reasons they will have to come to grips with. Does good teaching depend more on the person than the process?" (1986, x–xi). These are the kinds of direct and personal questions that research and theory cannot answer without teachers.

One of the most compelling arguments of feminist criticism is that theory is the province of everyone. If we see theory as "an enlargement of observation" (Coles 1989, 20) and a discourse that disputes previously accepted assumptions and concepts which once went without saying (Graff 1989), then teacher research is theory of the highest order. A feminist perspective on theory removes the capital letters from the concept and ascribes as much value to interpretive, provisional knowledge making as it does to grand, all-encompassing theorizing. From this perspective, the writing of teachers is just as important to knowledge making in composition as the model building of formalists, the controlled studies of experimentalists, and the abstract conceptualizing of philosophers and critics. It means that there is as much power in the particular as there is in the general. As Howard Tinberg argues in his article on theory building in the classroom:

> To be both on the inside and on the outside, to be both in the field and in the study, to be immersed in local detail and to be observing all from a theoretical perspective: such is what is demanded both of the ethnographer and the classroom teacher. The stories that are told by the classroom teacher, like those told by the ethnographer, can be seen as the construction of all these perspectives. They should be read as we would read allegories, containing many voices and many strata of voices. It is time, I think, that the stories of the classroom be read and that they be read as genuine meaning-making, not least of all by the teachers themselves. From such a reading, I believe, can come an "enlargement of observation." (1991, 41)

Current scholarship in ethnography, which informs much teacher research, supports Tinberg's claim that presenting the particular, in the form of protracted descriptions which emphasize local detail, is important to the making of knowledge. Geertz argues for the relevance of such thick description to the social sciences:

> The important thing about anthropologists' findings is their complex specificness, their circumstantiality. It is with the kind of material produced by long-term, mainly (though not exclusively) qualitative, highly participative, and almost obsessively fine-comb field study in confined contexts that mega-concepts with which contemporary social science is afflicted . . . can be given the sort of sensible actuality that makes it possible to think not only realistically and concretely *about* them, but, what is more important, creatively and imaginatively *with* them. (1983, 23; emphasis his)

Thus teacher research, in its particularity, can provide ways of thinking more concretely and imaginatively about and with the "mega-concepts" in composition, such as how discourse and meaning are socially constructed; what it means to "read" a text, including a student text; how reading and writing inform one another; how speaking and writing interrelate; how a text enters into a "conversation" of texts, including that of the classroom; how power relations are inscribed in texts and learning contexts; and how literacy education is and is not served by the institutional imperatives under which teachers and students live and work.

A common feature of ethnography, as Geertz describes it, and feminist inquiry, as Sandra Harding (1987) and others define it, is a tendency toward reflexivity—the willingness to observe oneself as the observer and to acknowledge the tentative, interpretive, and political nature of one's observations. Moi sees this prpensity as one of the major contributions of American feminist criticism, for it

> supports the basic feminist contention that no criticism is "value-free," that we all speak from a specific position shaped by cultural, social, political and personal factors. It is authoritarian and manipulative to present this limited perspective as "universal," feminists claim, and the only democratic procedure is to supply the reader with all necessary information about the limitations of one's own perspective at the outset. (1985, 43)

Although the feminist critic recognizes that she can never fully understand what motivates her, or grasp her own understandings, she makes an effort to do so, and she shares her thinking with the reader. This approach points "to the discomforting fact that we are unable to do much more than partially describe what it is we know or do. We know more than we can say and will know even more after saying it" (Van Maanen 1988, 123). Similarly, contemporary ethnographers often turn their attention to themselves as researchers, acknowledging the subjectivity of their work and making it part of their study of a particular culture. In the telling of what John Van Maanen calls "confessional" tales,

> fieldwork constructs now are seen by many to emerge from a hermeneutic process; fieldwork is an interpretive act, not an observational or descriptive one. . . . This process begins with the explicit examination of one's own preconceptions, biases, and motives, moving forward in a dialectic fashion toward understanding by way of a continuous dialogue between the interpreter and interpreted. (93)

Mary Louise Pratt, in "Fieldwork in Common Places," makes the convincing case that personal narrative has always been a conventional component of academe, including the social sciences. She calls it an "anthropological subgenre" that, "not having been killed by science," has persisted over a long history, beginning with early travel accounts, despite the "confusion and ambiguity" it causes among social scientists (1986, 31). Pratt's explanation for the endurance of personal writing is that it creates a necessary balance within the discipline between personal and scientific authority. Evidence of an imbalance is apparent in much traditional ethnographic writing, which Pratt finds "surprisingly boring," given the interesting people and situations on which it is based. Personal writing enlivens such ethnography, for it

> mediates [the] contradiction between the engagement called for in fieldwork and the self-effacement called for in formal ethnographic description, or at least mitigates some of its anguish, by inserting into the ethnographic text the authority of the personal experience out of which ethnography is made. . . . That is why such narratives have not been killed by science, and why they are worth looking at, especially to people interested in countering the tendency toward alienation and dehumanization in much conventional ethnographic description. (33)

In anthropology, the personal narrative typically introduces or is placed alongside a more traditional "realist" account of a culture, though narratives in book form have been published as well. Pratt concludes that, through these alternative representations, "anthropologists stand to gain from looking at themselves as writing inside as well as outside the discursive traditions that precede them; inside as well as outside the histories of contact on which they follow. Such a perspective is particularly valuable for people who would like to change or enrich the discursive repertoire of ethnographic writing" (49). Such a perspective, too, would remind us, as Ann Berthoff and Glenda Bissex do, that "research" means to look and look again and that this process takes on many forms. Bissex entreats us to "enlarge our gallery of images of researchers to include not only the white-coated scientist but also the naturalist in the salt marsh observing wild ducks, the parent carefully recording a child's monologues, the ethnographers in New Guinea observing and experiencing life in a different culture, and the teacher listening to tapes of his own writing conferences" (Bissex 1987, 14).

Teacher-researchers as individuals can gain a deeper understanding, and the teacher-research movement in general can develop a better sense of itself in terms of other research paradigms, by engaging in introspection and personal, reflective writing. Teacher-researchers might begin by asking themselves questions such as these: How have I come to know what I think I know? What values, beliefs, and assumptions about learning and teaching inform my work with students and colleagues? What other ways of knowing may conflict with my ways? How do I respond when I encounter these conflicts in my classroom? Asking such questions of oneself can be difficult, even threatening, but it can also be, as Patrocinio Schweickart says of the personal narrative in feminist writing, "a kind of therapeutic analysis. . . . The feminist reader hopes that other women will recognize themselves in her story, and join in her struggle to transform the culture" (1986, 50–51). One of the best ways for a reader to recognize herself in another's story—and perchance to act on that recognition—is to read an honest account of struggle in the face of intellectual and personal challenges. This is an important point for teacher-researchers to keep in mind as they attempt to motivate other teachers to conduct classroom inquiry.

In order to be self-reflexive, teacher-researchers could also begin to construct texts around what Young-Bruehl has called the "scrupulous observation of their 'I's'" (1991, 18). She uses the word "scrupulous" advisedly, pointing out that

> identity is not insight. And autobiography that ends where it began, that defensively or offensively armors an identity rather than journeys in search of one, is simply a weapon, not an education. Simone de Beauvoir once issued a warning about such confusions of être and écrire: "I think one must be able to say 'No: no, that won't do! Write something else, try and do better. Set higher standards for yourselves! Being a woman is not enough!'" (17)

Teacher-researchers need to develop the same self-critical perspective as feminist critics and to set increasingly higher standards for their thinking and researching. Bissex describes the necessary relationship between teachers and their research this way:

> No single research design, no single angle of vision or set of assumptions, will enable us to see the whole picture. We need methods that will allow us to use our empathy and intuition while giving us the distance to look critically, as a writer alternates between the roles of involved creator and critical reader of his own work. (Bissex 1987, 13)

Observation of themselves in the classroom is how teacher-researchers initiate the reflexive "autobiographical turn." And it is what can empower teachers, as well as enliven and enrich the field of composition studies. What has been true for feminists can also be true for teacher-researchers: "[E]fforts to define an authentic self have been, for many women writers and intellectuals, the most personally gratifying feminist activity of the last decade" (Young-Bruehl 1991,

16). And this is in spite of the fact that "to deconstructionists and semioticians, the notion that language could be about (or used on behalf of) the self is one of those old-fashioned notions that should be 'problematized'" (16). Those who resist the idea that research and theory making can be autobiographical might consider Donald Murray's claim (1991) that all writing, including scholarship, is autobiographical because it draws on one's past experiences, unique ways of looking at the world, and particular uses of language to communicate what is seen.

Personal writing in composition theory would lead to more accounts of teachers' own ways of seeing and knowing and would reveal their particular conflicts and confusions. These texts would question, challenge, and move beyond the discursive practices of current composition research. This is the kind of teacher research that Sandra Hollingsworth has recently called for in her addresses to the American Educational Research Association and the American Association of Colleges of Teacher Education, as well as in her articles on teacher training. It is not surprising that Hollingsworth comes to this perspective from Anglo-American feminist studies (she cites Mary Field Belenky et al., Carol Gilligan, Sandra Harding, and Sara Ruddick). In her introduction to "Learning to Teach the Culturally Diverse through Collaborative Conversation: A Feminist Pedagogy," Hollingsworth reveals the feminist influence in her self-reflective stance toward knowledge making in education:

> I have recently been experiencing quite a bit of self-doubt and confusion about my work as a teacher educator. I wonder if what I am doing is really supportive of many beginning teachers as they move through culturally familiar teacher education programs and into complex and—quite often—culturally different classroom settings. Or I wonder whether I've simply been attempting to be true to what is currently valued in teacher education, to see if they value my expertise by using what I've told them, and/or to support an academic career for myself by reporting the results of what *I* learn from *them*. Some of my friends call my confusion a mid-life crisis. Some of my colleagues call it a misguided movement away from the established principles of research and educational theory. Other colleagues, friends and many of my teachers and students call it progress toward a closer match between teacher education, educational research, and classroom teaching. (1990a, 1)

This is the kind of critical reflection that makes teacher research meaningful to those who practice it and motivating to those who read it. It is also an approach that realizes the potential of teacher-researchers to challenge, and even change, the roles that teachers play in the making of knowledge in composition studies. Exactly how teacher research, as a collective body of inquiry, challenges and brings about change in education is the subject of the next chapter.

Notes

1. In a recent article on "The 'Difference' of Postmodern Feminism," Teresa Ebert provides yet another response to the argument that, in deconstructing identities and experience, postmodernists render themselves unable to act socially and politically. She distinguishes between two kinds of postmodern feminists: "ludic postmodernists," who see all difference in terms of textuality and have dismantled the notion of politics as a transformative social practice outside of language, thereby becoming "postpolitical," and "resistance postmodernists," who see difference in terms of social conflict rather than textuality and seek social transformation through a politics of emancipation from gender, race, and class exploitation (1991, 887). At this point, Ebert's resistance postmodernism is a proposal which challenges totalizing views of postmodern feminist theory; it has not yet been realized as a working construct which informs feminist practice within academe.

2. It should be acknowledged that Tompkins's ability to assert her beliefs with such force, and to be heard and acknowledged for it by male and female critics alike, is in part made possible by her previous history as a more conventional critic. Thus one could claim that, having paid her dues to the patriarchy, colleagues allow that she has "earned" her right to exhibit a rebellious streak. Further, as an Ivy League academic, she hardly speaks from the margins. See Camille Paglia (1990) for another view of feminism and resistance to authority as written from outside institutional structures, rather than from within them.

II Articulating the Teacher-Research Perspective, K–12

3 The Argument
for Teacher Research

We produce through education a majority who are ruled by knowledge, not served by it—an intellectual, moral and spiritual proletariat characterized by instrumental competencies rather than autonomous power.

—Lawrence Stenhouse 1985

All of us should first define ourselves not as teachers or researchers but as persons who teach, read, write, discuss, and research (among other things), and learn from each other in the process of doing so. Consequently, we enter more easily into an interactive and interpretive learning community.

—Ken Kantor 1990

Something is missing in the way we create and disseminate knowledge in schools and universities. This is the primary message of teacher research. In an era when nationally normed test scores, exit-level proficiency exams, and reports from outside experts, rather than classroom teachers' professional judgments, are looked to as the "real" measure of students' learning, teachers are seeking change. They want to influence the development of curricula, have more say in decision making, make more choices about what goes on in classrooms. Teacher research, then, is a movement both intellectual and political in its impetus, motivated by a national need to professionalize teaching, thereby investing practitioners with more authority and control in classrooms, schools, and ultimately the fields of education and English studies at large. It is a grass-roots effort to address the problems of schools and universities from the inside out, starting with individual teachers documenting successes and failures, questions and answers, from their own classrooms.

A good working definition of teacher research is "systematic and intentional inquiry carried out by teachers" (Cochran-Smith and Lytle 1990). Also called "action research," particularly in Great Britain, the teacher-research movement began in the late 1960s with the work of Lawrence Stenhouse at the Center for Applied Research, University of East Anglia.[1] Stenhouse attributed teachers' low status, in large part, to a false dichotomy between teaching and research—

between what is taught and what is learned and known. He was particularly concerned that universities and school systems were producing teachers who do not play an active role in creating knowledge or initiating change based on that knowledge. His claim was that "we produce through education a majority who are ruled by knowledge, not served by it" (1985, 3). Although Stenhouse was arguing on behalf of K–12 teachers, what he says and what the teacher-research movement stands for is just as relevant to college and university teachers whose classroom experience is institutionally devalued and discounted as a form of knowledge making.

In this chapter, I describe the teacher-research movement as it has developed in grades K–12 and then draw parallels to the status of teachers and teaching at the postsecondary level. The argument for teacher research at the K–12 level is that it is a "quiet revolution" (Bullock 1987): it brings about fundamental change through individual acts, such as the teacher who stops using basal readers and workbooks as a result of her classroom inquiry or the group of teachers who use their own research to support an argument to the principal against a particular textbook-workbook series. "These small acts, these little rebellions add up to a quiet assault on the entire educational hierarchy through the actions of individuals and the assertions by teachers in individual schools that they, not their supervisors or textbook companies, should determine the curricula for their subjects" (Bullock 27).

The quiet assault of teachers overturns hierarchical ways of knowledge production and dissemination, too, and poses fundamental challenges to the construction of composition studies as a field. It demands change in the way compositionists perceive relationships between theory and practice, teachers and researchers; the way we conduct research; the kinds of research we value, promote, and publish; and the ways we orient new members to the profession. The potential of teacher research to motivate changes in the construction of composition studies is still in its latent stages, however. For teacher research to have that kind of influence, teacher-researchers now need to adopt a proactive stance in which they build on their collective strengths and actively argue for the importance and legitimacy of their work to composition scholarship. Teacher-researchers need to understand for themselves—and then assert this claim within the field of composition studies—that there are other forms of knowledge and other knowers, namely teachers and students, who are now demanding full representation in the construction of composition studies as a field. This chapter is my initial effort to assert that claim.

Teacher Research, K–12

A key concept for Stenhouse was "emancipation," by which he meant the "autonomy which we [teachers] recognize when we eschew paternalism and the role of authority and hold ourselves obliged to appeal to [our own] judgement" (Stenhouse 1985, 3). Stenhouse's proposed route to emancipation was teacher research, through which the classroom teacher develops a researcher's model of mind, characterized by intellectual uncertainty, a self-critical attitude, and openness to new ideas and practices. Through teacher research, Stenhouse reasoned, teachers would develop confidence in their own judgment, leading them to contribute to knowledge by first improving their own classroom, then the local curriculum, and finally their fields in general by demanding more from themselves and other researchers.

To better enfranchise teachers, Stenhouse and the many others who have promoted the K–12 teacher-research movement in Great Britain, Australia, and the United States (Hustler, Cassidy, and Cuff; Carr and Kemmis; Goswami and Stillman; Mohr and Maclean; Lytle and Cochran-Smith, among others) have argued for changes in the means and methods of educational research. From the beginning, teacher research has been defined *against* traditional means of producing knowledge. Stenhouse, for example, argued for "illuminative research" in the form of case studies and ethnographies and against what he called the "psycho-statistical paradigm" of scientific research, characterized by experimental design, sample and control groups, and claims of internal and external validity. He called for research which strengthens *professional* judgment, in addition to that which strengthens *research* judgment. In research judgment, a study is deemed valuable if its design and methodology are correct; such research is typically done *on* education by those viewing the classroom from the outside. In professional judgment, a study is deemed valuable if it "illuminates particular cases that can be judged against experience"; such research is done *in* education by those who are part of the learning environment. Stenhouse argues thus for "insider" research:

> I claim no more than that a research base offers the teacher a security for his authority in a mastery of seeking rather than knowing, and hence provides him with a necessary protection in the enterprise of educating those who will, he wants to hope, exceed his grasp. . . . The university stands—or should stand— behind enquiry in schools as the curator of that uncertainty without which the transmission of knowledge becomes a virtuoso performance in gentling the masses. (1985, 120–22)

Thus teacher research, as originally conceived, was a form of political as well as intellectual activism—an emancipation proclamation for classroom teachers from the ruling authority of administrators and university researchers.

Over the past twenty years, however, teacher research as conducted in the United States has come to be characterized more in terms of its methodology and practical outcomes than its emancipatory goals. It is seen primarily as classroom ethnography conducted to improve an individual teacher's pedagogy. This characterization, constructed by K–12 teacher-researchers themselves, has been both a strength and a weakness. On the one hand, in its interest in methodology, teacher research poses a healthy intellectual challenge to the positivist research paradigm which still prevails in most schools of education. It also brings to light the dynamic tension between action (teaching) and research (knowledge construction), blurring traditional boundaries and challenging old assumptions that teaching and research, acting and theorizing, are contradictory aims. Another strength of the movement has been its efforts to empower teachers through collaboration; it has clearly motivated educators to work together to bring about changes that may not have otherwise occurred. On the other hand, teacher-researchers have focused too much on research paradigms, namely ethnographic research versus experimental research, and too little on the epistemological assumptions underlying those paradigms and the larger intellectual and political implications of the teacher-research movement for knowledge making in fields such as composition.

A hallmark of the K–12 teacher-research movement has been its critical stance toward traditional education research. This positioning of "us" against "them," teachers against researchers, is clearly articulated in Ann Berthoff's now classic article entitled "The Teacher as REsearcher":

> Educational research is nothing to our purpose, unless we formulate the questions; if the procedures by which answers are sought are not dialectic and dialogic, that is to say, if the questions and answers are not REformulated by those who are working in the classroom, educational research is pointless. My spies tell me that it's becoming harder and harder for researchers to get into schools: I rejoice in that news because I think it might encourage teachers to become researchers themselves, and once that happens, the character of research is bound to change. (1987, 31)

It is significant that Berthoff's assertion, originally part of a 1979 address to the California Association of Teachers of English, should be referred to in nearly every book, article, and passage on teacher research in America. Perhaps it is because her statement is in fact a rallying cry, a call to arms against current educational research, which Berthoff says is based on the "fraudulent" claim that education can be studied in the same way we study the natural sciences and is grounded in the "absurd" belief that classroom teachers need to look to researchers' data-based studies in order to learn how to teach. Says Berthoff, "[T]he people [researchers] who call language 'verbal behavior' are the ones who call literature 'literary material,' just as they are the ones who call making mudpies 'earthplay.' They are not our allies" (29).

A problem with this stance of "us" against "them," evocative as it may be, is that it asserts the argument *for* teacher research by setting it *against* other forms of research which are more highly valued among university scholars. Teacher-researchers are placed in the difficult position of having to argue that their form of inquiry is superior to that of established researchers following other methods. This is one reason why teacher research has not significantly affected knowledge making in education and composition studies. Devaluing the scientific method is not the most effective way to legitimize teacher research. Teacher-researchers would gain more by arguing for the necessity of broader definitions of *research*, encouraging alternative forms of inquiry, and opening up the province of research to other inquirers. An effective approach would be for teacher-researchers to turn inward, acknowledging and addressing through reflection and critical self-analysis the limitations, as well as the strengths, of their own inquiry. As feminist criticism illustrates, the development of knowledge through self-reflection and personal insight leads to deeper understanding of a field and one's place within it. The advice of Maxine Hairston to composition scholars trying to establish legitimacy in English studies is just as relevant to teacher-researchers trying to establish legitimacy in education: "[W]e must . . . find our own values and listen to our own voices—values and voices that are not *against* someone else, but for ourselves" (1985, 278). In the discussion that follows, and at the risk of overstating and simplifying, I lay out some of the differences between teacher research and other forms of educational inquiry, not to pit one against the other, but to suggest how the different values and voices underlying these research paradigms might better converse with one another.

The Challenge to Positivism

Berthoff's assertions about "us" and "them" reflect, on one level, the differences between the positivist research paradigm valued in most colleges of education and the paradigm promoted by teacher-researchers. Because of these differences, teacher research has been called an "alternative research tradition" (Goswami and Stillman) and even a new "genre" of educational research (Threatt; Cochran-Smith and Lytle). I prefer to call it an "alternative *discourse*" within the field of education, emphasizing differences in language and epistemology rather than research methods; it is important to understand the two research paradigms, not just in terms of methodology, but also in terms of the assumptions about language and knowledge making that underlie them.

In *Actual Minds, Possible Worlds*, Jerome Bruner argues that

> [t]here are two modes of cognitive functioning, two modes of thought, each providing distinctive ways of ordering experience, of constructing reality. The two (though complementary) are irreducible to one another. Efforts to reduce one mode to the other or to ignore one at the expense of the other inevitably fail to capture the rich diversity of thought. (1986, 11)

Bruner's two modes, narrative and paradigmatic, are valued differently within Western society and certainly within educational contexts, where paradigmatic thought is often promoted as "a refinement of or an abstraction from the other" (11). However, Bruner argues that this distinction is "either false or true only in the most unenlightening way," for it fails to acknowledge the equal value of narrative thought. A more useful way to distinguish between the two is in terms of their form and function:

> Each of the ways of knowing . . . has operating principles of its own and its own criteria of well-formedness. They differ radically in their procedures for verification. A good story and a well-formed argument are different natural kinds. Both can be used as means for convincing another. Yet what they convince of is fundamentally different: arguments convince one of their truth, stories of their lifelikeness. The one verifies by eventual appeal to procedures for establishing formal and empirical proof. The other establishes not truth but verisimilitude. (11)

Bruner offers much of science, mathematics, and philosophy as examples of paradigmatic or logico-scientific thinking. This type of thinking is based in large part on the principled testing of hypotheses; it "deals in general causes, and in their establishment, and makes use of procedures to assure verifiable reference and to test for empirical truth" (13).

Paradigmatic thinking is reflected in positivism, a general term for a research paradigm which holds that valid knowledge can be established only by reference to that which can be manifested in experience and apprehended by the senses through "objective" observation, logical deduction, and rational argument. Positivist research, ostensibly free of any ideological or normative elements, is based on the premise that knowledge and truth exist and are "found" through research that can be tested and validated against other research findings. Reliable research, then, must be carefully controlled and decontextualized, theory-driven and generalizable; similarly, reliable researchers must be distanced and uninvolved emotionally or psychologically with the subjects of their study. The positivist paradigm "seeks to transcend the particular by higher and higher reaching for abstraction, and in the end disclaims in principle any explanatory value at all where the particular is concerned" (Bruner 1986, 13). This research paradigm "now enjoys a position of near orthodoxy" in schols of education, where issues of learning and teaching are typically seen as "technical" problems which can be solved "objectively" through "rational assessment of the evidence" (Carr and Kemmis 1986, 78).

The language of paradigmatic thinking is "regulated by requirements of consistency and noncontradiction" (Bruner 1986, 13) and is considered apart from that which is observed and known. That is, language is merely a sign system for transcribing or translating thought. In his discussion of objective theories of rhetoric, James Berlin describes paradigmatic language in this way: "[L]anguage is regarded at worst as a distorting medium that alters the original perception [of truth] and at best as a transparent device that captures the original experience so that it might be reproduced in the faculties of one's audience. . . . [The audience] is also assumed to be as objective as the writer, so that the language presented can stimulate in the reader the experience that the writer originally had" (1987, 8). In order to "transfer" thought without distortion, language must be "precise" and conform to standards of usage. Careful use of language verifies the credibility of authors and their thinking.

In contrast to paradigmatic thinking, "narrative thinking deals in human or human-like intention and action and the vicissitudes and consequences that mark their course. It strives to put its timeless miracles into the particulars of experience, and to locate the experience in time and place" (Bruner 1986, 13). In recent years, narrative thinking has been most clearly evident in ethnography, a research paradigm which attempts to account, as fully as possible, for naturally occurring events in their social context. Stephen Doheny-Farina and Lee Odell note that ethnographers

> stress the importance of closely observing the specific phenom-
> ena of the culture in which [they are] conducting research. Thus
> an ethnographer's observational notes . . . may contain detailed
> references to minute, even apparently trivial matters of how
> people dress and how they interact with colleagues; of whom
> they initiate conversations with and who initiates conversations
> with them; of the features of their nonverbal language. (1985, 504)

Collecting ethnographic detail, however, is not an end in itself but a
means toward understanding the larger significance and meaning of
a culture; it is a "thick description" (Geertz 1973) of the "ways of
living of a social group" (Heath 1983). Ethnography is often reported
or realized in the form of stories or "tales," as John Van Maanen (1988)
calls them.

One of the best examples of ethnographic research in education is
Shirley Brice Heath's *Ways with Words: Language, Life and Work in
Communities and Classrooms.* The following excerpt, part of a story
about a story about a story, illustrates Heath's "thick description" of
children's language learning in context:

> On one occasion when they were in the third grade, Roadville's
> Sally and Wendy expressed their understanding of the distinc-
> tions between "stories" at home and at school. On the school bus
> on the way home from school, Wendy had regaled her friends with
> a tale about how she was going to bring her dog to the end-of-
> school party. When they got off the bus, Sally, somewhat outdone
> by the story, decided to invoke home knowledge on her friend.
> Sally: That story, you just told, you know that ain't so.
> Wendy: I'm not tellin' no story, uh-er-ah, no I'm tellin' the kind
> Miss Wash [the teacher] talks about.
> Sally: Mamma won't let you get away with that kinda excuse. You
> know better.
> Wendy: What are you so, uh, excited about. We got one kinda story
> mamma knows about, and a whole 'nother one we do at school.
> They're different //*looking at Sally*// and you know it=
> Sally: =You better hope mamma knows it, if she catches you
> making up stuff like that.
> Here the girls took up the differences between story-telling, an
> event accepted and promoted in school, and tellin'-a-story, an
> event equated with lying and exaggerating at home. This exchange
> was a rare description of how the girls recognized the differing
> conventions and moral values home and school attached to
> stories. (1983, 294–95)

Heath's description illustrates the reliance on both dialogue and
narrative in ethnography and the importance of the particular in such
narratives. The purpose of ethnography is to describe a situation as it

occurs naturally, in the process explaining its social, intellectual, and political significance.

In their preference for ethnography, K–12 teacher-researchers are demonstrating a tendency toward narrative thinking. Marue English Walizer sees parallels between Bruner's paradigmatic and narrative thinking and "the different kinds of thinking and language used by researchers and teachers, respectively" (1986, 524). While university researchers, at least those following the positivist paradigm, typically think and express themselves paradigmatically (in terms of general principles and researched evidence), teachers typically think and express themselves narratively (in terms of specific cases and previous experiences). A high school teacher herself, Walizer offers the following anecdote as evidence: "Ask a teacher how he or she teaches a concept or handles a classroom problem; at some point in the response you will likely get the story of a particular class or student" (524).

In *The Reflective Practitioner,* Donald Schon makes a similar argument about the differences between the thinking of practitioners and the thinking of university researchers in the same field. Through an examination of experienced practitioners in the fields of education, psychotherapy, architecture, engineering design, town planning, and business management, Schon argues that, for the practitioner, knowledge is *in* the act of doing, not *applied* to it, as it is for the researcher. He shows that practitioners have a kind of "intuitive knowing" which is "primarily tacit, but which can be reflected upon in the midst of performing one's work" (1983, ix). Part of being an expert in a field is "knowing more than we can say." However, it is important for practitioners to be able to reflect on this knowledge through inquiry because most traditional research has failed to illuminate this aspect of knowledge making.

Practitioner inquiry, then, is an important complement to the positivist paradigm, which Schon calls the model of "technical rationality." The problem with exclusive reliance on positivism is that it never corresponds to actual practice in any field. The practitioner has to deal with many variables that the positivist paradigm cannot account for, such as "complexity, uncertainty, instability, uniqueness, and value conflict" (1983, 39). Schon offers a geographic analogy to distinguish between positivist and practitioner inquiry: positivists traverse a terrain of "high, hard ground" where they confine themselves to narrow research problems, avoid areas which cannot be controlled and carefully defined, and strive for technical competence and methodological rigor. Practitioners traverse "a swampy lowland where situations are confusing 'messes' incapable of technical solution." Practitioners in the lowlands "deliberately involve themselves in messy but crucially important problems and, when asked to describe their methods of inquiry, they speak of experience, trial and error, intuition, and muddling through" (43). Although researchers traveling the high ground achieve rigor and some measure of security in their findings, they often do not tackle the more difficult issues inherent in most fields. It is these issues that practitioners are most likely to perceive and address in their inquiry.

Thus teacher-researchers often use narrative thinking to represent the complexity of the classroom experience. Defined here as "a verbal memory of human experience, a record—a telling—of what life is like" (Knoblauch and Brannon 1988, 23), the teacher narrative

> aims not at selectivity or simplification but at richness of texture and intentional complexity. The telling . . . seeks instead to depict, to evoke, what phenomenologists such as Heidegger and Gadamer have called "the life-world"—that palpable, sensual, kaleidoscopic, mysterious reality that constitutes our material rather than merely intellectual existence . . . a close observation of the phenomenal reality of the classroom, what it looks like, the objects that define it as a material and social space, how the people in it look, talk, move, relate to each other, the emotional contours of their life together, the things that happen, intellectual exchanges, social understandings and misunderstandings, what the teacher knows, plans, hopes for, and discovers, how different students react, the subtle textures of the teaching experience, the subtle textures of the learning experience. (25)

Examples of such narratives abound in the teacher-research literature. Works such as the "research close-ups" in Goswami and Stillman's *Reclaiming the Classroom* (1987), the longitudinal and short-term case studies reported in Glenda Bissex and Richard Bullock's *Seeing for Ourselves* (1987), and many of the contributions to Donald Daiker and Max Morenberg's *The Writing Teacher as Researcher* (1990) are typical. Art Young's chapter in the Daiker and Morenberg collection is, in fact, a story about storytelling in the technical writing classroom. He explains what he sees as the purpose and significance of the classroom narrative for his students and himself: "[S]tories helped us make sense of our experience and understand what we were about, and stories helped us build our supportive, collaborative community" (Young 1990, 168). Other examples of ethnographic narrative written by participant observers who are not teachers include Alex Kotlowitz's *There Are No Children Here* (1991) and Tracy Kidder's *Among School Children* (1989).

Ethnography may well be a reflection of the teacher's unique way of seeing and responding to life in the classroom. In *The Practice of Teaching,* Philip W. Jackson asserts that "real teaching" (that done by experienced teachers) must be defined epistemologically, for it is more than what a teacher is *doing* (that is, standing in a classroom, talking to students, writing on the blackboard). A real teacher (as opposed to an imposter who is merely "playing teacher") *thinks* like a teacher. Jackson suggests that there is something like "a pedagogical outlook on things, a 'teacherly' way of viewing the world" (1986, 86). This outlook involves a "sense of 'being at home' in the classroom" and includes abilities such as noticing details, processing a considerable amount of information at a glance, perceiving irregularities and trouble spots immediately, thinking in a "future-oriented" way so as to see possibilities that others miss, and responding appropriately to a variety of behaviors. In short, real teachers perceptively "see more" than nonteachers:

> They are alive to the latent pedagogical possibilities in the events they witness. Within a classroom setting, they anticipate what is going to happen. They can spot an inattentive student a mile off. They can detect signs of incipient difficulty. Their senses are fully tuned to what is going on around them. They are not easily rattled. As younger students sometimes swear is true, they behave as though they had eyes in the back of their heads. (87)

If we accept that experienced teachers see and respond in these ways, teacher-researchers' propensity for classroom ethnography makes sense: in perceiving the particular, they mark its significance in their discourse. And my claim that teacher research makes a significant (and unique) contribution to composition studies makes sense, too: if teachers see things differently, they offer a perspective on the development of language and learning that university researchers cannot provide.

Teachers' language, as well as their thinking, may differ from that of traditional researchers. In discussing what he calls "transactional rhetoric," Berlin describes the language of narrative thinking in contrast to the language of paradigmatic thinking. He suggests that language and experience are deeply interrelated in narrative thinking:

> [T]here is never a division between experience and language, whether the experience involves the subject, the subject and other subjects, or the subject and the material world. All experiences, even the scientific and logical, are grounded in language, and language determines their content and structure. And just as

> language structures our response to social and political issues, language structures our respose to the material world. . . . All truths arise out of dialectic, out of the interaction of individuals within discourse communities. Truth is never simply "out there" in the material world or the social realm, or simply "in here" in a private and personal world. It emerges only as the three—the material, the social, and the personal—interact, and the agent of mediation is language. (1987, 17)

If what Berlin says is true—if the classroom narrative both constructs and is constructed by the teacher's response to the world—then teacher research has the potential to alter significantly a teacher's understanding of education. Yet teacher-researchers need to become more cognizant of the effects of their inquiry not only on their own teaching, but on their profession as well. An understanding of the contributions that teacher research makes to the knowledge base in education in general and composition in particular is necessary for the progression of the teacher-research movement. One such contribution is the insight that teacher research provides into the relationship between theory and practice.

The Dynamic Tension between Theory and Practice

One of the major strengths of teacher research is that it challenges the familiar division between theory and practice, a bifurcation that seriously weakens education and English studies in general and composition studies in particular. Teacher-researchers proceed on the premise that theory and practice are interrelated aspects of the same enterprise, namely knowledge making in education. In the early stages of the teacher-research movement, the theory-practice connection was facilitated by collaboration between university researchers and classroom teachers. Projects supported by the University of East Anglia in the 1970s involved teachers as "internal researchers" and university faculty as "external researchers" jointly involved in designing and conducting studies and interpreting and reporting their findings. Stenhouse described the teacher-researcher relationship this way:

> [I]n action research, the teacher has full and responsible control of the research act, while the researcher's responsibility is to ensure that the maximum learning is gained from the teacher's acting as he does—through an act at once an educational act and a research act. This relationship is the basis for the claims that I would make that in action research the researcher should be accountable to the teachers. (1985, 57)

This type of collaboration is still essential to the British model of teacher research, where "some form of dialogue with an 'outsider' is not only desirable . . . but almost one of its defining characteristics" (Hustler, Cassidy, and Cuff 1986, 15).

Collaboration between teacher and researcher, when done properly, creates a dynamic tension between theory and practice in education. In the preface to their edited book on *Action Research in Classrooms and Schools,* Hustler, Cassidy, and Cuff discuss how teachers and researchers can achieve what appear to be contradictory aims—conducting research that is relevant to other researchers yet still meaningful and practical to teachers. They suggest that teachers and researchers can meet these dual aims by "gaining access to each other's relevancies" (1986, 10). What is relevant to the researcher is meeting other researchers' standards for intellectual rigor and contributing to the knowledge base by building on theory. What is relevant to the teacher is meeting other teachers' needs and contributing to the knowledge base by building on practice. When teachers and researchers work together, they have an opportunity to negotiate these "relevancies" and, ideally, come to respect and learn from their different priorities. This point is made by Ken Kantor, a researcher in education at an American university, who has learned through his collaboration with classroom teachers that "the researcher and teacher educator need to diminish their roles as 'experts'—transmitters of prestige knowledge or welfare worker/missionaries—and begin to take on the roles of colearner and coparticipant with teachers" in order to break down hierarchical power relationships and create a shared vision of educational reform (1990, 64). Teacher-reseacher collaboration requires that both participants redefine their roles and their ways of interacting. Kantor concludes that, ultimately, "all of us should first define ourselves not as teachers or researchers but as persons who teach, read, write, discuss, and research (among other things), and learn from each other in the process of doing so. Consequently, we enter more easily into an interactive and interpretive learning community" (66).

But teacher-researcher collaboration has disadvantages when it does not involve such redefinition of roles. When researchers are perceived to have more power and status than teachers, cooperative research "often constructs and predetermines teachers' roles in the research process, thereby framing and mediating teachers' perspectives through researchers' perspectives" (Lytle and Cochran-Smith 1989, 3). As a result, the teacher's perspective and the teacher's "relevancies" may be minimized, trivialized, or even ignored.

In the American approach to teacher research, the dynamic tension between theory and practice is more often developed through an individual teacher's inquiry rather than through collaborative inquiry between a teacher and a researcher. In the United States, teacher research typically refers to the teacher *as* researcher, rather than the teacher *and* researcher, although a few collaborative studies between schoolteachers and university researchers have been conducted (Perl and Wilson; Kantor; Berkenkotter; McCarthy), and many teacher-researchers have worked closely with university researchers through such programs as the Breadloaf School of English and the National Writing Project.

Critics of the American version of teacher research typically cite the following disadvantages: (1) without benefit of an outsider's perspective, teachers themselves lack an understanding of what they do in the classroom; (2) teachers conduct "biased" research that does not meet the standards of established researchers; and (3) teachers do not have the theoretical perspective needed to interpret their findings for the research community (Stenhouse 1985).

In responding to the first criticism, teacher-researchers need to assert the relevance of practitioner inquiry and the proven benefits of self-reflective inquiry. Teachers do not need an outsider to tell them what they are doing if they practice the kind of critical self-analysis that Schon describes in *The Reflective Practitioner*. What distinguishes practitioner inquiry from simple practice is point of view. The inquiring practitioner

> allows himself to experience surprise, puzzlement, or confusion in a situation which he finds uncertain or unique. He reflects on the phenomena before him, and on the prior understandings which have been implicit in his behavior. He carries out an experiment which serves to generate both a new understanding of the phenomena and a change in the situation. . . . He does not separate thinking from doing, ratiocinating his way to a decision which he must later convert to action. Because his experimenting is a kind of action, implementation is built into his inquiry. (Schon 1983, 68)

The teacher engaged in such inquiry carries on a "reflective conversation with the situation," as well as with those involved in the situation, and learns from his or her personal involvement:

> [T]he professional recognizes that his technical expertise is embedded in a context of meanings. He attributes to his [students], as well as to himself, a capacity to mean, know and plan. He recognizes that his actions may have different meanings for his [students] than he intends them to have, and he gives himself the

> task of discovering what these are. He recognizes an obligation to make his own understandings accessible to his [students], which means he needs to reflect anew on what he knows. (Schon 1983, 295)

Stephen North notes, too, that teachers engaged in inquiry have an alternative perspective on the classroom (1987). He suggests that one of three scenarios must be present to distinguish teacher research from teaching: (1) the teacher sees the teaching situation as somehow unfamiliar and alters or adapts familiar strategies to address the situation; (2) the teacher perceives the situation as familiar, but sees standard teaching approaches to be inappropriate; or (3) the teacher perceives that both the teaching situation and the usual approaches are unsatisfactory. In any case, the teacher-researcher approaches the classroom as an opportunity for analysis and change, unlike the teacher who is invested in maintaining the status quo and therefore relies on "lore"—a common stock of practices, beliefs, traditions, and ways of perceiving, organizing, and limiting experience that are neither questioned nor analyzed. In distinguishing between teaching and teacher research, it is also useful to keep in mind Cochran-Smith and Lytle's definition: while teaching may well include occasional inquiry into one's practice, teacher research entails "systematic and intentional inquiry," which requires planned, sustained activity centered around a predetermined research problem or question.

The change in perspective that occurs through reflective inquiry can be liberating, for in assuming the status of learner, practitioners no longer feel the heavy responsibility of presenting themselves as the "expert" beyond reproach. Although the traditional role of "expert" can make teachers feel secure, after a while it becomes boring, and they begin to look outside their work for gratification:

> When practice is a repetitive administration of techniques to the same kinds of problems, the practitioner may look to leisure as a source of relief, or to early retirement; but when he functions as a researcher-in-practice, the practice itself is a source of renewal. The recognition of error, with its resulting uncertainty, can become a source of discovery rather than an occasion for self defense. (Schon 1983, 299)

Thus reflective practice, unlike simple practice, can counteract job burnout, increase enthusiasm and motivation, and help teachers better understand themselves and their profession.

There are at least two appropriate responses to the criticism that teacher-researchers are not "rigorous" enough in conducting their inquiry. The first response is to question the assumptions underlying the criticism—that teacher-researchers should be held to the criteria of more traditional educational research, that they are *accountable* to the research community. The reality is that K–12 teacher-researchers are not aspiring to be "apprentice researchers" within the established research community, and teacher research is conducted primarily for teachers, not researchers. Thus it is teachers' criteria for rigor, not researchers', which must be met. The standard for evaluating teacher research, then, is its relevance to teaching and its credibility among experienced practitioners, not researchers.

A second response to the criticism of rigor is that teacher-researchers, *if they choose* to align themselves more closely with the established research community, can base their classroom inquiry more closely on the practices of ethnographers. Specifically, they can strengthen the validity of their findings to the research community by engaging in triangulation and by constantly questioning and moving beyond their own findings. There are at least three types of triangulation: theoretical triangulation, whereby individual researchers interpret their findings from several theoretical perspectives; investigative triangulation, whereby a team of researchers uses the same procedures to collect information; and methodological triangulation, whereby a single researcher uses a variety of methods to gather information, rather than relying on a single source (Doheny-Farina and Odell 1985). It is quite possible for an individual teacher-researcher to engage in any or all of these forms of triangulation to enhance the credibility of the work. For example, a teacher-researcher can interpret findings in terms of various theories of learning and teaching; can conduct research in collaboration with other teachers at the same school or in different schools; and can develop ethnographies which use a variety of data-gathering methods, including interviews, surveys, classroom observations, and discourse analyses of students' speech and writing. "The underlying logic of triangulation is this: ethnographers seek patterns in the data they collect. Triangulation at any level tests emerging patterns by increasing the possibility of finding negative cases and countering the bias of any one approach. Thus triangulation fosters more rigorous research" (Doheny-Farina and Odell 1985, 510). Classroom inquiry, then, *can* meet the criteria of the research community, if teacher-researchers choose to evaluate their work in terms of those standards.

Anticipating the third criticism, Stenhouse (1985) argued that teachers *do* have a theoretical perspective, although they may not always articulate it in the ways expected and validated by traditional researchers. What teachers lack is experience (and in many cases the desire or need) to relate their theoretical understandings in ways that the research community values. A similar point is made by Lytle and Cochran-Smith, who argue that, although teachers' research questions "are not framed in the language of educational theory, they are indeed about discrepancies between theory and practice" and that "although they are not always motivated by a need to generalize beyond the immediate case, [teachers' questions] may in fact be relevant to a wide variety of contexts" (1989, 2).

Another response to the claim that teachers lack the requisite theoretical sophistication to conduct research is to challenge the ways in which the term *theory* is used in such arguments. If theory is a lens, a philosophical perspective, or a stance, then teachers surely rely on theory. This definition requires a willingness to view theory as function rather than form, as process—a way of seeing and thinking—rather than product—a body of information. Unfortunately, when many critics use the word theory, they are often referring to bodies of knowledge—isms such as poststructuralism, deconstructionism, Marxism, new historicism—rather than to current perspectives for understanding the world. Thus we talk about writing the "theory section" of a paper or "putting theory into practice," as if theory were an object in the physical world. Scholars assign values to these bodies of knowledge, asserting that some theories are politically and intellectually correct, while others are not. As a result, theory becomes tyranny, a superior type of knowledge that is imposed upon others as a form of authority.

In his discussion of literary theory and its relationship to the teaching of literature, Robert Scholes proposes a better way to see theory which begins with an examination of our assumptions: "We must mount a critique of what we do when marching under our traditional banner with the strange device that says, 'Teaching Literature.' . . . To step outside the line of march, to scrutinize the device and see it as strange for the first time—defamiliarized, as the formalists put it—is to become, perforce a theoretician" (1985, 11). Those who focus on the device—the object—see theory as an established body of knowledge; those who focus on their perceptions of the device see theory as a process of knowledge making. Teacher-researchers clearly fall into the second category.

Empowerment through Collaboration

One of the greatest strengths of teacher research is that it involves a form of collaboration that participants find empowering. I define *empowerment*, following Patti Lather, as the process one undertakes *for oneself* to understand the "causes of powerlessness, recognizing systemic oppressive forces, and acting both individually and collectively to change the conditions" of one's life (1991, 4). K–12 teacher-researchers involve students, teachers, administrators, parents, school board members, and others in their study of the social, cultural, intellectual, and institutional influences on their lives and the lives of their students. Research of this kind is a community effort which generates the motivation and commitment needed to bring about change.

Students involved in teacher research are not merely subjects or statistics, as they are in other kinds of educational inquiry, but co-researchers and key sources of knowledge and insight. Rather than imposing meaning on classroom situations, teacher-researchers construct meaning in negotiation with their students. The result is empowerment for both teachers and students. An example of such collaboration is Jeffrey Schwartz's study of computer networking among high school students. In one project, two students helped Schwartz, then a teacher at Sewickley Academy in Pittsburgh, collect and analyze computer conversations. As a result of this shared inquiry, Schwartz found that students came to discoveries through their data analysis that he alone would not have seen. He also found that the teacher-student collaboration made students more responsible for their own learning because "it redistributes the power of the class, not equally, but so that it's not exclusively in the hands of the teacher" (1990, 166). Harste, Woodward, and Burke, through their ethnographic studies of children learning to read and write, reaffirm the claim that classroom-based inquiry empowers both teacher and student:

> The research attitude of "I can find out" is absolutely liberating, not only for teachers and researchers, but also for children. For us this new attitude allows a change from testing our language hypotheses to giving children an opportunity to test theirs. For children it allows a change from being tenants of our texts to owners of their own texts. (1984, 223)

Teachers also collaborate with other teachers to plan, conduct, and present research. Across the country, groups of teachers from different school systems are meeting together to assist each other with individual projects. Among the best-known examples are the National Writing Project, the Breadloaf School of English, and the Northeastern University Institute on Writing. Teachers involved in this type of collaboration see its primary benefit in terms of the interactive sharing of ideas and the intellectual growth that result from it. Indeed, Susan Threatt, who has worked to build and maintain communities of teacher-researchers, asserts that one way to ensure the future of the movement is to establish an elaborate computer network that significantly increases opportunities for teacher exchange. She foresees teacher-researchers consulting with each other across countries and creating an evolving "shared text" of questions, observations, theories, and personal findings (personal conversation).

Another form of collaboration among teachers is shared inquiry, in which a number of teachers work on the same research question or problem. Nancie Atwell describes a project involving fourteen teachers, representing grades 1–8 in the same school system, who worked together to develop a new writing curriculum based on their findings. Following the inquiry procedures of Emig, Goswami and Odell, and Graves, for months the teachers collected data, which included observations of students in the process of writing, histories of students' reading and writing experiences, daily logs of classroom exchanges, and analyses of students' written texts. Their purpose was to find patterns in those data which would suggest direction for local curricular change. According to Atwell, "Rather than design a writing program based on prior practices and assumptions, publishers' materials or mastery checklists, and then evaluate its effect on students' written products, we are . . . developing a curriculum based on what we learn from the writers in our classrooms" (1987a, 88–89). Not only has the group revamped its writing curriculum, but each project teacher has also "dramatically altered" his or her approach to teaching writing as a result of a shift in focus from disseminating knowledge and evaluating outcomes to learning from students and reflecting on teaching. One seventh-grade teacher, for example, gave up her minutely detailed lesson plans for a more spontaneous approach in which she discovers from students what they need to learn next. As a result of their close observation and documentation, the teachers have also developed an awareness and appreciation of students' differences: "Rather than emphasizing mastery or ranking our students, we [now] look for individual writers' growth over time" (90).

Atwell also notes that teachers' altered perspective on students has significantly affected the quality of teacher-teacher interaction, as well as teacher-student interaction: "The nature of teacher-talk shifted away from discussions of specific children's problems and attendant teacher frustrations toward excited descriptions of students' resourcefulness and accomplishments, as well as question-raising concerning the logic behind a particular writer's particular behavior" (1987a, 91). Further, teachers' interactions within the field of education have changed:

> Our roles and functions in the larger community of educators are
> redefined. No longer the peripheral recipients of others' theories,
> findings, and programs, we have become professionals essen-
> tially active in and central to the improvement of writing instruc-
> tion. We are more knowledgeable about curriculum design. We
> are writing descriptions of our research for educators' journals.
> We are serving as resources to teachers outside of our district and
> presenting our research findings at state and national confer-
> ences. And we are seeing a change in our community's percep-
> tions of our professionalism and expertise. (1987a, 91)

As they turn to the procedures and findings of others' research, the
teachers are also discovering that they approach this literature with
more knowledge and authority, as well as with a more critical eye.
They have found all of these changes to be positive, energizing forces
in their lives and careers.

It is not surprising that teacher research improves teachers' practice. Indeed, a standard argument in academe is that faculty members
in research institutions are better teachers because they are also
researchers. However, when most university faculty members talk
about improved teaching through research, they are referring to the
content of teaching; research assures that they are familiar with
current theories, use updated materials, and teach the latest research
methods. In contrast, when teacher-researchers talk about improved
teaching through research, they are referring to the *process* of teaching; research assures that they approach the whole teaching enterprise as a form of inquiry, analysis, and reciprocity with their
students. Focusing on the process helps teachers discover their
weaknesses and build upon their strengths. Schon (1983) points out
that reflective inquiry of this kind gives practitioners the opportunity
to consider what in their work gives the most satisfaction and how to
create more of these experiences.

An additional form of collaboration comes when teacher-researchers share their findings with colleagues. For Stenhouse, a full definition of research requires that it be made public—exposed to the
critical response of a larger intellectual community. There are many
ways to "go public" beyond communication of ideas through national conferences, scholarly journals, and books. Teacher research,
for example, is often published locally rather than nationally, a
situation which Stenhouse deemed appropriate: "[P]erhaps too much
research is published to the world, too little to the village. We need
local cooperatives and papers as well as international conferences
and journals. And in any case we need more face-to-face discourse"
(1985, 18). Examples of face-to-face discourse range from impromptu

discussions with colleagues in the faculty lounge and at staff meetings to more formal presentations at districtwide workshops or state and regional conferences.

Stenhouse envisioned an alternative model of distributing teacher-research based on Gramsci's (1971) deliberative college, where "cultural circles" involving members of several specialties work through discussion and joint criticism to "improve the collective competence" and create "conditions for the rise of a homogeneous group of intellectuals" (Stenhouse 1985, 17). The significance of the deliberative college, aside from its collaborative nature, is its dedication to action. Research can also be expressed in performances or actions "if its force is to make action hypothetical or problematic. To the extent that a substantive action is an expression of a research enquiry, it tests the hypothetical outcome of the enquiry; and this is one understanding of action research" (18). It was his strong belief in the importance of action research that led Stenhouse to conclude that "researchers must justify themselves to practitioners, not practitioners to researchers" (19). This stance represents a significant change in the concept of audience and purpose for teacher research: the inquiry is conducted by and disseminated to an audience of practitioners in order to promote action, rather than to an audience of researchers in order to promote further research.

Collaboration among teacher-researchers creates not only an improved intellectual environment, but also a stronger political base. A support group of practicing teacher-researchers is needed to empower its members to continue their work amidst possible resistance. It must be acknowledged that not all teacher research is received positively within schools. As Bullock notes, many K–12 teacher-researchers claim that their peers, feeling threatened by classroom inquiry, have negated the significance of these studies and dismissed them as illegitimate or irrelevant. Indeed,

> when one or two teachers in a school show that they care about their professional development beyond accumulating state-mandated credit hours, when they refuse to capitulate to the despair born of powerlessness that engenders attitudes of defensiveness and time serving, they do make their colleagues look bad, because they model professional behavior through seizing authority for their subject matter and activities. (Bullock 1987, 23)

One of the best ways to respond to this negativity from colleagues is to draw them into the collaboration, encouraging them to conduct their own inquiry and to experience what it means to take control of the classroom and contribute to their profession as scholars.

The Contributions of Teacher Research to Composition Studies

The teacher-research movement will become more influential when teacher-researchers *claim* the knowledge that they are making in the field of composition studies. Because most K–12 teachers have not considered the potential impact of their research beyond their own classrooms and schools, they have not always articulated their assumptions or framed their work in ways that convince composition scholars of their significance. As a result, teacher research has, as yet, had little impact on the field, even though it exemplifies a reciprocity between theory and practice that composition studies most needs: teachers, informed by theory, think about what they are doing and why, observe the effects of their thinking and doing in the classroom, raise more questions about their thinking, do something different or do the same thing in different ways, observe some more, and reexamine their findings in terms of what theory suggests and what practice demonstrates. The teacher-researcher works through this process again and again in the span of a single class period, a week, a semester, a school year, a lifetime of teaching and learning. The pedagogical stance is ever-informed by theory, and the theoretical stance is ever-informed by practice. Teacher research is proof of Scholes's claim that "practice is never natural or neutral; there is always a theory in place, so that the first job of any teacher . . . is to bring the assumptions that are in place out in the open for scrutiny" (Scholes 1985, xi). Articulating and questioning these assumptions is what Berthoff refers to as "knowing our knowledge," and determining the relevance of this knowledge to English studies is very much like determining the relevance of literature:

> The knowledge that literature offers is not cumulative in the way that physical knowledge is: one does not "know more" as each story is added to the others. But one knows "better"; one's instincts and values, expectations and judgments mature. One's ability to read the world grows. Literature enhances the *quality* of understanding without presuming to add to its "content." Also unlike physical knowledge, literature is not self-corrective: that is, one story does not falsify another. It is instead dialogical: stories beget stories; voices mingle and interanimate. (Knoblauch and Brannon 1988, 26)

In this way, teacher research informs our understanding of the type and quality of student and teacher experiences, helping us better "read the world" of the composition classroom.

Patricia Harkin argues that the knowledge practitioners create is, in fact, superior in some ways to that created by university researchers in established disciplines. Free of the constraints of disciplinary practices and the ideologies which make university researchers blind to alternative explanations for phenomena, teacher-researchers are "postdisciplinary" in their ability to admit contradictions and deal with "overdetermined" situations in which complex phenomena are typically reduced to single, cause-effect relationships:

> Unlike the linear, cause-and-effect relations that are represented by disciplinary techniques, [practitioner inquiry] arranges its data serially, spatially, paratactically, like a rhizome, however they work. A practitioner can say that basic writers have restricted codes, that restricted codes cause secondary orality, that secondary orality causes situations in which people do not (need to) read, that class and race cause a writer to expect to err, that the expectation of error causes restricted codes, that poverty causes secondary orality, and so forth. When a practitioner like Shaughnessy "solves" for all these variables at once by taking into account a multitude of structural determinants of a given problematic situation, she may—and I think must—be said to have produced knowledge. (1991, 134)

Further, for Harkin, that knowledge is theory, "elid[ing] without denying the opposition between theory and practice. And the informed intuition that produces that elision may, I would assert, be called theory—not in the sense of a metadiscourse, a generalized account of a practice to which all instances of that practice can be referred, but rather as a way of coping, contending with the overdetermined words of knowledge production" (134).

That knowledge is also power in the classroom. Teacher research forcefully illustrates a political reality: most significant changes in education occur not from the top down through dissemination of new theories generated by university researchers, but from the bottom up through the questioning and experimenting of teachers attempting to solve real problems in their own classrooms. As more and more teachers become involved in teacher research, their impact on composition studies will inevitably grow. They will begin to question and challenge the "overdetermined" research in composition and the ideologies underlying it. Teachers will become more critical consumers of composition theory. As they come to see themselves as legitimate knowledge makers, teachers will look more to each other and less to university "experts": "As time goes by, teacher-researchers will prevail in more and more curricular decisions as they become recognized as authorities in their classrooms. In effect, the locus of academic planning will move from central administrations to the teaching staff, because expertise and authority will lie with the teachers" (Bullock 1987, 26). University researchers will have to come to terms, eventually, with these challenges that teacher-researchers are posing to the field of composition studies.

Teacher Research, Postsecondary

All of the arguments for teacher research, K–12, apply to post-secondary education. College and university faculty members, including part-time and nontenured faculty members who choose to focus their efforts on teaching, can achieve the same benefits from the teacher-research movement: a sense of their own professionalism, status within educational institutions, and empowerment to effect change through a broadened definition of what it means to do "research," what constitutes "knowledge," and how teachers contribute to knowledge making in their fields.

It is time for college writing teachers, as well as K–12 teachers, to assert their importance both politically and intellectually to the field of composition studies. At this time in the history of the field, knowledge making is within the purview of researchers and theorists, and there is little or no recognition of the knowledge constructed in college classrooms and disseminated by teachers. Yet there are stirrings in higher education that a change in this perception of teaching is needed across the disciplines. As reported in *The Chronicle of Higher Education,* faculty nationwide are unhappy with the hierarchy that privileges research over teaching and other forms of scholarship. "The New American Scholar," a 1990 report released by the Carnegie Foundation for the Advancement of Teaching, argues the need to overturn old conceptions of scholarship in order to better represent what most college faculty actually do. The report acknowledges as myth the claim that all professors are researchers: a 1989 Carnegie Foundation survey determined that 71 percent of the college faculty members surveyed saw themselves as teachers rather than researchers; that 57.5 percent had never published or edited a book or monograph; that 28.2 percent had never published in a professional journal; and that 46.6 percent had had no writing accepted for publication in the past two years (Lacey 1990).

Given these findings and other indications that the current concept of scholarship does not fully represent what most faculty members actually do and value, the Carnegie report recommends that scholarship be more broadly defined to account for professional activities other than traditional research that contribute to knowledge. Applying knowledge and relating existing forms of knowledge through such activities as course development and curriculum design and communicating knowledge through such activities as teaching and consulting would be considered scholarship under the Carnegie proposal. In addition, the report also recommends that the new definition of scholarship should encourage faculty members to shift interests and support their desire to change scholarly endeavors; under the current system, faculty members are often discouraged from taking up new intellectual pursuits if these will not lead to publication in the foreseeable future.

The publication of the Carnegie report suggests that university faculty and administrators are open to new perceptions of research, including classroom-based inquiry conducted by college teachers. Indeed, the Carnegie report seems to be calling for a return to what Paul Lacey calls the "scholar-teacher" model of the professoriat, in contrast to the more typical "researcher model." Lacey, a thirty-year veteran of academe and professor of English at Earlham College, supports the scholar-teacher model, drawing on Wilbert McKeachie and Kenneth Eble's 1985 book, *Improving Undergraduate Education through Faculty Development,* to support his argument:

> From the research literature and our own experience as teachers, we can create a model that will support the professional growth of current faculty members and also help prepare future ones. That model starts by affirming that faculty members are primarily teachers. It builds its activities around the research evidence showing that individual growth is most enduring when it enhances such intrinsic satisfactions in teaching as "feelings of competence, achievement, mastery, autonomy, intellectual curiosity, and engagement," and when there are institutional structures that increase communication, enlarge the faculty member's sense of participation in the institution, and raise the institution's standards of teaching. . . .
>
> Research for publication is neither the sole nor the most effective means of enhancing those intrinsic satisfactions. Most of us need to feel them where we are most engaged professionally, in our teaching. Our satisfactions derive from whether something good happens to students, whether we are effectively communicating the best new thinking in our discipline, and whether our engagement with our material and our students helps them find their own intrinsic satisfactions as learners. (Lacey 1990, B3)

Lacey goes on to argue that scholarship at the college level, which means keeping abreast of one's discipline and the profession of higher education, also involves designing and teaching new courses, writing textbooks, preparing lectures for students and colleagues, experimenting with new technologies in the classroom, and teaching with other faculty members across disciplines. A further benefit of the scholar-teacher model is that, because it embraces different styles and paces of scholarly activity and different personal goals, it appeals to a wider range of faculty, including women and members of minority groups whose work is often more inclusive and diverse than that traditionally promoted by the researcher model (B3).

Teacher research provides an excellent means for documenting and analyzing the kind of scholarship Lacey describes. It also provides a means for college writing teachers to make visible their significant contributions to the field of composition studies. In her article on the value of teaching, Jane Peterson argues that current constructivist theories of reading, writing, and learning necessitate that we see teaching as inquiry and that we support it as such, both institutionally and professionally:

> Much has changed in these past 27 years [since the beginning of composition as a research field], and it is time to explore the implications of those changes for us as teachers—as learners and knowers. The new demands of teaching simultaneously require and develop the same habits of mind that we have long associated with research and scholarship. If we expect students to be active learners, engaged in conscious theorizing and open to being transformed, we must also approach teaching as active, committed learners and knowers. . . . Because these habits of mind, required when we act upon our theories, parallel those of the scholar who works with more traditional texts or the researcher with data, I believe that teaching writing today is not only another way of learning and knowing, another mode of inquiry, but one that offers the same intellectual stimulation and personal satisfaction that research and scholarship bestow. (1991, 32)

Composition teachers themselves, as well as university administrators and scholars, at this point still need to be convinced that their classroom work is as valuable to the field of composition as the more traditionally conceived research and scholarship. My own arguments for teacher research in this chapter are first attempts at convincing; read in conjunction with the discourse of other teacher-scholars, I hope they provoke an informed response.

What, then, has been missing in the way we create and disseminate knowledge in schools and universities? Marilyn Cochran-Smith and Susan Lytle, consummate teacher-researchers who are active proponents of the movement in education, provide a fitting summary for my argument in this chapter:

> What is missing from the knowledge base . . . are the voices of the teachers themselves, the questions teachers ask, the ways teach-

ers use writing and intentional talk in their work lives, and the interpretive frames teachers use to understand and improve their own classroom practices. Limiting the official knowledge base for teaching to what academics have chosen to study and write about has contributed to a number of problems, including discontinuity between what is taught in universities and what is taught in classrooms, teachers' ambivalence about the claims of academic research, and a general lack of information about classroom life from a truly emic perspective. (1990, 2)

Teacher research helps fill this gap in our knowledge base, as will become clear in the next two chapters, where I offer more concrete, data-based evidence to support that claim.

Notes

1. The works of Lawrence Stenhouse have been influential in Great Britain, but have received little attention in the United States. Comments in this chapter are drawn from *Research as a Basis for Teaching: Readings from the Works of Lawrence Stenhouse* (1985).

4 Comprehension from Within: K–12 Teacher Research and the Construction of Knowledge

> It's about time that somebody recognizes that what we have has validity and can surely be used to redirect the course of education.
>
> —Alicia, high school teacher

> I think too long we have gone to the experts, to the theory and drawn from them . . . and now we're going to find that people will be drawing from what just ordinary teachers have said. And the practitioners now become a little more important than the theorists, perhaps.
>
> —Loraine, elementary school principal

These are hopeful words to begin a chapter on K–12 teachers' role in the making of knowledge in composition. Not everyone believes those words, not even teachers. But it is the contention of a small but growing number of teacher-researchers that practitioners will figure prominently in the continued development of composition as a field. If most teachers have not been fully convinced of their part in creating this future, most composition researchers have not even acknowledged the possibility. The prevailing view of the theory-practice relationship in composition—indeed, the motivating force which has driven composition as a research field—is the view that formal theory is the only legitimate guide to practice: "Leaders of the reform in composition thought it self evident that rigorously developed knowledge—the 'theory' produced by disciplinary inquiry—would provide a better guide to teaching or discourse practices than incoherent, inconsistent, unreflective beliefs and maxims, the content (according to the new rhetoricians) of the textbook tradition" (Phelps 1988, 206). However, twenty years ago these leaders did not anticipate the growth of a teacher-research movement which would articulate a practice that is, in fact, coherent, consistent, reflective, and theoretical.

As a result of the influence of the new rhetoricians, most contemporary composition theorists have so far eschewed the possibility that teaching could be a form of serious inquiry and have thus overlooked the powerful implications of this inquiry, both practical and philosophical, for composition as a research field. Two composition theorists, though, have just recently begun to discuss practitioner inquiry as a serious form of knowledge making.

Stephen North's position, which acknowledges that a vast majority of professionals in composition are and always have been practitioners, is that the future of composition as a coherent field depends on its ability to reconceive practice as inquiry and to return practitioners to a position of status and influence equal to that of researchers. He claims that, over the past twenty years, the various methodological communities—historians, philosophers, critics, formalists, clinicians, experimentalists, ethnographers—have made a concerted effort to legitimize composition as a discipline at the expense of practice. As a result, in divesting practitioners of all intellectual and political authority, the researchers and scholars have fragmented the field to such an extent that "composition as a knowledge-making society is gradually pulling itself apart" (1987, 364). To assure the future health of the field, then, "radical change" must take place involving, among other things, a reorientation toward practical inquiry or lore:

> What is required here . . . as the basis for a transformed Composition, is a full recognition of and appreciation for lore: an understanding of what it is and how it works such that other kinds of knowledge can *usefully* interact with it. . . . Practitioners will have to make the same efforts as other communities to become methodologically aware and egalitarian, while the other communities must treat practice with much greater respect. (372)

North's argument here is not just intellectual; it has major political implications as well, given the fact that teachers far outnumber theorists and that teacher lore, by North's account, is far more influential among practitioners than the formal research conducted by methodological communities. Unless composition theory recognizes and embraces "its inextricable entanglement with practice" (374), it denies a part of itself and its purpose, severely limiting its potential for growth and evolution.

Although North makes these claims assertively, in the end he offers no insight into how the widespread acceptance of practice will be brought about, a limitation which he has since acknowledged as a "failure of imagination" on his part (1991). He does briefly refer at the end of his book to the National Writing Project, which he considers "an important prototype" because of its premise that experienced K–12 teachers are among the best sources of knowledge and authority among other teachers. For the most part, however, North does not distinguish among several types of practitioner inquiry (for example, research conducted collaboratively among university researchers and K–12 teachers in elementary and secondary school classrooms, research initiated and conducted by K–12 teachers independently in their own classrooms, and research conducted by postsecondary teachers in college classrooms). His argument for practitioner inquiry seems to be based primarily on the knowledge produced by K–12 teachers in their own classrooms (the group generally represented by the National Writing Project). North does not even begin to consider how practitioners in different school contexts might vary in terms of their purposes for researching, the audiences they address, the knowledge they construct, and the potential effect of this knowledge on composition as a discipline.

Louise Wetherbee Phelps constructs an argument similar to North's in *Composition as a Human Science* (1988), where she asserts that a new relationship between theory and practice must be developed:

> For some disciplines such as mathematics, praxis is not part of their self-understanding *as* disciplines. This is not the case for composition, whose distinctiveness lies in the experimental relationship it establishes between the general principles of inquiry posited and systematically pursued in science and philosophy, and the normative practice of these principles in ordinary discourse and everyday life. The role of Theory and personal theory in a teacher's life is therefore a crucial question for composition's very definition as a discipline. (237)

Phelps's greatest contribution to redefining the field in terms of practice is her insight that the theory-practice relationship, like knowledge and knowledge making themselves, is organic and ever-changing; it "is contextually defined and varies from one situation to another. Each specific case of practice raises anew the question of what theory, if any, is relevant, and how in particular it applies, and with what changes, caveats, and consequences" (207–8). Composition teachers, then, play a significant role in deciding how, where, and to what extent theory "counts." Without teachers and the governance of daily teaching practices, composition theory in the abstract has little meaning or purpose.

Phelps offers this contextualized theory-practice relationship in place of the more common view which has motivated the "reform" of composition since Braddock, Lloyd-Jones, and Schoer (1963). Most composition researchers currently accept, without question, the assumptions that theory governs practice in exactly the same way, regardless of the teaching situation, and that theory is inherently superior to practice in terms of its overall importance to the field (Phelps 1988, 207). She calls these assumptions into question and enforces the point that too often they lead to oppression and intimidation rather than enlightenment and knowledge making:

> Freire's characterization of banking education translates with
> uncomfortable precision into a description of what is too often the
> relationship that teachers form with Theory: (a) Theory instructs
> and the teacher is taught; (b) Theory knows everything and the
> teacher knows nothing; (c) Theory thinks and the teacher [prac-
> tice] is thought about; (d) Theory talks and the teacher listens.
> (213)

Drawing on John Dewey's critique of philosophical thinking that is
divorced from practical experience (*Experience and Nature* [1929]),
Phelps provides an alternative characterization of the theory-practice
relationship in composition that has the following features: (1) theory
originates in "primary experiences of discourse (by people in the roles
of teachers, learners, writers, readers, speakers, listeners) that set
problems to be solved and circumstances to be explained"; (2) theory
is constantly tested and retested in daily teaching; (3) teaching itself
"is an arena for reflection and theorizing, including experimentation
to test reflective concepts developed directly in and from primary
experience"; (4) theory and teacher education function, in part, "to
articulate and deepen teachers' reflective powers within praxis,
making these more systematic and sustained"; and (5) by virtue of
these relationships, "teachers' personal and collective experience
logically has priority over the products of systematic inquiry, since
such experience is both source and ultimate testing ground for
theoretical conceptions" (1988, 211).

In order to accept that teaching is a form of inquiry and that it is a
necessary and inevitable part of knowledge making in the field, most
composition researchers will need more evidence than either North
or Phelps provides. While Phelps constructs a compelling philosophical argument, she leaves the real proof of it to other researchers.
In a later work, however, she does lay the groundwork for future
research that would more specifically support her theory.

In an article written three years after *Composition as a Human
Science*, Phelps extends the argument presented in the final chapter
of her book, offering more direction as to how compositionists might
conceptualize and study practical inquiry. "Practical Wisdom and
the Geography of Knowledge in Composition" outlines a phenom-
enology of teaching that entails the "essential, defining qualities of
practical wisdom, along with its knowledge sources and knowledge
products" (1991, 868–69) and that construes teaching as "an expertise
based on experience that is understood as a complementary form of
knowledge" (869). By her definition, teaching becomes disciplinary
knowledge when it "makes a public claim on others for attention,
belief, or appropriation, rather than merely announcing private

experiences" (869). This public knowledge is "rhetorical" in that it "seeks universality or generalization through representation and communication in expressive forms" (869). Phelps explicitly names teacher research as an example of practical inquiry that leads to disciplinary knowledge. One of her main points is that teacher research produces a *different kind* of knowledge rhetorically than that produced by formal research: "In particular, practical and formal inquiry differ by choosing to make themselves responsible to a local and cosmopolitan community, respectively; this choice correlates with differences in method and standards of rigor, audience, genre, and so on across the classical dimensions of rhetorical analysis" (880). Phelps names some of these differences by referring to the Syracuse Writing Program as a general example of practitioner inquiry. Because she does not make the Syracuse community or its writing the direct object of her analysis or discussion, her argument is still essentially hypothetical. It is also rather one-dimensional because it conflates, as does North's argument, all types of practitioner inquiry in suggesting that the Syracuse Writing Program, which includes university researchers and graduate teaching assistants training to become university researchers, is reflective of teacher research communities in general. Thus Phelps's work has some of the same limitations she sees in North's work: in arguing that practitioners are capable of creating new knowledge when confronted with problems in their own teaching that require creative thinking, she "is unable to play out that possibility in much detail phenomeno- logically" (872).

My purpose in this chapter and the next is to provide some of this missing detail by presenting the findings of my own teacher research on teacher-researchers. Through specific reference to the work of seven teacher-researchers who were part of a 1989 National Writing Project summer institute, I illustrate in this chapter Phelps's two main philosophical points: (1) that there are some conditions and qualities of teacher research that distinguish it rhetorically from formal aca- demic research and (2) that teacher research has the generative power to force compositionists "to rethink our understandings of the- oretical knowledge-making as a rhetorical activity" (1991, 882). In providing evidence for these two points, I am, in effect, answering the larger question of what kind of knowledge practitioner inquiry produces and how it is relevant to composition as a discipline. I draw conclusions exclusively on the basis of K–12 teachers who are independently researching their own classrooms. The knowledge that these National Writing Project teachers create differs in some ways from the knowledge created by teacher-researchers working in university communities. The differences between the perspectives of these two communities and the knowledge they create and communicate will become more apparent in the next chapter, where I describe the workings of another community—graduate students in a seminar on teacher research that I conducted during the winter 1991 semester at Wayne State University in Detroit. For now, though, we will be concerned with the outcomes of practitioner inquiry conducted by K–12 teachers.

The National Writing Project Participants

The details provided in this chapter come from interviews with and analysis of the writing produced by seven teachers enrolled in the Metro-Detroit area National Writing Project Institute II, a course designed to train experienced teachers to become researchers in their own classrooms. Overall, the participants represented grades K through 12, although one participant was a retired elementary school principal teaching a college composition class at the time. All had been involved in a previous National Writing Project course (Institute I), which focused on developing teachers' interests in and experience with writing. However, none of the teachers had conducted practitioner inquiry before; in fact, most of the participants, with one exception, had had little or no contact with teacher research before enrolling in Institute II. The primary motivation for these teachers was to upgrade their skills and retool intellectually for the coming school year, in the process receiving four graduate credits from Wayne State.

Conducted as a seminar, the class met three days a week, three hours a day, for five weeks in the summer of 1989. These meetings were organized around discussion of assigned readings and teachers' responses, as well as discussion of teachers' initial research questions. After the five-week session was over, the group met once a month on Saturdays during the 1989–90 school year to discuss their research in progress and to respond, in the early months, to each other's ideas and questions and, in the later months, to each other's drafts and revisions of a final paper reporting the results of their study. The meetings ended in March 1990, when participants presented their papers at the Fourth Annual Conference of the Michigan Writing Project in Detroit.

Institute II was taught by a full-time faculty member who is also assistant director of composition in the English department at Wayne State. Although I was not present for most of the group's meetings, I conversed regularly with the presiding faculty member, participated in a Saturday meeting in January when the group discussed semifinal drafts, met individually with each teacher at the end of the school year for a lengthy interview, and analyzed the teachers' final papers in terms of their interview comments. (See interview questions, Appendix A.) My conclusions about this group of teacher-researchers, then, are largely based on a retrospective analysis of their talk and texts. This approach is justifiable because I am primarily concerned here with characterizing a particular type of practitioner inquiry. I want to illustrate the unique characteristics of teacher research that is primarily oriented to the K–12 classroom, as evident in the conversation and writing of the seven National Writing Project teachers. My purpose is to substantiate and elaborate on Phelps's claim that teacher research can be distinguished from formal, academic inquiry by the types of knowledge it creates. I organize my conclusions around two terms that Phelps uses to characterize this knowledge—"local" and "global"—and include a third, "personal," which interpenetrates both local and global knowledge.

Personal Knowledge

Any discussion of teacher research must acknowledge the fact that most practitioner inquiry begins and ends with personal knowledge. Personal knowledge is what teachers construct about themselves, their teaching, and their interactions in the classroom. A standard argument for K–12 practitioner inquiry is that it improves the self-understanding and self-esteem of teachers, thereby improving teaching. All of the National Writing Project teachers assert that the research they conducted did indeed enhance their own learning and positively affect their teaching. Nancy, a high school teacher in a rural community about an hour's drive from Detroit is a good example. She claims that the note-taking, journal keeping, reflection, and recursiveness required to conduct practitioner inquiry was a major factor in her intellectual development. In the first and last paragraphs of her final paper, Nancy describes her own learning process over the school year:

> Looking back on my early journal entries written during the first week of school, I found I had noted that recursiveness is as vital in education as it is in writing. As educators, we must return regularly to earlier thoughts, expanding, comprehending, and developing new offshoots, tying them to earlier ideas, and with these bridges, develop meaning for our classrooms and our worlds. . . .

> As my students were able to verbalize their own learning when writing about their writing, keeping journals and writing about my teaching has allowed me to see what I've learned about my students and my classroom, revealing what I've taught effectively, recording effective and ineffective techniques, showing me where I've been, and pointing me where I need to go. The process has also created far more questions, piqued my interest to do more reading, and helped me to see how I can most effectively help my students to learn.

Nancy's comments are typical of teacher-researchers, who believe that self-discovery and personal development are prerequisites for improved teaching. Another illustration of this point is Ron, a high school teacher in the same rural school system as Nancy. Conservative by nature, Ron claims that his year of researching "kind of freed me about taking risks. . . . I was more willing to try different things in the classroom that were not really compatible with my teaching methods before." Thinking of his research year as an experimental one, Ron became less concerned about failing in the classroom because he "had a reason to fall back on"—the fact that he was doing something totally new (practitioner inquiry) that few of his colleagues had tried. Although his year was sometimes frustrating and his teaching experiments not always successful, Ron now says that practitioner inquiry will have a lasting effect on both his self-perception and his performance in the classroom. For this reason, he urges that teacher research "be incorporated into any type of graduate program in teacher education because you take more risk and you begin to have some introspection about yourself and your teaching methods. You are very concerned with how your methods, or what's going on in your classroom, relate to what's being learned by students. . . . It [research] now just seems a logical step in the teaching process."

Most revealing for Ron is the fact that self-reflection and introspection led him to challenge some strongly held beliefs and assumptions, such as the necessity of a teacher-directed classroom for high school students. His final paper focuses on this self-discovery, as reflected in the research journal he kept on his tenth-grade English class. He had not anticipated that his writing would take this direction. At the beginning of the school year, he had intended to focus exclusively on the outcomes of his teaching, documenting the effect of particular "mini-lessons" compared with teacher-directed mastery instruction on students' learning, but he became dissatisfied with this research direction and doubted his ability to follow it. In his final paper Ron explains:

[Negative] thoughts about my ability to be an academic researcher were soothed by my interest in doing the best for my students. I wanted to do what worked. Ethics became more important to me than the findings. Yet I still had a research project [to do] and I was still recording my observations.

I began searching for a new focus. . . . During a class discussion with my fellow researchers about my difficulty, they suggested I do a case study about myself. The result of this was that the next three school days I did not write any observations in my journal. I had trouble accepting the idea that there was anything about myself worth writing. I had thought the content of the research was important. I had not yet realized it was the process itself that makes the difference.

Eventually, Ron got used to the idea that he himself was changing as a result of his research and that other teachers might learn as much or more from this personal change as they could from the research findings. His final paper, entitled "Journaling to Learn," chronicles Ron's relinquishing over the course of the school year his self-defined role as "benevolent dictator" and his working to develop an environment where students take more responsibility for their learning. One of his discoveries was that

by keeping notes, I not only changed my teaching strategies, but I also changed the way I reacted to my students. I found myself recording observations of my students' behaviors and not reacting so quickly to them. . . . In going through my journal I found many reminders to myself: "Be patient—take your time. REMEMBER: LEARNING IS A PROCESS." So the journal helped remind me to act on a personality fault of mine—impatience.

Ron raises the significant point that the end product of teacher research may not be as important to the inquiring teacher as the personal process of getting to it. Phelps makes this claim in the form of a hypothesis, suggesting that, if the process of practitioner inquiry is more important than the results, as a consequence "much of the knowledge developed from practical inquiry is short-lived; it is really a sophisticated form of feedback that needs constant updating" (1991, 881). This possibility does not, however, negate the long-term effects that practitioner inquiry has on teachers' thinking and self-perception.

Nancy talks further about the importance of teacher research in terms of improving teachers' self-image: "Teacher research allows you, the teacher, to look at yourself more as a scholar. . . . American teachers I don't believe consider themselves to be scholars. If you ask the average classroom teacher anywhere in the USA and say, are you a scholar? most of them would look at you like you were crazy."

Raising the self-perception of teachers through research is, according to Nancy, a crucial first step in the professionalization of teachers:

> Teachers don't perceive themselves as professionals because teachers, especially in larger systems ... don't have a tremendous amount of control. Now in small schools you do. ... I know all of our board members on a first-name basis. It's the type of system ... where you can have a tremendous amount of input without having a horrendous amount of [trouble]. Not that you don't have to justify what you're doing, but we don't have to go through committee after committee after committee for a taxable change. We just get together after school and look at what we want to look at, decide where holes are, what we need, and do it. We go to the board, and the board asks us what we want to change, and we tell them. ... We're allowed quite a bit of input. I guess I'm feeling from many of the teachers I talk with that they don't really have that input. They're told to be on page 95 on September 30 and that's it. I guess I see this [teacher research] as helping teachers' self-esteem. I guess what it boils down to is if they believe they have input, if they believe that they can make a change, they do. ... I think we need to have teachers have input as to what goes on, and in order to have input into what goes on, I think teachers need to justify some of the things they believe. Teacher research allows that.

Teacher-researchers experience this personal development themselves and also assist their colleagues in developing self-esteem by providing positive role models for other teachers who initially doubt their scholarly potential. Loraine, an elementary school principal, makes this point when she suggests that "other teachers [will become] interested [by] reading teacher research. ... They will begin to think 'Gosh, I did that in the classroom. What's the big deal? Maybe I'm better than I thought I was!' "

Another way in which teacher research increases self-esteem and leads to personal knowledge is through the questioning process. Asking the right questions (those that address their major concerns) in the right way (in a manner that is focused narrowly enough to allow for systematic inquiry) became a major issue for all of the National Writing Project teachers in the course. Each noted that the process of choosing and forming a single research question was one of the most important and exasperating aspects of practitioner inquiry. Yet the very fact that they *had* so many researchable questions and that these questions led to even more questions was confirmation of their own knowledge, experience, and scholarly potential. For example, when asked if she experienced any problems as a teacher-researcher, Nancy responded:

> It's not really a problem—I think it's maybe more of a revelation—
> that you think you have your questions, and then you go further,
> and more questions evolve from the questions. Pretty soon you're
> sitting there thinking, "What do I want? Which direction do I want
> to go in?" So many avenues open up that you almost become
> overwhelmed.

Although frustrating, this expansion of inquiry is also what excites
teachers and motivates them to continue researching. As Loraine
wryly noted during a Saturday session, "Now that we've started, we
can never stop researching. Our last paper will be on writing in the old
folks' home!"

Local Knowledge

Through the construction of personal knowledge, teacher-researchers come to the construction of local knowledge, defined here as
knowledge for the community of teachers within one's department,
school, community, district, or state. Clearly, for the National Writing
Project teachers, development of personal knowledge was primary.
Then, as a result of increased self-understanding and improved
teaching in their own classrooms, they began to think about presenting their findings to the local teaching community. Knowledge
created within the classroom may be slow to circulate, but when the
word does get around, it can have a significant impact. Alicia, a high
school teacher in inner-city Detroit, discusses this influence when
she addresses the question: Who, if anyone, benefits from teacher
research?

> The teacher, the students, and—if the whole school understands
> and can see the validity, can see the end results of teacher
> research—the whole school [benefits]. If the findings are really
> important and are published, whoever is in the field of education
> can benefit. If anybody is really interested in restructuring and in
> meeting the needs, anybody who cares can benefit, whether that's
> a politician, an administrator, a parent, or a fellow teacher.
> Anybody who's interested in forging ahead can benefit.

The benefits she speaks of come not so much through formal publication of a written paper as through curricular change which begins
with individual teachers:

> It [publication] is an appropriate result, but it in itself is not the
> end result. Implementation is the end result to me. So far as
> presenting it to my colleagues is concerned, fine, but if I never had
> a chance to present it to my colleagues, if I tried it in my own

classroom and had it spread to other classrooms, to have students take what I've done with them and go out into the larger world, that to me is the end result.

When asked to elaborate on how this implementation is communicated within a large public school, Alicia describes the process this way:

It happens on my own level. It has to start with me. I have to find a way and be creative enough to do what I need to do in my own classroom. And then, if it has merit and I'm going in the right direction, it will spread. . . . Students take it with them; they do what we've practiced in this classroom, or they try anyway. When another teacher sees somebody doing something differently . . . or his writing begins to take a different turn in someone else's classroom and that particular teacher can see what he's doing and see that he has some degree of success, then maybe that teacher will also accept the same thing from other students or try to teach other students, or ask the youngster who's succeeding, "Where did you learn this?" and take it from there.

Other National Writing Project teachers agree that slow but steady changes occur among teachers locally when they see in students' and colleagues' work the results of another practitioner's inquiry. Nancy, for example, observes that teacher research "really does lend itself to sharing, not as in going out and telling everybody, 'I've got a great idea!' but if people see the results, you can share that. They wonder what you're doing. It's a slower share, but I think perhaps it has more impact." Loraine mentions that she began to have more influence on the teachers in her school after she presented the results of her study, which concludes that the fifth graders she surveyed and observed liked to write much more than their teachers thought they did and were not being given as many varied opportunities to write as they wanted. Communicating these findings to students and faculty, in Loraine's words,

had an overall positive effect, a small effect, but still I began to see more writing being done within the building. And I'd always encourage students to bring down good work and teachers to send down good work. . . . I mean, change is very slow, especially with a staff that has been [together] for a number of years in one place and has not changed their teaching habits for a number of years. So I feel this is a kind of accomplishment, and perhaps we can do more next year.

These teacher-researchers suggest that informal publication of practitioner inquiry through observable changes in students' and teachers' behavior has a more lasting impact on a local writing curriculum than any conference presentation or formally published journal article ever could. For them, the necessary step past words is always action—research leading to changes in teaching, however slow or subtle. Teaching leads to researching and back to teaching in a self-perpetuating cycle. One reason why the various forms of "publishing" are effective is that K–12 teacher-researchers typically identify with and address the concerns of teachers in their own communities. Thus many teachers have come to value practitioner inquiry over formal research because it is relevant to them on many levels: it is based on real teachers' questions, generated in actual classroom situations with which teachers are familiar, framed in teachers' language, and directed specifically to an audience of teachers. Nancy notes that

> the single biggest complaint I hear from teachers when they read educational material is, "They don't have my kids. They don't deal with my classes. They're in their own little world, and they've never seen kids who've had to milk cows for two hours in the morning and three hours at night," or whatever. Teacher research is accepted more by teachers because the teacher-researcher is the same type of teacher, and she's dealing with a lot of the same problems.

As a result of their similar situations, teacher-researchers ask the kinds of questions that most teachers want to know the answers to. The following questions from the seven National Writing Project studies, for example, have surely occurred to most writing teachers: Exactly what thinking difficulties do students experience while writing? Does a connection exist between the quality of students' writing and their attitude toward writing? Do students who dislike writing share any common elements or experiences? If individual students can speak fluently in class, why don't they write as fluently? How can students be taught to switch from neighborhood speech to standard written and spoken English, while maintaining positive feelings about themselves and their communities? How might weekly student evaluations affect teaching? How do students' self-perceptions affect their writing? How do their self-perceptions change over the course of a semester or school year? These questions reflect universal teacher concerns. Indeed, Fredie, an assistant middle-school principal and codirector of Institute II, asserts that "most of the questions asked by individual teacher-researchers are probably asked by teachers all over the world. . . . Teachers' concerns are global, not just local. We all have similar, typical problems: keeping students interested in learning."

In some cases, the National Writing Project teachers considered the *process* of formulating and revising their research questions important enough to highlight in their final papers. Fredie, for example, focuses on the questioning process in her introduction:

> During the first week of August, a former National Writing Project fellow called to chat. He discussed how he had assisted a group of special education youngsters with a difficult writing task. I commented on the positive results he described and questioned him about his own writing efforts. I asked if his method of writing had influenced how he taught the children. He hesitated for a while before replying, "I haven't written much lately, and I am not sure if how I write influences how I teach writing."
>
> At that moment, I knew the area I wanted to find out more about.... I wrote many versions of what later became the question, "Is there a correlation between how teachers write and how they teach writing?"

The significance of this narrative is that it places Fredie's study within the community of practitioners by describing how the research question arose, not from other theorists' work (as formal research suggests), but from talking with another teacher about teaching. In so doing, it illustrates how teachers' values and priorities are inscribed in the framing of their research questions. Fredie's discourse suggests that she sees the authority of her work coming, in part, from the personal, collaborative situation from which it arises.

Indeed, for K–12 teacher-researchers in general, there seems to be a natural relationship between the creation of personal knowledge and the creation of local knowledge. Nancy describes this relationship in terms of the theory-practice connection:

> I think teacher research is a way to move ideas from the theoretical into the practical, and I think in that regard it breeds success. When you succeed in transferring part of it [the theory] over, and you can prove to people that this [theory] works—I guess I've been increasingly sharing material, probably more than I ever realized, because so often in a classroom you close the door and nobody sees what anybody else is doing—I think that's another really positive aspect of teacher research and the whole National Writing Project. You start to realize that what you have and what you're doing might be of value to someone else, and you also seek out what they're doing because you know it's going to be of value to you.

The work of the National Writing Project teachers, then, substantiates, at least in part, Phelps's hypothesis that "knowledge developed in practical inquiry is bound in origin and by purpose to its community, though not primarily or at all to the individual practice of the inquirer. Its fate is to return to that community in order to inform further decision-making" (1991, 881). As Loraine writes in the implications section of her final paper: "The major goal of this study was not to provide answers for others (though, if sought, perhaps they might be found here), but to examine a local situation to determine the status of student writing and if improvement was needed." This local focus occurs, in part, because most K–12 practitioners do not aspire to become members of professional organizations that work to create a more "global professional culture" (Phelps 1991, 880). K–12 teachers are not as highly motivated as formal researchers by the desire for recognition that comes from membership in a global culture. The fact that most K–12 teacher-researchers make the rhetorical choice not to situate themselves and their work within the traditions of formal research communities, such as empiricists, historians, critics, and philosophers, also indicates the difference between their beliefs and values and those of formal researchers. While most formal researchers are committed to the idea of change occurring from the top down—from the global to the local level by way of theory—teacher-researchers are committed to the idea that significant, lasting educational change occurs from the bottom up—from the individual classroom to the larger community by way of practitioner inquiry.

Global Knowledge

Global knowledge refers to knowledge which is constructed for the field of composition, which includes formal researchers and theorists as well as nonresearching teachers and teacher-researchers. Contrary to Phelps's suggestion, some K–12 teacher-researchers do think of their work in global terms. They do not, however, separate personal, local, and global knowledge the way formal researchers tend to do. For teacher-researchers, these forms of knowledge are indistinguishable; they intermingle, animate, and inform one another.

The interests of K–12 teacher-researchers in contributing to global, field-based knowledge is evident in the way they talk about methodology, including the level and scope of their research questions and the validity and reliability of their findings. The comments of Melvania, a second-grade Detroit public school teacher, illustrate her concerns about focus and validity:

> It was difficult for me to narrow my range, because I had so many things going on [in my head]. But eventually I did, and then I had

a difficult time trying to figure out, well, how am I going to measure this? What ways are there to measure this? And finally I decided, well, you can do this and this. And even at that, I'm not sure it was an accurate measure because ... there are certain kinds of things that are going on when children write, you know, in the brain and in the hands and all that. So I was thinking perhaps I wasn't really getting accurate measurements by using the writing and the tape player, but that was all I had as a teacher.

Melvania's concern about validity is in large part a reflection of her previous experiences in the college of education. As a graduate student working on a master's degree, she had been trained to value the positivist model of research widely promoted in the global community. She wants to make sure that her study will gain the approval of this community and perhaps affect its thinking. This influence is also apparent in the comments of John, the retired elementary school principal who conducted his research in a college English class:

This [teacher-research seminar] was important for us as educators because we've gone through the traditional training for research as part of our higher education, so it was really important that we had some retraining and reorientation into ethnographic research and teacher research in a place like the classroom, as opposed to what we imagined research to be from our past courses. It was a very important thing to think ahead, [to consider] validity, and to respect it [teacher research] as a legitimate process . . . to know what the structure of the process is and that it *is* orderly, that it *does* have to make sense, that you *do* have certain things that you need to think through and go through, that you *do* need a continuity, a consistency. All of these things are important, and then to go out and do it, because it's like experiencing the writing process; experiencing it is part of the confirmation of it.

Melvania's and John's concerns for the legitimacy of practitioner inquiry and the validity of teachers' findings are much like the concerns of formal researchers. The primary difference is that the community they envision reading their work and evaluating its authority consists primarily of teachers and administrators rather than researchers. Most of these readers have been trained to view research from the perspective of a global educational community which has traditionally valued quantitative, experimental inquiry over qualitative, interpretive inquiry, so teacher-researchers feel compelled to address methodolgical issues. For teacher-researchers, though, validity is measured not so much in terms of adherence to formal research procedures, as in terms of what can be done practically and unobtrusively in the classroom and what would yield information of use to teachers and students working in similar situations. Given these priorities, K–12 teacher-researchers tend to define *methodology* less rigidly than do formal researchers. Their methodological flexibility is a positive contribution to the field, according to John, who sees teacher research

> as lending itself to some fluidness and a little less rigidity than what I associate with a traditional research project where everything has to be spelled out totally in the beginning. That [kind of research] has its place, but when we're dealing with real, live people in a real, live setting, I think that there is equal validity when you discover something that is significant to go ahead and bring that in, or to take something out, because you're trying to discover something in the end that I don't think will be invalidated by modifications as you go along.

From this perspective, method is merely a means to an end, and the end (better teaching and learning) justifies some modification of the means. Thus John considers his final study valid, even though he started out in September planning to measure students' thinking formally, using Bloom's taxonomy, and ended up in February drawing informal conclusions based on students' journal writing.

Phelps argues, too, for the legitimacy of such methodological flexibility on the basis of her observations of university-based teacher-researchers in the Syracuse Writing Program:

> One might expect that either practical inquiry would have its own unique "method," less rigorous than those of disciplinary inquiry (North's claim), or would select one or two appropriate research methods to follow as precisely as possible. Instead, we have been surprised to find in projects at Syracuse that practitioners develop strategies for informal inquiry that bear an *analogic* relationship to an array of formal methods. Teachers use available forms of research and scholarship, but practice them in characteristically different ways with potential for their own kind of rigor. The differences are not arbitrary, careless, or ignorant (some teachers have research training); rather, our practitioners are adapting approaches to fit the circumstances of practical activity focused on curriculum. (1991, 878; emphasis hers)

Phelps goes on to explain this analogic relationship in terms of Aristotle's discussion of rhetoric as a counterpart to dialectic. She suggests that practitioner inquiry (like rhetoric) is a counterpart to formal inquiry (akin to dialectics) in its attempts to serve different audiences and purposes and its liberal use of several methods, including case study, participant observation, interview, stylistic analysis, and phenomenological description. Further, it must be emphasized that this flexible, eclectic approach does not make teacher research any less valid or rigorous than formal inquiry:

> Rigor lies, after all, not in rules and techniques, but in the values that inspire them—values like honesty, heuristic passion, control, objectivity, or openness to the truth of a situation (Polanyi). We need to examine in detail how such values translate from theoretical to practical worlds of knowing, in aspects of inquiry like framing problems, observing carefully, validating results, attributing ideas to others, and following conventions for representing truths and arguing them to others. (1991, 878)

In other words, teacher research shows us that "the interpretation of rigor is a rhetorical issue," just as the interpretation of many other aspects of research is, or should be, dependent on the context in which the research is conducted and the audience for which it is intended.

Methodological eclecticism leads inevitably to rhetorical eclecticism. As a result, it is often difficult to put the written products of teacher-researchers into established research genres. By *genre* I mean "a set of rules and strategies for encoding and expressing knowledge, which usually include epistemological, methodological, communicative and linguistic standards and conventions" (Phelps 1991, 882). Although Susan Threatt has suggested that teacher research is a "new genre" distinct from other forms of inquiry (1990), we might more accurately say that it combines existing genres for its own distinct purposes. Although their general preference for qualitative or interpretive approaches is well documented (Berthoff; Carr and Kemmis; Bissex and Bullock; Knoblauch and Brannon), teacher-researchers also make frequent use of quantitative approaches such as surveys, questionnaires, and test results, often within the frame of a qualitative study. As a result, teacher research ends up being a kind of hybrid text—part narrative, part case study, part experiment, part ethnography, part discourse analysis.

There are some practical problems with this rhetorical eclecticism. For one, as already indicated, most teachers have been trained to read and value more traditionally developed research and may initially feel uneasy about the lack of a prescribed structure for reporting classroom inquiry. For this reason, when asked what she would do if she were training teachers to become researchers, Melvania focuses on providing more structure for writing:

> I'd give them a little more insight into methods of writing up the research, because what happens is, if you've gone to [a university education school] and they have given you a format for writing,

> you think that's the way everyone wants a research project written up. Then when they come and say, "We want you to be our teacher-researcher, and we want you to write whatever it is that you find," you've got in your head this framework that you got from the university, and it doesn't work. So I think if they spent a little more time perhaps reviewing a research situation and then practice writing it up—how would you write this, how would you express this, what did you see—I think that would be helpful.

In Chapter 5, I follow through in more detail on the rhetorical issues raised by teacher-researchers' eclecticism, particularly when it involves the construction of personal knowledge. The point for now is that written reports, however difficult to categorize in terms of genre, do figure prominently in teacher research. In reading North, one would not reach this conclusion, for he defines practitioner inquiry largely in terms of its orality: practitioners are distinct from formal researchers in that they communicate their findings in face-to-face conversation carried on in hallways and staff lounges. Phelps, in contrast, does acknowledge that "writing for the local audience is equally important in a teaching community: for reflective practice (making proposals, drawing up course plans, thinking back over a teaching experience, exchanging observations, and so on); and for reporting, debating, and acting on local knowledge derived in practical inquiries" (1991, 880).

On the one hand, the National Writing Project teachers' emphasis on writing is not surprising: all of the participants are English teachers who have chosen to be in the project, thereby accepting its philosophy that teachers can teach writing better if they are writers themselves. On the other hand, the seriousness and intensity with which they talk about their own writing seems unusual for a group of full-time practitioners whose primary job is teaching and who are not expected to write or publish as part of their profession. Something about practitioner inquiry appears to increase teachers' *need* to write, even for a global audience.

Several of the National Writing Project teachers indicate that, through personal inquiry and various forms of local publishing, teacher research may lead to the desire to contribute to global knowledge. The following exchange between Loraine and me suggests how this happens:

> *Ruth:* How did you share your results? Did you pass around the written product or do some oral presentation?
>
> *Loraine:* No, no I did an oral presentation with the students and with the teachers.

Ruth: Oh, in front of the students too?

Loraine: Mmmhmm. Yes, oh yes. I told the students, and of course everything [I said] was positive. I told them how interesting it was, how I found that so many liked writing. I used terms that, you know, would get all the fifth graders involved. And I told the teachers about it, and when they questioned me, I answered. If they had requested a copy of the writing, I would have given it to them. No one requested; I didn't think they would. . . .

Ruth: So now you're planning to publish this a little more formally in a journal?

Loraine: I would like to.

Ruth: Uh-huh. You mentioned that you liked to write. Is this something now that you'll be doing in the future—teacher research and then reporting it to your colleagues and other professionals?

Loraine: I should hope so. I think I would like to. In fact . . . perhaps you've seen in my final written statement that I did mention a lot of questions that arose in my mind—mysteries since then that I'd like to pursue. So hopefully I'll find time.

Ruth: Do you think the [formal] publication of teacher research results is an important aspect of the process?

Loraine: I think it's very important. It's especially relevant nowadays when people are feeling a lot of pressures within the classroom. I think it makes the teacher who feels isolated or frustrated feel like a more important contributor to education. I think it gives teachers an opportunity to . . . go beyond the classroom and actually reach out to educators in general, no longer as a teacher who just has the authority within that room for those children, but now the teacher becomes an authority involved with the method. They are the authority because they actually were there when this [research] was going on, and they reported it. . . .

   I think before, when teachers felt the need to rise above the classroom, they went into administration . . . but I always see teachers now who like teaching and want to remain in the classroom fulfilling themselves more by becoming teacher-researchers, especially if they get some input from people who read and share their results and perhaps try things because of the studies they have done. I think it's a new dimension in teaching, almost another side of teaching. It's exciting.

Loraine raises an important point: conducting and publishing teacher research gives practitioners a new avenue for professional advancement that allows them to continue teaching yet experience the challenge, change, and rejuvenation that come from new work. In learning about themselves and their own teaching and in communicating this knowledge within their local communities, teacher-re-

searchers expand their world, and they find themselves more interested in contributing to a larger community of scholars. This is why
Donald Schon, in his *Reflective Practitioner* (1983), claims that
practitioner inquiry is one of the most effective means of professional
development and one of the best preventive measures for professional
burnout.

Knowledge Making as Rhetorical

The thoughts and feelings of these seven teacher-researchers—and
the directness and intensity with which they are expressed—provide
the best evidence available that "our understanding of the tensions
and ties between theory and practice can be framed fruitfully in terms
of the rhetorical demands of each community, reflecting their different commitments with respect to knowledge and their different
relationships to the experiences and claims of other thinkers" (Phelps
1991, 882). The work of the National Writing Project teachers reveals
that teacher-researchers conduct inquiry for some of the same reasons
that many formal researchers in composition do: to generate and test
new ideas about the teaching of writing and to communicate those
ideas to others for the purpose of encouraging change. But there are
some differences, too: K–12 teacher-researchers begin with the pri-
macy of personal knowledge, which motivates and informs the
creation of local and global knowledge. These forms of knowledge are
communicated in various ways, both spoken and written, and are
characterized by methodological and rhetorical diversity.

It is imperative that composition theorists see these differences
between formal research and practitioner inquiry as assets rather than
liabilities in the making and disseminating of knowledge in the field.
Where formal researchers have been unsuccessful in transforming
classrooms through theory, teacher-researchers may succeed in doing
so through practical inquiry. The time has come for composition as a
discipline to accept the fact that, at least for K–12 teachers, "the
research most likely to improve teaching and learning is that conducted by teachers on questions they themselves have formulated in
response to problems or issues in their own teaching" (Cross and
Angelo 1988, 2). Most teachers know the truth of this statement
intuitively; most researchers have yet to be convinced of it.

It is also necessary to recognize that the importance of practitioner
inquiry in no way undermines the importance of theory. In composition, theory and practice exist—or should exist—in dynamic tension,
counterbalancing one another. Theory provides the "infusions of

intellectual energy" necessary to sustain good practice: "A writing program becomes capable of novelty and change because it is open to the surprises of theory. *Theory galvanizes and disrupts the system, changing its very questions, undermining long-held beliefs, introducing ambiguities, revealing complexities, setting new tasks, forcing risks*" (Phelps 1991, 883; emphasis hers). In return, practice challenges, questions, interprets, supports, and refutes theory within individual contexts. Practitioners realize, on a daily basis, the full implications of theory for the teaching and learning of writing in particular classrooms. How this interanimation of theory and practice works is described by John as he reflects on his own practitioner inquiry:

> *Ruth:* When I say the word "theory," what do you think of?
>
> *John:* Well, a general idea that we don't know the truth of or have a specific application for. But it seems to provide some general answers for some general problems or general observations.
>
> *Ruth:* Okay. Now do you see any relationship between theory or theories and teacher research?
>
> *John:* A fair relationship, because we have a lot of things we assume, that we don't check out, and there's value in checking out some of these assumptions. Teacher research can be one of the ways to do it. It's also finding out whether what works in other contexts can work in my context. . . .
>
> *Ruth:* Okay. So you see the teacher research-theory relationship as the teacher moving from some generalized theory or maybe even an unarticulated theory, an assumption, to the testing of that theory in the research and then confirming it, or calling it into question, or somehow challenging it?
>
> *John:* And it—right—that's one way [it works]. There's also the reverse. Sometimes teachers have done a good deal of observing over a period of time, and they've begun to hazily formulate some theory or theories of their own but have not taken the time, made the effort, or reflected on it enough to formulate it specifically. Sometimes, if they move into the mode of being a teacher-researcher, that might be motivation to really formulate their thinking into a more specific idea or theory and then say, "Now I will check this out specifically to see how it is and how I might benefit students more by attending to it and using its implications as a regular classroom practice." So you can check out things that your experience has suggested to you, but you haven't really put together and made as much of as you could.
>
> *Ruth:* Which direction did you move in your project? From theory to practice or practice to theory?
>
> *John:* I have a feeling I moved back and forth.
>
> *Ruth:* So that leaves a third possibility then.

John: Let's see . . . I was interested in metacognition and how the mind works while a person is writing, but that was pretty hazy. Then I began to single out, what is this going to mean in practice and how can I get some handles on it? And then I got into looking at practice, and then from practice I kind of went back to the overall context of what I was trying to do in theory. It seems to me I was flowing really between the two and discovering all the way. . . .

In her argument for teacher research, Eleanor Duckworth describes the "flow" John talks about between theory and practice in terms of the making of knowledge in clinical psychology:

My view of teaching suggests an analogy to the work of a psycho-therapist with a research interest. She is both a practitioner and a researcher. She could not possibly learn anything significant about psychodynamics if she were not genuinely engaged in the therapeutic process. It is only because she knows how to do her job as a practitioner that she is in a position to pursue her questions as a researcher. I would like to propose that similarly, through teaching, one is in a position to pursue questions about the development of understanding that one could not pursue in any other way. (1986, 490)

Feminist critics have said essentially the same thing about the importance of personal investment in relating literary theory and the practice of feminism. As Elaine Showalter reminds us, "Observation from an exterior point of view could never be the same as comprehension from within" (1985a, 261).

As a final caveat, I should make it clear that, although I argue strongly in favor of widespread practitioner inquiry and believe that all graduate students in composition should learn how to conduct it (see Chapter 6), I do not believe that teachers *need* to be granted the title of "researcher" in order to acquire status and authority in the field. I am not of the opinion—as are many of my colleagues in composition, according to North—that writing pedagogy lags far behind its potential because teachers resist, misinterpret, misuse, and oversimplify theory. Good teachers should be respected and consulted for the expertise and insight they have gained from the daily experience of teaching; they do not need to conduct research in order to "earn" this respect. Teacher research is merely an added dimension that can help practitioners realize and articulate their enormous potential as change agents. The claim that teachers need to become researchers before they can be heard and acknowledged as "legitimate" knowledge makers in composition is met by self-respecting teachers with indignation.

My time with the participants in the National Writing Project and other teacher-researchers has shown me that dignity and importance within one's field come not from research itself, but from the spirit and intellect that motivate it—from the desire to continue learning and improving one's work and one's world. Alicia is a good example of such motivation. In addition to teaching English five days a week in one of Detroit's most troubled high schools, she serves as student adviser, teaches Sunday school, conducts an adult education class of working women on Saturdays, teaches summer school, and raises her own family of four children. She bespeaks a professionalism which has nothing to do with research:

> If we had to do something such as formalize teacher research to recognize the merit of teachers, that does not say very much for us as a society. If I had to be recognized or catered to because I now have the ability to do research in my own classroom, then that has really put this nation down in a hole. You have entrusted me to teach your children for all these years and you have not recognized me and my responsibilities, but now all of a sudden you're going to do that? What does that say about us? If I had to do research to be considered an important factor in the development of this country, I don't think too much of that.

It is significant that Alicia speaks of her work in terms of its larger contribution to society, rather than in the more narrow terms of composition studies as a formal researcher would. Her comments suggest that it may be teachers, after all, who are thinking globally and researchers who are thinking locally.

III Toward
Theory-Based Practice
and Practice-Based Theory

5 Contextual Constraints on Knowledge Making: Graduate Student Teacher Research

> The role of Theory and personal theory in a teacher's life is . . . a crucial question for composition's very definition as a discipline.
> —Louise Wetherbee Phelps 1988

As shown in the last chapter, knowledge making in composition is a rhetorical activity as well as a social construct. Knowledge constructed through research can differ considerably across contexts: the purposes for conducting research, the methodology selected, the focus of the study, the way findings are communicated, and the audience addressed are all determined by the discourse communities to which the researcher already belongs or aspires to belong. A number of composition researchers have recently made this point. Lee Odell, for example, notes that "ultimately, we must recognize that we are part of a professional community, and our research will reflect our awareness of that community" (1987, 137). Thomas Newkirk asserts that, if Donald Graves (one of the original teacher-researchers) "were to be consistent with his claims for 'context,' he would look reflexively at the discourse community the researcher works in and explore the ways in which narrative conventions predispose the researcher to account for data in a particular way" (1992, 132). And Deborah Brandt makes the point that, because writing is "a profoundly social enterprise," in order "to understand any writing act we must look to the context of situation in which it takes place to see how a writer enacts that context or brings it to life through the functional resources of language and through various composing strategies" (1988, 153).

Thus we would expect differences between the research and writing of university-based teacher-researchers and that of K–12 teacher-researchers. The National Writing Project teachers conducted research as a means of personal development, first and foremost; they saw their classroom inquiry as a basis for increased self-understanding and self-esteem that translated directly into better teaching. They also believed that the personal knowledge developed through their teacher research provided a compelling example for other teachers at the local level to bring about change through classroom inquiry. Motivated by the need to influence these local readers, most of whom have been trained to evaluate research from the global perspective of education schools, the National Writing Project teachers sought to make their research as rigorous and methodologically sound as possible. It is apparent, then, that K–12 teacher-researchers *do* want to be heard outside their own classrooms, for they are confident that their personal knowledge is relevant to others. As practitioners, they come to take an authoritative stance on the field of composition, testing, challenging, and extending theory by reflecting on and analyzing their own teaching.

What, then, of university-based teacher-researchers? Do they consider the construction of personal knowledge as critical to professional growth? What are the relationships among personal, local, and global knowledge within this community? What kind of authoritative stance on theory and practice do university teachers come to articulate through classroom inquiry? How do they negotiate the methodological and rhetorical issues of teacher research? In this chapter, I address these questions by describing the work of another group of teacher-researchers: those who are graduate students at a research institution and are therefore both teachers-in-training and researchers-in-training. Although graduate students represent only one segment of the population of college writing teachers (part-time teachers representing the largest segment), it is my contention that the field of composition can learn a great deal about itself and its potential by observing graduate students, for in juggling their multiple roles within the university as students, teachers, and researchers, graduate students must negotiate, on a daily basis, a personal relationship between theory and practice. I illustrate in this chapter that, by conducting teacher research, they develop a stronger rhetorical stance in terms of this relationship. Further, in communicating this stance through their writing, graduate students learn how knowledge is constructed in the field and how one might play a significant part as *both* teacher and researcher in this knowledge making.

The Participants in English 702

The details in this chapter come from the talk and writing generated in a composition theory course, English 702, Researching Teaching, which I developed and taught for the first time during the winter 1991 semester at Wayne State University. There were seven students in the class, the only prerequisite for which was graduate standing and ongoing experience as a teacher or tutor. The course was an elective for all students. The class was comprised of Gay and Andrea, Ph.D. students in composition theory and teaching assistants in the English department; Jill and Alex, Ph.D. students in education who had a variety of teaching experiences between them at both the secondary and college levels; Elaine, a second-semester M.A. student in professional writing and a tutor in the English department's tutoring lab; Mary, a post-M.A. student who, as an adjunct faculty member, taught a full load of five writing classes, dividing her time between a local community college and Wayne State; and Bill, a newly admitted Ph.D. student in literature who was returning to college at the age of fifty for a new career after selling his successful tooling business.[1] Although Bill had not yet taught college English (he had just been awarded a teaching assistantship for the following year), he oversaw a seminary course for his church and regularly observed and taught the class himself.

All students were informed when they registered for English 702 that they would be required to conduct research on their own teaching. None to my knowledge had ever heard of teacher research or conducted classroom inquiry themselves. The previous semester Andrea had taken my course in which we had written case studies and ethnographies on the uses of computers in various contexts. Jill had had a seminar on composition pedagogy with me the previous year. I came to know the rest of the students through their talk, writing, and research for English 702. We met one evening a week for three hours to discuss the assigned readings and students' ongoing research.

As articulated in the syllabus (see Appendix B), the stated goals of the course were for students to learn about classroom inquiry by reading about the methodologies relied on in this body of research and determining its value and relevance; to become reflective, analytical teachers who consider the classroom a place of learning and change for teachers as well as students; to challenge, through research, their own and others' beliefs and assumptions about aspects of writing or teaching that arise out of interactions with students; and to conduct original studies which allow them to test the methodological issues raised in class against their own experiences. The course description focused on research methodology and the theoretical and epistemological premises underlying classroom inquiry. Students were formally introduced to ethnography and case study through the work of John Van Maanen, Clifford Geertz, James Clifford, Shirley Brice Heath, Glenda Bissex, and Thomas Newkirk, among others. They also read about the teacher-research movement, as represented in my own work (a draft of Chapter 3 from this book) and selections from Don Daiker and Max Morenberg's *The Writing Teacher as Researcher* (1990), Dixie Goswami and Peter Stillman's *Reclaiming the Classroom* (1987), and Glenda Bissex and Richard Bullock's *Seeing for Ourselves* (1987). (See complete course bibliography in Appendix B.)

Each week, the students reacted orally and in writing to the assigned readings in terms of their own and each other's research in progress, thereby developing over the course of the semester a set of criteria for evaluating each other's final papers. I saw my role as that of facilitator; I attempted to pose questions, challenge responses, elaborate on students' observations, summarize, encourage, and suggest. End-of-term evaluations indicate that I did, in fact, play this role: the students commented that my approach "never intimidated students," that I served "as a mentor, guide, and peer," that I was "knowledgeable and challenging, but supportive toward [my] students and accessible," and that I "didn't 'tell' [but] suggested a number of different alternatives and pointed the way."

Finally, all students were aware that I too was conducting classroom inquiry on the seminar, just as they were researching their own classrooms. I often took notes during and after class sessions and, with their permission, tape-recorded the final workshop sessions in which we discussed drafts of students' papers. Toward the end of the semester, the students were given the option to sign a release form allowing me to quote from them and their work in my research. I assured them in writing that I would use pseudonyms when referring to them and that my analysis of their talk and writing for research purposes would occur well after the class was over and would have no effect on their graduate standing or their final grades. Further, I assured them that, if they chose not to sign a release form, this decision would be respected and would in no way affect my assessment of their class work. (See Appendix C for release form.) All students in the class chose to participate in the study, and most later read drafts of this chapter.

My being a participant-observer in English 702 was advantageous for all involved. It modeled for the students the research approach I was attempting to teach, and it continually forced me to challenge and question my own pedagogy and the theory and politics underlying it. Several times I had to stop and reassess my priorities during the semester. What I present here as findings reflect what I learned from my graduate students about the teacher-research process. Without having taught the course, I could never have anticipated these findings. Specifically, I did not suspect that the methodological pluralism I had seen in the work of the National Writing Project teachers would be just as pronounced in the work of graduate students. This was a surprise, because I had carefully constructed the course around ethnography and case study exclusively. Initially, I had assumed that each student would select one of these approaches and follow it rather strictly, in the end writing a "realist tale" of ethnography, as Van Maanen defines it, or an extended case study of the type written by Bissex or Newkirk. The work of these published researchers, I thought, would provide rhetorical models that the students could easily emulate. However, instead of writing realist ethnography in the social science vein, they wrote interpretive texts of a more literary nature that included narrative and personal reflection. And their case studies turned into critiques of institutional practices, examining how tutoring labs fail to account for the personal needs of staff and students, for example, or how colleges fail to meet the needs of nontraditional and differently abled students. In short, when encouraged to establish their own rhetorical strategies, graduate students wrote texts in which genres naturally "blurred," in the best Geertzian sense of the term.

I also did not anticipate the high anxiety that English 702 caused for most of the students, largely because I did not fully realize the emotional impact of what I was asking them to do: to analyze their teaching when they already felt inadequate in the classroom and to do so in the context of a graduate seminar, where they often felt intimidated and insecure. Sections of many class periods were spent talking through the students' anxieties: How do I decide on a research focus? What if I change my mind at midterm and want to focus on something else? What if the students in my study drop the course or tutoring session and leave me with nothing to research? What should I do when students skip class for weeks at a time or when the people I want to interview decline or don't show up? What if, after all of this work, I don't find anything significant? What if I find out at the end of the term that I haven't collected enough data or that I've collected the "wrong" kind? How do I make sense of all the data I *have* collected?

These and other issues, which troubled every student during part or all of the semester, reflect a final-product orientation toward research. They are the kinds of concerns harbored by students who have been evaluated exclusively on the basis of final papers submitted under the fiction that their research is "complete." One of my goals for the class was to move the students away from this product orientation, at least temporarily, in order to open them up to the experience of conducting research which is always in process, never

complete. It was not an easy task. My reassurances to "trust yourself
and your work," to "be confident that everything will turn out all right
in the end," and to "focus on the process of inquiry rather than the
final product" did not always help, despite my good intentions and
firm belief, given my own experiences with classroom inquiry, that
the human mind has an inherent ability to make sense out of chaos,
even that which it has itself created.

The students expressed their anxieties in various ways, both in and
out of the seminar. In class, even though a generous amount of time
was allotted for discussion of research in progress, the students
expressed serious doubts about their abilities to carry out their
individual projects. At one point around midterm, after we had spent
more than an hour discussing audience and purpose for the final
papers, it seemed to me that we had covered every possible contin-
gency. Nevertheless, Jill said to me on the way out of the classroom,
"I can't *believe* how anxious I still am about this paper!" During that
same class period, Gay had spoken of the nervousness she suddenly
felt during student conferences now that she was taping them for
research. This surprised me because she was an experienced student-
centered teacher who had taught writing part-time for several years at
the university before entering the Ph.D. program and becoming a
teaching assistant. When asked what she was nervous *about,* she
replied, "Not doing it right—students not learning what they need to
learn and then having to document that." Andrea expressed a related
concern, saying at one point, "I'm not sure I want to make this study
public." When asked why, she noted how politically charged the
research was for her: "Well, teaching assistantships haven't been
decided for next year yet, and the director of composition is reading
this!"

The students expressed other anxieties in frantic telephone calls to
me or in frustrated journal entries. Around the sixth week of the
semester, for example, Alex called one afternoon to say that his
research just wasn't working and he wanted to drop the class. He had
been hoping to interview and observe teachers of blind students at a
local secondary school where he taught part time, but the administration refused to give him permission to conduct the study because, in
Alex's words, he "wasn't a legitimate member of the staff." His
research log included a litany of other complaints: problems arrang-
ing his personal life to do interviews and follow leads; confusion
encountered in doing simultaneous research on different topics for
different classes; not getting the class readings done or feeling
intimidated and overwhelmed by them ("academic writing may be

above intellectual capacity" he wrote); mechanical setbacks ("interview tapes—ribbon of tape spews out," "microphone didn't work—nothing on tape or too much noise—voices are unintelligible"); hours spent in the library peering at blurry microfiche without finding anything to substantiate his research; and negative emotions ("depression, worry—do not know direction of research"). We talked about the problems for a while, as well as his other part-time teaching jobs that semester, and I convinced him that he still had time to work up an alternative research plan focusing on another student population. I suggested that he give himself one more week to see if he would come to feel more positive about himself and the class. He was back the following week, having decided that, since he had been through so much work and worry already, he might as well finish the term.

Other students' research logs revealed similar frustrations. Jill wrote what she called "panic attack entries," and Elaine spent the first month trying to come to terms with her insecurities. In her first entry, written during the second week of class, Elaine wrote, "When I left class last Wednesday, I was thoroughly confused. While the idea of learning from my teaching (and how to improve it) greatly appealed to me, I felt extremely limited by my position in the Tutoring Lab." In the following week's entry, she referred to suggestions made during the previous class session that she research the effectiveness of her tutoring: "There was and still is no way that I alone can research the effectiveness of tutoring. After all, who am I but a tutor who still struggles with her *own* writing?" Other entries show the conflict Elaine felt between the "bona fide scientific research" she had learned to value as a psychology undergraduate major and the need to conduct a study for English 702 that to her seemed "highly subjective." Her fourth entry, entitled "Do I Stay or Do I Go?" discusses the personal issues involved in deciding whether to drop the class:

> Last night I left class in tears. True, Dr. Ray assured us that the frustration we are all experiencing is normal. (I don't feel any better.) She also said that perhaps we are all apprehensive because we are scared that in the long run our research may suggest that we, as teachers, are ineffective. Yep, this is definitely me. Last night I wanted to drop this class, drop grad school, and get a job. Unfortunately, I am not qualified to do anything. . . . I want to drop this course because it's threatening me. . . . Ruth said the frustration is OK, that it's part of the research. However, I can't see her justifying a grade in a seminar course based on my learning that I am not effective.
>
> This year I have been questioning whether I even belong in grad school. I feel like such a misfit in class. I feel immature, inexperienced, young, and extremely—the major problem—threatened.

That's why I want to run away. I feel that the English Department
thinks that the Tutoring Lab is ineffective. I know some of my
classmates do. Students think we're ineffective. Logical conclusion—I am ineffective.

This morning I didn't even get consent forms from my two
students because tomorrow I was dropping the course. Then I had
two student sessions that were effective. They even said so. That
is why I want to be a teacher. Now I am confused again. Do I stay
or do I go now?

Elaine brings up a conflict that many graduate students feel:
insecurity about their qualifications to be either teachers or researchers, weighed against an equal or greater insecurity about their qualifications to succeed outside academia. An obsession with final papers
and grades is only one of the ways this issue is played out. In Elaine's
case, at least during the first month of the semester, everything she did
for English 702 was based on fear of failure. Fortunately, however,
that fear had positive as well as negative potential. Encouraged by
classmates, she decided to complete the course and make her personal
concerns a part of the research. Thus, in her final paper, she discusses
how tutors should have more control over the physical environment
in which they work, how they need a better understanding of the
relationships between personality and the development of student-
tutor relationships, and how a better understanding of personal
dynamics would improve tutors' and students' attitudes and expectations for the tutoring process.

These experiences indicate that graduate students have been
taught to see "research" as another opportunity for faculty to judge
and critique them, rather than a means of personal inquiry. They point
to what is wrong with the way we induct graduate students into
scholarship and introduce them to the role of the scholar: scholarship
is done to please others, and scholars are externally motivated to seek
approval and recognition. The graduate students in English 702 had
not yet considered the possibility that scholarship can be done for
oneself, first and foremost, and that scholars can be internally motivated to seek relevant knowledge and personal growth, which leads
to keen insight and high-quality research, *thereby* bringing recognition in the field. Why does teacher research bring up these issues?
Because it forces us to examine our thinking and behavior, to become
self-reflexive and self-critical. This is a difficult process for graduate
students because they have few role models. They have not learned
how to observe themselves and their teaching and learning without
judging. After all, their previous experiences in graduate school have
suggested that a perfect finished product is the goal of all writing and

thinking, but that the process of trying to perfect—which is actually far more interesting and relevant to their learning—is irrelevant.

By the tenth week of the semester, all of the students in the class had come to realize that they were actually *doing* the research they had proposed, and they had finally committed themselves fully to completing it. Just when they were beginning to feel comfortable thinking about research as a process, however, I began prodding them to think about writing a final paper. Our discussion of audience and purpose for these papers initiated a new set of frustrations that extended through the end of the semester. The students' major problem was finding ways to analyze their findings as they went along and to organize their writing in a way that would provide compelling and informative reading for their projected audience. Rhetorical issues weighed heavily upon them. As Gay told me when she handed in the final draft of her paper, "To be honest, I was afraid to touch this because there was so much more material than I'm used to. Obviously, when you do a typical library research paper, you also have more material than you can use, but in this case, you have MEGA material. . . . It was just scary thinking, 'How am I going to *do* this? How am I ever going to sort all this *out?*'"

During our final class session, students were still joking about "sorting it out," as the following excerpt from Mary's workshop session indicates:[2]

> *Bill:* You're going to have a lot more tables here when you add the rest of the class [material] and then do the error analysis on all those other papers.
>
> *Mary:* Should I just quit the class? [laughing] Drop? Can I get my money back?
>
> *Alex:* [I tried that already.]
> *Elaine:* [I wish.]

Mary's good-natured angst and that of the other students at this point is due in part to the fact that they are making sense of their findings as they go along—that the "writing up" of research is no more definitive than the process of conducting it. They have discovered that there are no fixed meanings in this type of research, no "ah hah" moments in which great truths are realized and gloriously reported. Instead, their studies take shape only at the point of utterance, and the significance of their work is inscribed in the act of writing, not "found" in their classrooms or conclusively explained by the theories they have been reading. Further, their research has challenged some previously held beliefs and assumptions, and they are struggling with the rhetorical issues of whether and how to report this new self-knowledge. Egos are bruised.

During Mary's workshop session, for example, the class laughs about the fact that her research is still incomplete, that she does not know what the final outcome will be, and that she may yet find that teaching grammar is not as effective as she had originally thought:

> *Mary:* What I was looking at was what was happening in this one class [in terms of learning grammar] because I have a sense that what is happening in my one class is happening in other classes. And it's like your thing [referring to a case-study paper of mine the class had read] where you have an idea that what's his name improved, you know . . . and she really didn't. Well, I might find out that [class laughter] three-fourths of my students—I mean, shit. [laughing] I'm just going to leave altogether, you know! This is just—
>
> *Jill:* Yeah, but still that's an important finding.
>
> *Mary:* Yes, it is. Oh it is.
>
> *Bill:* Absolutely.
>
> *Jill:* Just never do it *again.* [class laughter]
>
> *Mary:* But then it [my study] substantiates the gall darn research that I read that says they don't get any better [when you teach grammar] and I always say, "Well, *they do!*" You know?
>
> *Andrea:* I'd be interested in that because I don't teach grammar anymore.
>
> *Jill:* I don't either.
>
> *Mary:* I know, because I have a sense that they do [get better]. But then, am I thinking about the ones that I . . . those people who stand out?
>
> *Ruth:* Maybe selective attention.
>
> *Mary:* And I make promises to them at the beginning of the semester. I tell them, "You will all get better." . . . So I don't know what I'll find out. . . . Now in Rob's case, we will see a dramatic change. But whether it will be on everybody or not—If it's the majority of people, I'll be pleased.
>
> *Ruth:* Let me just reiterate the point I've made many times this semester. Even if you don't find positive reinforcement for your method, it's still a very successful study.
>
> *Mary:* Right, right.
>
> *Ruth:* And, uh, we don't do research just to affirm that we're great teachers. [class laughter]
>
> *Mary:* I know, I know.
>
> *Ruth:* Just try to keep that in perspective.
>
> *Mary:* Yeah. And that's why it's *exciting* to me, because I don't know what I'll find out, and that's exciting.

Mary's last comment is telling, for it indicates the mixed emotions that teacher research evokes: fear tinged with excitement, resistance coupled with a strong desire to know. The exchange also suggests that the class is still struggling to accept the perspective that teacher research is best seen as a process rather than a product. Therefore, no matter what the findings, the research is "successful" if it has led teachers to question, challenge, and learn from their experiences in the classroom.

My reason for documenting the students' anxieties in such detail is this: they illustrate the real concerns of graduate students and the constraints—intellectual, physical, psychological, emotional, temporal—under which they work. When researching the classroom, teachers' awareness is heightened: they become more sensitive to what students and colleagues are saying, how classroom dynamics are working, and what effect they are having on students. Thus, when we consider the context of graduate student research and writing, we must account for anxiety. I had not anticipated how frustrating teacher research would be for graduate students until their frustration became a subtext for our weekly seminar meetings. The research logs definitely helped defuse some of those feelings, as did classroom talk and private conferences. Although anxieties remained to some degree right up until the end of the semester, nobody dropped the class, and everyone handed in a final paper which represented a higher level of thought, effort, and personal engagement than I had ever seen in graduate writing before. As writers, each had dealt with personally constructed knowledge and had begun to see its relevance in terms of some aspect of composition theory.

Personal Knowledge: Two Cases

As it was for the National Writing Project teachers, personal knowledge—that which teachers construct about themselves, their own teaching, and their interactions in the classroom—was of primary concern to the graduate students in English 702. The impact of the research experience was explained by a student in the final course evaluation: "My research will not end here. This class has influenced me to think differently so that I will be actively searching and working on my area of interest. A valuable course—you bet. How many courses have changed your life?!" What changes, exactly, occurred in these students and why? One significant influence of the research process was that it led the students to take a personal stance on some aspect of composition theory.

Andrea

Andrea is a good example of a student who came to terms with composition theory through her personal experiences with classroom inquiry. At age thirty, Andrea is about the average age of Wayne State graduate students. Like many of her classmates, she has not followed a straight trajectory toward graduate school; instead, she has held various jobs between her degree programs, including a position as a journalist. She is an outspoken feminist and describes herself as "politically very active," saying, "I take my personal powers under democracy very seriously. It would be fair to say that this strongly informs and is reflected in my teaching style." She began the semester, as she noted in her research log, with a plan "to base my study on the teaching processes I discovered and liked through last semester's [composition theory] seminar." More specifically, she "set out to discover if a student-centered approach to the teaching of composition would affect my students in the way James Moffett proposed in *Teaching the Universe of Discourse* (1968)." She was also influenced by James Berlin's discussion of transactional teaching in *Rhetoric and Reality* (1987).

Using the ideas of Moffett and Berlin as a theoretical base, Andrea developed a freshman composition syllabus which she hoped would "empower" students personally, intellectually, and politically. She arranged the class time to emphasize journal writing, a free exchange of ideas, and group work. On the first day of class, she had her students form a circle with their desks, and she sat among them. After the students had introduced themselves, she opened up the discussion to any topic. Andrea later wrote in her log that

> they quickly began to ponder the possibilities of war in the Persian Gulf. It would seem that most of the students are gung-ho about the prospect of a war. Only two women, Kim and Lydia, voiced their opposition to the war. I must say that I was shocked and scared by these attitudes. All of the young men in the class were registered for a draft—as required by law—but were not at all disturbed about being drafted to go to war! Since no one has yet shown me a voter's registration card, I am also upset that many of these young people are willing to go to war for their country, but are not willing or at least interested in voting for the representatives who in cases such as this are the ones who will decide the fates of these young people. Maybe my goal to empower these students within the democratic process is, indeed, beyond my grasp? Aren't young people supposed to be rebellious? anti-establishment? and passionate about resisting the status quo? Or did this attitude die with the seventies?

There are clues, even in this first entry, that suggest Andrea will experience some personal conflicts with the student-centered class she has created. The language and tone of the entry suggest that she does not really see herself as "one of the class," even though she has constructed a syllabus which stresses the free exchange of ideas and has situated herself physically to suggest that she and the students are "equals" in terms of this exchange. Her use of "these students" and "these young people" indicates her perceived separation from them, and the tone of the passage makes it clear that she objects to their personal politics.

The political differences between Andrea and her students cause her to question, early in the semester, the appropriateness of the facilitator-peer role she has assigned herself in the classroom. It becomes increasingly difficult for her to follow "the plan," especially when the problems in the Persian Gulf escalate and when many other issues constantly present themselves for discussion, such as the sexism she sees in television programming and a local television station's advertising of a series on campus rape that "seems to say, and not so subliminally, I might add, that the best way to protect your daughters is not to let them go to college, especially to colleges where they must live away from home!" Although she writes in her log that "both of these problematic media messages should—or perhaps I'd better say would—make interesting discussion prompts for class tomorrow," she must hold back because her syllabus calls for in-class writing on a topic she has already assigned. So she decides to "stick with the plan" and not initiate the class discussion that she very much wants to hold. Andrea articulates her frustration at this decision in a log entry written the next day:

> Finally, a reflection on world events. We are quickly approaching the deadline set by the United Nations (in other words, the United States of America), for Iraqi troops to leave Kuwait. Any time after midnight on Jan. 15, 1991, the allied UN forces will have "permission" to launch a war against Saddam Hussein and Iraq. As I mentioned in an earlier entry . . . I seem to be more concerned about the prospect of war than my students. When I mentioned to my students that an anti-war rally was scheduled for 4:30 p.m. this afternoon, they just sort of looked at me and each other. I had a feeling that I wouldn't see any of them there.
>
> I attended the rally, but left by 5:30 p.m. (my 703 seminar met at 6 p.m.). There were about 200 people there, mostly radicals and anarchists whom I recognized from previous rallies protesting the Detroit incinerator and the Fermi Nuclear Power plant in Monroe . . . as well as numerous pro-choice rallies and clinic defenses. There were, however, also considerable numbers of people from

mainstream society (with which I am identifying more and more
each day). . . . Two things struck me as being useful for my 102
class. One had to do with the problematic of context: when is it not
a good idea to provoke the establishment/authority structure?
And [the second] had to do with media representations, again. On
the evening news, only the violent part of the rally was shown,
thus representing one hour of peaceful demonstration via 10
minutes of emotional conflict. . . . I feel compelled to make this an
issue for discussion in tomorrow's class. I know, I know, I will be
usurping the authority to drive the discussion. How am I ever
going to reconcile my need and desire to bring up topical issues
for class discussion with the students' ambivalence and ignorance
of these same topics? If this is truly to be a student-centered
classroom, then I can't push them into this, but then how will we
ever discuss anything worth thinking critically about? ARRGH!
This is not working out the way I planned at all! I sense another
research study falling through the cracks!

After writing this entry, Andrea raises a question in her log that we
had been discussing in the 702 seminar: "Can an individual hold
seemingly conflicting theories within oneself?" Her response is "oh,
yes. While I like the student-centered approach to teaching, I realize
now—only 3 weeks into my course and my study—that I am essentially unable to carry it out. It is not suited to my temperament or
personality as a teacher, as one who knows and wants to pass my
knowledge of learning and thinking strategies on to students. Perhaps
it is also not suitable to students who have never learned to cope with
maintaining their own responsibility for learning and studying." She
also asks herself, "Can one take a technique without buying the theory
behind it?" Her response: "Maybe I'll be able to answer it when my
study comes to a close. Although my first impulse is to say 'yes,' I'm
realizing through my problems with the student-centered approach
that maybe it should be 'no'."

Andrea does eventually answer that question for herself, after
surveying her students three times at various points during the
semester on the effectiveness of the course, altering her syllabus on
the basis of student feedback, bringing in another teacher (her hus-
band) to observe the classroom dynamics, reflecting on her teaching
in the research log, and discussing her findings with the seminar
class. At one point during the term, when Andrea was reporting to
classmates on her findings to date, she noted that there was "definitely a group dynamic missing" in her composition class and
admitted that, in making critical judgments about their attitudes and
politics, she was probably communicating "that I didn't have respect
for my students." This was a revelation for her, as was the fact that this
finding made her "as much a subject of the study as they are" because

it forced her to examine the effects of her own beliefs and attitudes on classroom dynamics.

The impact of this personal knowledge on Andrea's understanding of both composition theory and pedagogy is apparent in the following excerpts from a workshop session held during the fifteenth week of the semester in which we discussed a draft of Andrea's final research paper, entitled "One Teacher's Research: An Odyssey of Self-Discovery":

> *Gay:* I seem to recall that you shifted direction in your class, didn't you, in terms of what you were going to do?
>
> *Andrea:* Yeah.
>
> *Gay:* Ok. Are you going to bring that out at all?
>
> *Andrea:* Uh-huh. Yeah. That's going to be part of the results. After the first two surveys we had, I, uh, there were a lot of things I went through. I restructured the class—new syllabus—talked to the students, and found out that what I had really wanted to abandon, they really wanted to do. And so I found that I wasn't listening as carefully as I should have. What I came away with here is that you can't impose a methodology on a class. And, even though [her previous composition professor] had brought this up last term when I read Moffett, I was excited about Moffett and the student-centered approach. And she said make sure that there isn't some kind of inherent contradiction between the aspect of teacher authority and student authority.

This excerpt illustrates that Andrea came to understand through her own inquiry a theoretical point she had read in a graduate course the previous semester. It was not until she conducted her own research, however, that the point about conflict between student and teacher authority became truly meaningful in the context of her own teaching and learning. Through teacher research, Andrea discovers her *own* perspective on authority:

> *Ruth:* I'm not real clear yet how you're going to show how your personality and philosophy influenced what happened in the classroom.
>
> *Mary:* Without the examples, I'm not too clear on that either.
>
> *Ruth:* First of all, I need to know more about your personality and philosophy and then I need to know what kind of examples you will use to show cause and effect.
>
> *Andrea:* I have . . . notes from class sessions that we had, and one of the things that [my husband] pointed out when he watched the class is that I sat in one spot on the desk during the whole hour. The students are in a circle, and I started out being in a circle with them, and then found out that I didn't have enough control over what was going on, that I needed the control, that the students

needed the control. So I started standing up behind the desk, but then I found there was this barrier between me and the students. Then I started sitting on the desk, facing them . . . and I thought that worked really well, but [my husband] pointed out that that just made me a focal point when I didn't move, and that that exerted a kind of blanketing effect on the discussion.

I also found that when students don't come up with the answers, I jumped right in with the answers. And that was part of my wanting not to have empty spaces, wanting to fill up every minute, feeling, again, I would lose control if I let them sit too long without saying anything. So I found out that even though I wanted to have a student-centered classroom, that I was very much steeped in the teacher-centered, and that I do have a strong sense of authority that somehow must be exercised. So lately, I've been trying to sit in different spots in the classroom, next to different students. I had them shrink the circle . . . into a more intimate setting. I've practiced shutting up, which is not easy, and I have examples of it. I have a tape and some dialogue. I think I can show that when I'm set up as the authority, they always look to me for the answers, but if I don't jump right in, someone, lately, has always jumped in at some other kind of remark, and that they get more into the fights, you know, the discussions. . . .

Ruth: So actually are you saying, more specifically, that, not so much that your research question changed, but that you realized it was an environment in which your personality and your need for control and other aspects of your personality kept the kind of learning from happening that you were intending to document?

Andrea: Right.

Ruth: OK. So actually it may not be two different research questions. It may be that you had this first research question that you didn't get the answer to that you thought you'd get—

Andrea: Right. That's really what—

Ruth: —That you ended up challenging your research question and yourself rather than changing your research question.

Andrea: Yeah. What I kind of meant by a changed focus was that I stopped looking at the methodology as the main focus of my research and started to look more at myself and [my] interaction with the students as the focus, but still trying to see what engaged the students in the things that I wanted them to do. And that was a problem for me. I definitely had a goal for what *I* wanted them to do, and it wasn't, it did not work out that this is what the students always wanted. So, I'm still very, oh you know, a little confused.

Ruth: And what are the implications of that [outcome]? Does it mean that if you believe in a student-centered theory you can't also be goal-oriented? Does it change your understanding of the theory?

Andrea: What it does is it changes the way I would approach implementing the theory. To say—it challenges the role of the theorists who came up with the theory and my role as the teacher in adopting some theory and in being inexperienced and not knowing how to adopt the theory to make it work. I think what I want to show with this is that there's a learning process to teaching, and I think this is where my problem comes out. I think I'm trying to show that this teacher research is important to beginning teachers and not, essentially, the question I started out dealing with. Does that make sense?

Mary: Yeah, because you operated from a methodology before ever having read about methodologies. You were in that classroom operating from a methodology, right? And then from reading about the methodology of Moffett, you started to try out these techniques. But you *had* a methodology, which now we could, you know, whether we could attach it to current-traditional or whatever authoritative position you came from, but I realized that last semester when I started reading about methodologies, and that's what I meant in that last [written critique] when I said that attaching a name to something—actually reading about the theory made me question the practice. All along I had operated from a methodology. My upbringing, my schooling, I turned around and did the same things. . . .

Gay: It seems also, what I'm getting out of this, is that as great as some approaches sound, they aren't going to work for every teacher and/or every group of students.

Mary: Or in isolation from one another. You know, what Ruth was saying, do you necessarily change everything when you do something else? I mean, does the philosophy totally change? Do you have to, then, not be, going back to what you said, not goal-oriented because you want the students to take more charge? Well, no, it doesn't have to cancel out. So, then, what is the methodology that comes out of this? There's going to be a third one, the Andrea paradigm. [laughs] Maybe you can write a book. [class laughter]

Andrea: You mean the con*fusion* paradigm. [class laughter]

Andrea's experience illustrates the power of personal knowledge to effect changes in one's theoretical knowledge. By reading Moffett the previous semester and writing an academic paper on his theory of discourse, Andrea had developed one level of theoretical understanding; by "reading" her own classroom and writing a paper in which she develops and articulates personal knowledge about her own attempts at using Moffett's theory, she developed another level of theoretical understanding. This second level integrates personal and global knowledge in ways that Andrea will continue to draw upon and expand. In fact, in subsequent semesters, Andrea surveyed students and developed her composition classes further around the initial findings of her teacher research; she organized discussion classes based on Moffett's theory of discourse as interaction, but she also allowed herself room to influence these discussions and to exercise more authority in the classroom.

Alex

Alex's research experience is interesting because of the problems that personal knowledge caused him. Alex, who appears to be in his early forties, is a Ph.D. student in education. He has taught in the public schools and, at the time he conducted his teacher research, was a tutor at a local community college. He is soft-spoken and reticent in class, partly because he lacks confidence in his academic abilities. When he does speak, he is hesitant and often self-deprecating. Alex felt intimidated by the more outspoken members of the class, particularly Andrea; in fact, during a midsemester conference in my office, he confided, only half jokingly, that sometimes he'd like to "smack her in the face" because she was so articulate. (Paradoxically, Andrea had also confided during her conference that *she* sometimes felt inferior and underprepared in class and made up for it by "talking too much.") As these comments indicate, graduate students are competitive, despite faculty members' efforts to create an egalitarian "community of scholars" in the seminar room. Students constantly compare themselves with, and judge themselves against, one another, and these feelings are a significant aspect of the context of graduate students' learning. Alex's comment illustrates, too, his high level of frustration with the course. As already noted, he experienced many setbacks in his research project on tutoring blind students, including resistance from the school administration to his original research plan, failed taping sessions, and problems getting tapes transcribed.

Alex ended up writing a case study of one student, Jane. Throughout the semester, he had been interested in the social context of differently abled students' learning. As he talked of his sessions with Jane, the class was struck again and again by the unusual dynamics between the two of them: they argued, they criticized each other, they agonized together for twenty-two hours once over a single essay, and they worked under many unusual constraints. To illustrate, Alex described one of their meetings as taking place in the living room of Jane's parents' home, in the presence of her boyfriend (also blind) and her mother, amidst the noise of the television (Alex and Jane were watching a video to prepare for writing a movie critique), the ringing telephone, and the barking and jumping of two leader dogs. The class encouraged Alex to focus on how the personal dynamics between the two of them affected the writing they produced collaboratively (Jane dictated while Alex put the words on paper and then read them back). This research approach, however, required that Alex would have to reveal much of himself and his own insecurities in working with Jane, an idea that made him very uncomfortable. As a result of this discomfort, his first draft of the final paper was heavy with literature review—of ethnographic methodology, social constructionism, and studies on teaching blind students—but thinly written in terms of Jane and their actual sessions together. Alex's conflict about revealing himself was apparent in the awkward shifts between first and third person and the lack of coherence between the literature reviews and the case-study sections. He was aware of the disjointed nature of his writing and began the workshop session on his draft by asking the class to comment on general organization and "how I tried to put myself in the case study."

The following excerpts from the ensuing discussion show the class trying to get Alex to come to terms with personal knowledge by writing a more detailed and reflective case study of Jane:

Mary: If you filled in some of the details on maybe a few of these instances, you might start getting more direction, because I did have a strong sense of your friendship with Jane—that did come through, even though you were trying to stay out of it. The friendship there did come through strongly. In fact, I think you did say it really specifically in a few places, although you're "the tutor" again . . . [reading] "The process of Jane's interaction with her tutor seems to go beyond an ordinary academic tutoring session" etc., the lunch, the cafeteria, the social life, taking her to the bank, you know, the friendship part of it.

Alex: That's why I had a problem, that's why I wanted to use "the tutor" instead of myself. . . . It was easier for me the observer, the researcher, to describe than to describe it as myself.

Mary: But what happened in those sessions between you and Jane that did or did not result in a paper or a sentence or whatever? I thought that was what you were writing about when you talked about it during the semester. I thought that was really *it,* and maybe if the focus goes back to that a little bit when you look at some of the details maybe that you could fill in—the friendship and the interaction—the focus might be clearer, I don't know. My sense is that sometimes when I go back to the very particular, I start to see the big picture. You know, it's going back to the little stuff that fills it in for me.

Andrea: Alex, you might take a look at Shirley Brice Heath and how she incorporates—you know, that time when she's in the car, waiting?

Mary: Yeah.

Andrea: That's a social interaction with her subjects, and she relates it just as that. You know, "we were sitting in the car," and it also goes to show how the research extends outside.

Mary: MmmHmm. That would be a good one to look at.

Ruth: And it doesn't in any way mitigate the findings or call into question the researcher's credibility. In fact, for some of us, as I recall, it enhanced the study.

Mary: It did. It did.

This interchange shows how the class members, as interested readers, assert their desire for more personal detail in Alex's study and how Alex, as the "researching I" maintains his reluctance to provide that detail. He assumes that a simple switch to third person will ease the burden of telling personal knowledge, but his classmates point out that it is particularity, not the shift of pronouns, that will make his study credible. They offer some practical rhetorical advice: look to Shirley Brice Heath for an example of how to represent the self in an ethnographic account.

Another segment of the workshop on Alex's draft illustrates, even more forcefully, the rhetorical issues raised when graduate students attempt to articulate personally constructed knowledge through academic writing:

Jill: I think you did a marvelous job of not—we know obviously that you were very frustrated—and you didn't let that come through [in your writing], really as a personal kind of thing. And I think because of that it had a lot more credibility.

Gay: Is there anything wrong with expressing frustration?

Jill: No, but I meant, like when she [Mary] said, why don't you elaborate? I could see if he elaborated *each time,* it would probably become clearer and clearer to us that he was so frustrated that it might overtake, that it might overpower everything else that he was trying to say. Do you see what I'm saying?

Andrea: But don't you think we need to *know* some of that?

Jill: Uh yes, I do think *some.*

Andrea: If you could bear me out, on page 20, then—well, this is the reason I bring it up. We've got, as Mary mentioned, the shift from the trip to Florida to writing about being blind upon awakening at a hospital. And then we have the tutor mentioning . . . [reading] "However, the first tutoring session, which lasted five hours, produced little result in terms of a written piece of work. Jane cried, became very emotional, at one point, the floor became littered with shredded slivers of white tissues." You know, and I'm thinking, well what *happened?* If there isn't frustration implied here, I don't—you know what I'm saying? I want to know what made her *cry.* What was going on here that this was—

Gay: Ahh, I got—that didn't bother me. In fact, I wrote "this is powerful." I really liked that passage. I got the impression that talking about the experience upset her.

Alex: Yeah, it did.

Andrea: I didn't get that. I got the impression that somehow the conflict, five hours—

Gay: Oh, yeah. I got the impression that just talking about the, reliving the experience—

Alex: She mentioned that she couldn't do that at home because she didn't want to get her parents upset. So a lot of times she gets emotional, very nervous. She picks personal topics and she gets very emotional and has an emotional release.

Andrea: ⎡ Well, see that would be perfect. ⎤
Gay: ⎢ That would be *good.* ⎥
Mary: ⎣ MmmHmm. MmmHmm. He said that here. ⎦

Ruth: But then, how does that make you feel as Mr. Ditto King?[3] [class laughter] I mean, we don't get that.

Alex: The emotion that I feel?

Ruth: Yeah.

Alex: There was a lot going on there.

Ruth: Do you feel frustrated or out of control?

Alex: With what?

Ruth: When the students get very emotional, crying and taking these personal topics and working them out with *you.*

Jill: How do you handle it?

Alex: Usually, I try to be—we talk about our own personal experiences together, and it's, it's—I see that it helps her to get emotional. It goes beyond the writing process, and I guess I see her as a friend, so I, so it's natural for that to happen.

Gay: Then why did you say, [reading] "She didn't realize that she was driving her tutor to the brink of *excrescent moaning* due to her unreasonable crying" before? [laughs]

Alex: Well, I did say "unreasonable" crying, you know, after an *hour* of crying—

Gay: But excrescent *moaning?* [class laughter]

Ruth: We just don't know how to *read* you, Alex, because you're not here. We don't know how you figure into this learning situation.

Jill: So are we asking him to be more confessional?

Ruth: I don't know. Do you think he should be?

Jill: And if we're asking him to be, does that mean that *we* ought to be then, also?

Andrea: I—yeah!

Jill: [laughs, mumbles]

Andrea: Well, I think that if you are a teacher-researcher, you're in that picture, and if you try to be that third person watching, you can run the danger of [readers] wondering, "Well, what was our researcher doing during all of this?" You know, like whenever you see on a TV documentary, the scuba diver is going through a very dangerous hole, but you know the cameraman got there first? [class laughter] You start to wonder about this (or maybe I do). You start to wonder, what was the researcher *doing* in this picture? If Alex is the researcher, we see how the connection is made and how the roles intertwine. If I ever have to tutor a blind student or somehow "other" student, it would help me to understand how those roles kind of shape lines [of communication].

Ruth: Let me answer your question from another perspective though, Jill. It may be that we're responding to Alex and asking for confessional because he set us up for it by using the first person explanation of his earlier teaching experiences. We established an expectation that he would continue that. Now, there are other ways to set up an ethnographic study. If you choose to do a realist tale, and you don't bring in the personal at the beginning, then you're not compelled to write a confessional later in the tale. I think you can do another kind of more social science study if you choose to, but just understand that that's your choice, and there are implications for it, and you must follow through on them. Does that answer the question you were having about your own research?

Jill: MmmHmm. Yeah.

Gay: Well that raises a question for me, because when we went through our thick descriptions [an earlier assignment in the semester], you were encouraging us to leave the first person out of those, so—how do we resolve this paradox?

Andrea: [laughs] Oops!

Ruth: You decide what kind of tale you want to write: either a first-person, confessional, interpretive kind of literary ethnography à la Clifford and Geertz, or you write a realist tale, more social science[like], with the appearance of objectivity, à la Berkenkotter et al. Fine—whatever you choose. Just be consistent in carrying out the genre.

Andrea: And remember that your audience in this room consists of people who are slavering for confessional! [class laughter]

In this excerpt, again the class probes Alex for more personal details, leading into a discussion of the appropriateness of "confessional" information, which some students, like Jill and Alex, feel uncomfortable relating in their academic discourse but which other students, like Andrea, value very highly. "Confessional" is an adjective used by Van Maanen in *Tales of the Field* to describe enthnographic writing that is "intended to show how particular works came into being, and this demands personalized authority. No longer is the ubiquitous, disembodied voice of the culture to be heard. . . . There is an intimacy to be established with readers, a personal character to develop, trials to portray, and . . . a world to be represented within which the intrepid fieldworker will roam" (1988, 75). Van Maanen argues for the importance and validity of the confessional in ethnography, but he also admits that it does not usually stand by itself, but instead accompanies a more traditional "realist" tale, and even then it is not fully accepted in the social sciences as a valuable form of knowledge. In terms of the dynamics of the English 702 class, it is significant that Andrea is the student who most assertively prods Alex to consider the intellectual and rhetorical possibilities of personal confession. Perhaps this is one reason why Alex has been so frustrated in her presence all semester; she believes in and pursues an aspect of learning (the articulation of personal knowledge) that he resists. Where she finds the "confessions" of personal knowledge empowering, he finds them intimidating.

In the final draft of his paper, entitled "A Case Study of Collaborative Writing: A Blind Student and a Tutor," however, Alex does acknowledge some of the conflict he feels about representing personal knowledge. He decides to become more confessional, at least about his own learning experiences in English 702, if not about his relationship with Jane. The first three paragraphs of his paper read as follows:

> I have a story to tell. It began as an ethnographic case study of a blind girl named Jane. The study is completed. And now, as I look back over the last four months, I see how foolish my fears and apprehensions were. I feel confident and happy about my experiences as a teacher despite the problems. I haven't produced a study that shows any hard scientific data, nor have I made any discoveries that might seem relevant to the educational community. I have only the momentary facts of a relationship between two people who met as strangers and then developed a commitment to each other as they struggled to find a common goal.
>
> The study began as part of a graduate course in English at a four-year university. The theme of the course was teacher-research in composition. The class consisted of seven students, five women and two men. We met in a sparse room on the third floor of an old liberal arts building once a week. Usually the room was either too cold or too hot. The windows couldn't be opened and the poor lighting made the room seem even more oppressive and dingy than it really was during the dark winter months of our first meetings.
>
> As I sat at the corner of the large wooden table that filled the center of the room, I realized that the persons in my class were no ordinary group of graduate students. All were teachers and most

had numerous years of teaching experience. We had a common interest in composition and research so that the focus in class was immediate to doing research on writing. However, I soon became intimidated as I listened to their comments on the reading assignments. As the instructor asked for our critical insights on the discussion about ethnographic research, I wondered if I should confess that I didn't really understand all that everyone was talking about in class. My nervousness finally led me to try humor as a way of relaxing. Perhaps, my one-liners would elicit some sympathy from my instructor for my emotional insecurity. In any case, as Ollie would say to Stan, I told myself, "Here's another nice mess you have gotten me into!"

Alex's case-study section is still thin in terms of detail, and his paper has some coherence problems; the parts of his description do not fit together to form a smooth narrative, and his integration of the social constructionist literature with the case-study findings is stiff and awkward. Yet various sections of the paper are outstanding in terms of their honesty and vigor. A particularly strong addition, also confessional, is five new paragraphs describing scenes Alex has witnessed that made him want to teach and research the special needs of differently abled students. The following paragraph, taken from this section, shows a deep sensitivity to others, tempered by the familiar self-conscious humor:

On one particular day, I was walking down the center aisle as I heard the noise of a wheelchair behind me. A large German shepherd was pulling a woman and her wheelchair along haphazardly. Later I learned the woman's name was Mitzi. She was paralyzed except for her left arm and hand. As the wheelchair brushed past me, I saw that the dog's leash was tied to the left side of the chair. Mitzi would tug with her left hand as a signal to the dog to pull. However, the dog kept losing traction as his paws kept slipping on the slick tile floor. Mitzi's body leaned to one side of the wheelchair as she attempted to give the leash a few more jerks. Whoosh—off Mitzi went as the dog finally sped away at full run. Mitzi's body rocked back and forth as the wheelchair raced crazily down the aisles towards the other end of the building. Each wheel alternately tilted to one side and the other because the German shepherd was pulling the wheelchair to one side rather than straight ahead. I wondered if somehow this ride could be duplicated at the Cedar Point Amusement Park. People would pay money for this kind of thrill. For Mitzi, it was a daily occurrence.

It is this kind of observation and engagement, also evident in his interactions with Jane, that motivates Alex's research, as well as his teaching. It is what leads him to conclude that the social construction of knowledge may differ for handicapped students in college:

Each individual has a different set of needs according to his own particular situation. Teachers and administrators should not attempt to force a handicapped student to accept any support services until the student has gone through a process of self-determination. Most handicapped students need a period of adjustment to college. Academics are of secondary importance to students who need to learn coping skills and survival techniques. Eventually, each special needs student will make a decision on her role as a student.

It is difficult to say what exactly Alex learned from his teacher research about the relationships between theory and practice, because he does not fully articulate this connection either in class discussions or in his writing. But he does seem to have learned something about himself, the ways he interacts with students, and his orientation toward knowledge making. He has learned, for example, that he is uncomfortable revealing "confessional" information in his writing, and he has been pressed by his peers to examine why. That experience alone is valuable knowledge for a graduate student trying to determine what kind of researcher he aspires to be and how he will establish personal authority in his field.

Local and Global Knowledge

The students in English 702, like most graduate students, initially had a difficult time seeing their research and writing as being significant beyond the immediate confines of the class. Caught up in the logistics of conducting a self-initiated study and making sense of the results in a period of sixteen weeks, at first they felt it was all they could do to get through the experience. At about midpoint in the semester, however, during the class in which we spent time talking about the projected audiences for their final papers, things began to change. Although I had not told the students to whom to direct their writing, I originally assumed that, because it was a graduate seminar, they would think of their work as "contributing to the field" and would therefore project a global audience. This was not the case, at least initially. Once they got beyond the idea that their research was more than a graduate school exercise, each saw his or her study primarily in terms of its relevance to a local audience of teachers. Andrea wanted to write for other teaching assistants in composition; Alex for teachers and tutors working with blind students; Bill for others in his church who wanted to teach a seminary class but were not trained to do so; Elaine for fellow tutors; Mary for community college teachers; and Gay for composition teachers in general. The only student who considered addressing both a local and a global audience which included composition researchers and theorists was Jill, who is coordinator of basic writing at an outreach division of Wayne State. Jill said she wanted to "explain the maze of my program" to other faculty members in her division to help them meet students' needs, but she also wanted to write for composition specialists in general, because she hoped to present her paper at the Penn State Conference on Rhetoric.[4]

The decision to write for a local audience of teachers had obvious rhetorical implications. In Bill's case, for example, it meant that he had to include a section at the beginning of his paper on ethnography as a research method. In the following excerpt from our workshop session on his first draft, Bill justifies his rhetorical choices after several students mention that the first and second sections of his paper—the latter a discussion of ethnography—do not seem connected to the rest of the study. His research describes the results of encouraging students to take more authority in the seminary classroom by teaching selected Bible lessons.

> *Bill:* Well, I guess the reason I wanted to talk about ethnography is I wanted to just—I was trying to justify probably as much to myself as possibly to others who might read this who would not be teachers of composition in universities, what an ethnography is and even what case studies are and the fact that they're subjective versus objective, and so forth. And that's a legitimate method of gaining knowledge.
>
> *Ruth:* Do you feel like you did justify it to yourself?
>
> *Bill:* Well, I think it probably could be expanded a little bit, more than taken out. I sort of needed that for myself, I think.
>
> *Ruth:* Well, in that case maybe you could tie it into your *study* in such a way that your study presents the justification for ethnography. You know, you've got all this information on pages 1–4 about arguments for ethnography, qualitative research, so then the transition into your study is what? So I decided to test these assumptions? Or how do we move from that body of literature into the seminary at the Blue Water Ward?
>
> *Bill:* OK. MmmHmm.
>
> *Mary:* 'Cause I remember when we talked about how we saw the parts of our paper in class one time, I remember you did mention the ethnography as setting the background, and you got verification for that being probably an important way to lead in. I remember we talked that day . . .
>
> *Bill:* Yeah. I probably would feel more comfortable expanding the ethnography section a little bit and tying it into what I'm about to do, and it—

Mary: Yeah, and it might only be a paragraph you end up adding. It might not be that big a thing.

Bill: I see people reading this or going to some other seminary teachers and so forth who have never even *heard* of the term ethnography and who have never—and who possibly, like me, have come in contact now with this type of research which is not what we know as research—totally different. We've known for years that you gain knowledge by piling up all the red balls on this side and the yellow ones on that side, and then you count 'em. And that tells you where you stand. So I'm trying to just do a little background in the beginning, kind of setting up the fact and establishing the fact that ethnography and case studies and things that are subjective and things that are narrative are all right.

By this time in the semester, Bill had decided that he was going to show the final report of his research to other church authorities who were responsible for organizing seminary classes in local districts. He felt they could learn from his experiences and perhaps encourage other teachers to involve students more actively in the classroom. This was a particularly important issue for seminary classes like Bill's which ran from 6:00 to 7:00 a.m. on weekdays before regular school classes started. Seminary teachers were always looking for new ways to motivate students to participate more actively at that hour.

Interestingly, discussion of Bill's rhetorical choices in writing for a local audience leads into a discussion of both personal and global issues. After Bill explains his decision to include a section which defines ethnography in terms of methodology, the class presses him further:

Gay: Well, even though, as you say, it's hard to define ethnography, do you think you should totally sidestep it altogether? I mean, if you're going to talk about ethnography, then I think you should try to come to terms with what it *is* as well as what it *does*.

Ruth: Especially given the audience you've projected.

Gay: MmmHmm.

Andrea: And why you employ it in your classroom—not to say it was required for a class, [but] what sold you on it? What made it so suitable for what you wanted to find out? That might allow you to bring yourself into the study a little bit more, too. I mean, I can appreciate your distance in the study, but there came a point where I got curious—and someone else might not, because we know you as a teacher—[but] on page 7, where you talk about Ron the seminary teacher, I was a little confused. I thought maybe, were you talking about yourself or what? And it came out a little bit, I think, on the next page when you introduced the teacher as someone other. You might want to let us know that you are an observer in this classroom or that you are a co-teacher, so that we can place you in your study.

Ruth: I think that would go in the introductory section when you
define what ethnography is and specifically what it was for the
purposes of this study, and what role you played—that you were
a participant-observer, but also simply an observer. And define
your role in the system there, what part you play in terms of the
church hierarchy, etc.

Following this exchange, we suggest how Bill might reorganize his
paper to make it more readable for seminary teachers. We also begin
to question some of his conclusions:

Gay: You know, something that just occurred to me . . . if you gave
some constructive criticism to those who didn't do so well the first
time, and they improved, I wonder if the absence, if that's the case,
of constructive criticism of those who did well gave them the
message that they didn't have to do as well [the second time].

Andrea: MmmHmm. That's a good point.

Bill: W-e-l-l, I don't know. Uh, what I found out, when I transcribed my first interviews, is that I really talked an awful lot more
than I should have, and I should have listened. That was really
amazing. But I think when they did good, I think part of the
interview was the fact that, as we talked about it and I asked—one
of the questions was, how did you feel about your presentation,
what was the reaction of the other students to your presentation?—when they did well, they knew it. And then we usually
talked about what it was that was good about what they did, and
those same questions usually led into the criticism, because the
students sensed when they didn't do well, and they lost the class,
or the class had wandered off, as I mentioned there at one point,
the students *knew* that, and we talked about why or how that
happened.

Andrea: You know, Bill, in that sense I really liked reading it. It
flowed really well, and you have a very nice style of expressing
yourself. But now that you mention it, I think it's the same kind
of thing all of us noticed in mine is that the acts of the research are
missing and that maybe if you include a sample of those discussions and con*fessed* to maybe talking a little too much—

Bill: Me? Confess? [class laughter]

Andrea:—that that would further enrich this. I'm already tempted
to try this [teaching technique] in one of my classes, because it
seemed like it was a good exercise, but—

As these excerpts indicate, the class considers again, this time
through the acts of Bill's research and the discourse he constructs
around them, several issues which have been raised throughout the
semester in our discussions of the theoretical readings: What legiti-
mizes ethnography as a form of knowledge making? What place, if
any, does personal knowledge have in the writing of ethnography?

What gives an ethnographic text authority (inclusion or exclusion of the researcher's limitations)? What makes a researcher's analysis and interpretation of the findings credible?

In some cases, discussion of local issues led to discussion of local politics and how graduate students' discourse may be constrained by institutional forces. For example, in our workshop session on Jill's draft, entitled "Basic Writers and Cross-Curricular Instructors: Expectations and Responses," we discuss some of the politics underlying her rhetorical choices. In her research, Jill had determined through interviews with students and faculty, as well as analysis of faculty-generated assignments and student papers submitted for freshman courses in speech, Africana studies, history, political science, and sociology, that faculty members in her division sometimes have unrealistic expectations for student writing. This was particularly true of the writing produced by students who were simultaneously enrolled in content-area classes and Jill's developmental reading and writing course, ENG 001. In our session on Jill's draft, Alex responds by raising a local political question:

> *Alex:* I had some questions about—I remember this has been a controversy since they started the program in the 70s. . . . It's been a continuing controversy that the university wanted extra money for the program, but the students couldn't, [faculty] felt the students couldn't do the classroom work, and [there were] professors from the liberal arts and so on who couldn't deal with the students, and there was a controversy about whether they [the students] should get credit for these courses. So I know there's a history of that, and so I wanted to know why is this [conclusion] an important issue?

Jill responds by describing how her division has a community-oriented, open-enrollment policy based on the philosophy that everyone should have a chance at college and that faculty should be able to meet nontraditional students' needs. After a class discussion of the fact that, in Mary's words, Jill "has about a hundred papers here" and that the classroom implications of an open-enrollment policy is just one of them, we return, at my initiation, to the issue Alex has raised.

> *Ruth:* Could I just ask you one last philosophical question? You draw this conclusion that . . . [reading] "the study reveals that ENG 001 students should not take certain writing-laden classes—content-area classes—concomitantly with ENG 001." Well, that raises a whole lot of questions about what you think happens with basic writers and how they really need sort of a controlled curriculum, and it also assumes—Well, first of all, there's the question that all writing-across-the-curriculum emphases sug-

gest: that *every* course is writing laden, or should be. So are you calling into question the whole WAC emphasis? Number one question. And number two, it doesn't seem—another way of looking at the problem is that instructors of writing-laden courses need to rethink their assumptions and their expectations for students.

Jill: That would be *nice.*

Ruth: Rather than saying students shouldn't take the courses, we could also conclude that, well, these courses are good courses and they *should* be taken, but instructors perhaps should have more realistic expectations.

Jill: You know why I don't even make that suggestion? Because the college and departments and divisions across the university supply part-time instructors for our division, and there's absolutely no way that you could begin, although . . . I'm beginning to create a liaison between me and what I'm trying to do and the [content-area] instructors, but, see, they rotate . . . and there's no way that that can be controlled for at this point. Although, later on down the line, if I gain some trust or whatever, I could see if I could start having maybe seminars or something where I call groups together and do that kind of thing. But still, with part-time instructors, you can't expect them to give up their time and say, "Ooooo this is fun on Saturday! I work forty hours a week, you know, I think I'll come in for a seminar!" [class laughter]

Bill: Was the history instructor who wouldn't cooperate with you because he wanted to get paid [to be interviewed] a part-time instructor?

Jill: Oh, yeah. They all are.

Gay: But you didn't approach him in this one—

Jill: No because, yeah, I didn't approach him again because he had made it very clear that he wasn't doing anything outside of his assignments that was not compensated.

Ruth: Well, could you talk about it in terms of how we as teachers of nontraditional students in *general* may need to reconsider our expectations? Not just those instructors. If in fact they're representative of instructors in most programs, maybe we should—well, one of the assumptions we need to consider, reconsider, is that students understand everything they read and can respond to their reading from the first day of college, that we don't have to teach reading.

Jill responds by saying that she is reluctant to draw conclusions for *all* composition professionals on the basis of her limited experience within her division, and given the small number of students she is describing who struggle much more than most students in the university. She wants to limit her conclusions to her particular program, claiming only that those students enrolled in ENG 001 should not take certain content-area classes in her division. The class responds, however, by pressing her to consider the global issues underlying this local conclusion:

> *Andrea:* But it raises a really, really complicated question in terms of the university, and politically, you know, you can say, "What are these people doing in the university if they're not quite up to par? Do we have to make an effort to let them in?" So here you are in this kind of extension program, through the community, open enrollment—what you might want to point out is that this is not "real" college, you know, and that maybe these professors who are teaching these extension courses are expecting too much of this kind of student and that they have to understand the context in which the students are in that program.

> *Jill:* Maybe I should make clear that the students are enrolled in math and computer courses that they do well in. What I'm saying is that, perhaps, during the time they are in this course with me, they should not be in all of the heavy content writing-laden courses. I'm not saying that it's not real college, because they *are* succeeding in other courses perhaps that are not this intensive in their writing.

> *Ruth:* But some people would say it's not real college if they can't read and write in these writing-intensive courses immediately.

> *Jill:* What I'm saying is that we have a developmental *program* here, similar to those at community colleges, that *prepares* students and that—while it's not our decision, it's a political decision that's been made—that we are going to have an open door and that people are going to have access, just as they do at the community colleges. And our division serves that purpose at the university.

> *Andrea:* All I'm saying is what I see in your study is a very serious implication that you have this open-enrollment policy that is yet still very difficult to deal with in the context of the course load of these students. You know, it's very nice to say, "We shall open the doors and all ye come in here," but then if you're put in the position of having to *deal* with them, what these people are doing, you might want to raise some of those issues about . . . ways of solving this problem. . . . There is a social issue.

> *Jill:* Yeah, and I think that, really, it's a national curricular issue.

> | *Ruth:* | ⎡ Oh yeah. ⎤ |
> |---|---|
> | *Mary:* | Really. |
> | *Andrea:* | Definitely. |
> | *Gay:* | ⎣ MmmHmm. ⎦ |

Despite having acknowledged that her study raises a "national curricular issue," Jill is still reluctant to write about this issue. She wants to remain at the local level, even though her conclusions have global implications. In this sense, Jill feels a conflict between local and global concerns. Locally, she is concerned with helping her ENG 001 students succeed in college, and her study has suggested to her that restricting the content-area courses they enroll in during the first year may be the best way to encourage this success. Globally, her study raises serious issues about the philosophy of remedial education within research institutions, but they are issues which Jill is not prepared to talk about, given her personal and local emphasis, and does not feel qualiied to address, given her lack of experience, status in the university, and apprentice position as a researcher within the field of composition studies. Jill resists addressing a global audience on these issues because, at this point in her education and experience, she doubts whether she has anything credible to say.

Some of the English 702 discussions also suggest that graduate students doubt whether their writing can influence even a local audience. This point comes up in our workshop session on Elaine's paper, which focuses on the effects of students' and tutors' personalities on tutoring sessions. Before the excerpt that follows, we have talked about Elaine's personality traits and those of her students, as determined by the Myers-Briggs Personality Profile, which she administered as part of her study. It has been suggested that the tutoring lab itself has a personality, which Elaine describes as "sterile" and which one of her students likens to a doctor's waiting room.

> *Andrea:* But one thing I want to add before we stop, I really want to know why the English department's tutoring lab is like it is. Was it a conscious decision or, without getting anyone into trouble, uh, why is it, if it's supposed to be a nurturing environment, that you're not allowed to show personalities? What is the rationale behind that?

> *Elaine:* Well, there was, in the literature I was reading, there was also some really interesting stuff that a lot of tutoring labs . . . are working with the students' feelings and saying, "Why do you want to write about this?" and that kind of [thing]. And we're not supposed to do that. We're not supposed to even get involved with the student or anything. See, a lot of them will talk about personal stuff. . . .

> *Gay:* Who says you're not supposed to do this? It's in the research?

> *Elaine:* It's something you're told when you start.

> *Gay:* It's what? Oh, oh, in your orientation?

> *Elaine:* That we're not to get too involved with the students. Yeah. Like what to do if somebody starts crying. I can see the line that we're not involved in counseling, but I think it's kind of hard to distinguish between the two.

> *Ruth:* Well, that's a specific philosophy about teaching and tutoring that, you know, you're working with the intellect, this is a cognitive activity, we're not psychologists here, we can't get into personalities. But, in fact, and your research is premised on this fact, we *are* working with personalities. This is a human exchange

here, there's no getting around it. And no matter what you do with your environment, you can't change the fact that you have two warm bodies there who have come to this meeting with all kinds of emotions and problems and psychological issues and family background, and whatever. It's there in the room between the two of you.

Elaine: It's especially hard if you're talking about ideas. I notice with some of the . . . students talking about what ideas are in a passage, when you're talking about general ideas like that, you can't help but express what they're thinking and that kind of gets into the personal realm.

Andrea: Well, to put it into another perspective that we've been reading a lot about in [another composition seminar], what you seem to have discovered is that there's a process view of tutoring and that, in a sense, your lab is dealing with a tutoring situation as a product still, as a kind of an official, cold kind of interaction, as opposed to what Ruth said—two warm bodies with emotions, with histories, with personalities, different ways of knowing, coming together to try to solve a problem. That might be a good implication—that you have to recognize these findings do exist, and from what you've said, the situations that work best for you are the ones where you've gotten along with your student.

Elaine: But then, according to Myers-Briggs, that's part of what my personality does anyway.

Mary: Get along?

Elaine: Yeah.

Ruth: But according to the director of your tutoring lab, or the institution which has established this tutoring lab, your personality is irrelevant and so is the student's. All that's important is that paper there between the two of you, and what the teacher said the student was supposed to write, and what the student wrote.

Elaine: I mean, there are a lot of good points in not getting involved, but, I mean, I really don't think it hurts anything.

Gay: I would feel very comfortable if I were a student going to a tutor like you, because you're so cheerful and upbeat. I think that would put me at ease, and I do think that's an issue. If they were going in there feeling unconfident about their writing in a sterile environment and they had some person saying, "Well that's it, open your paper," I just think that would be a double whammy.

Elaine: A situation I find myself in a lot is I have a tendency to kind of coach them, [saying] "Oh, that's a good idea!" and that kind of stuff. I do get real enthusiastic, but to a certain extent we're not supposed to do that too much because there's the problem of a lawsuit. I mean, yeah, it's a little different circumstance, but there's one of the tutors who told a student that he would probably pass the [university's writing competence exam], you know. . . .

Ruth: Do you want another suggestion about how to frame this paper?

Elaine: Sure.

Ruth: Well, you can talk about it in terms of the larger issues in the field of composition studies. There's one approach to the teaching of writing which is cognitive, intellectual, rigorous, hard-nosed: we look at the writing, we train students how to think, we're not working with people or personalities here, we're working with academic discourse. There's another approach in the field that says we're working with people here, we're working with feelings. This is personal and interactive. You know, kind of a soft approach to the teaching of writing. And you could say, well, here are these two perspectives on the teaching of writing, and these are pretty clearly articulated in Peter Elbow's *What Is English?* There's a chapter on soft studies or whatever he calls them, and he argues very strongly for that personal approach to the teaching of writing, as many people do. And then say, well, this issue is manifest in the tutoring lab where I work. My physical environment supports the hard-nosed, rigorous, intellectual, nonpersonal approach to teaching. As a person, I support the other approach, and this is my personality, and I believe that personality is important, and here are these vignettes to illustrate that they are. And so, you present these vignettes, do the Myers-Briggs personality information, and then make your argument that, in fact, in your experience as a tutor working with individuals on a daily basis, there's no way you can avoid the personal. That's another option.

Andrea: You could blow the lab out of the water with this!

Ruth: Well, that's OK. [class laughter]

Andrea: I really like the way—

Gay: Do you want to keep your job?

Elaine: Yeah, that's a good question!

Andrea: No, but what you're doing is you're showing that you did research to prove a point, and here's the point: look at it!

Gay: It might even bring about change, who knows.

Andrea: Yeah!

Elaine: I doubt it.

Bill: Maybe you'll get your picture on the wall or something. [class laughter]

In this exchange, both Andrea and I suggest that framing the study from a global perspective would provide a way out of Elaine's perceived inability to effect change at the local level. Composition theory, we are saying, would allow her to critique the conditions under which she works by generalizing beyond the immediate situation and focusing on a larger philosophical debate within the field of composition. The class discussion of Elaine's paper suggests that, although self-generated acts of research can empower a student personally, theory can empower a student to articulate that research more confidently and assertively by opening up global avenues that help defuse the politically charged nature of personal and local findings.

Knowledge Making as Rhetorical Act

As I have illustrated in this chapter and the previous one, knowledge making in composition is not a fixed activity, but a rhetorical act which takes on many forms, depending on individual researchers, their audience and purpose. For composition to thrive as a field, researchers must come to see these rhetorical differences as strengths rather than weaknesses. We must realize that there are many knowledge makers other than university researchers and theorists, including K–12 teachers and graduate students, and recognize as beneficial the many forms of knowledge they create. Specifically, we could begin by acknowledging the role that personal knowledge plays in the conducting of research and the making of composition as a field. Teacher research illustrates how teachers' personalities, beliefs, feelings, and political views affect the learning environment, as well as how researchers interpret and write about their findings.

The English 702 class also illustrates the power of discourse communities to shape research. Clearly, the class itself was a discourse community, as is any graduate class. Through shared readings and class discussions, we came to value, as a group, the articulation of personal knowledge and to promote each other's research as a process of discovery rather than an impersonal search that is "written up" at the end of the semester. Theory for us became a practice rather than a content, where the making of knowledge was "participatory and experiential and process-oriented" rather than "content-oriented in the sense of asking students merely to learn and absorb the theories of others" (Elbow 1990, 81). As a discourse community, we also came to share language, adopting and freely using terms from the readings as well as terms and phrases from each other's own spoken and written discourse. References to Shirley Brice Heath, John Van Maanen, and my own writing about teacher research in the class transcripts suggest the influence of the course readings and my perspective on students' thinking. Finally, as a community we became deeply invested in the outcomes of each other's research; at the end of the semester students requested that I collect the papers in an informal publication so that everyone could read all the final drafts.

English 702 was a discourse community that students wanted to join because they saw membership as beneficial to their teaching, as well as to their graduate studies. For all of the students, the class offered a principled way to examine and improve their teaching. For some students, such as Jill and Gay, the class provided a means of collecting information they would use in writing conference papers and, quite possibly, dissertations in composition theory. Despite these benefits, there was also some resistance to the community and its perspective, as the case of Alex suggests. He did not fully enter into the discussions and resisted the group's repeated requests for "confessions" of his personal interactions with Jane. Yet teacher research allows for resistance in its eclectic approach and its blurring of research genres. Many other alternatives besides the confessional tale were available to Alex for interpreting and writing about his findings.

Indeed, teacher research provides a means of communicating to graduate students the concept of epistemological diversity because it illustrates, on a very practical level, how knowledge is constructed personally, locally, and globally and how these three inform one another differently in the experience of every researcher. Teacher research also provides a concrete way for graduate students to consider their "situatedness" within the sociopolitical context of the university and how this position affects their thinking, writing, and researching, as shown by the experiences of Andrea, Elaine, and Jill. As I will argue in the next chapter, these are all important lessons that graduate students must learn in order to understand the choices before them as professionals and their potential influence on the evolution of composition studies.

Notes

1. Students have been given pseudonyms.

2. A simplified version of class conversations is reported here without hedges and false starts. In most cases, one-syllable affirmative responses such as "yeah" and "uh-huh" have also been omitted. Bracketed speech indicates that two or more people are speaking simultaneously.

3. In his draft, Alex had included a section in which he talked about an early student-teaching experience with an English teacher who relied so heavily on mimeographed worksheets for grammar practice that students called her the "Ditto Queen." Alex, knowing no other way at the time, adopted her teaching methods completely and thus acquired the name "Ditto King."

4. The appropriateness of graduate students writing for a local rather than a global audience and for teachers rather than researchers is an issue that I myself was ambivalent about and had to confront directly through my teaching of this course. It is also an issue that the field of composition must address if we are truly to acknowledge alternative forms of knowledge making and teach graduate students to respect and pursue them.

6 Toward a Teacher-Research Approach to Graduate Studies

> All truths arise out of dialectic, out of the interaction of individuals within discourse communities. Truth is never simply "out there" in the material or the social realm, or simply "in here" in a private, personal world. It emerges only as the three—the material, the social, and the personal—interact, and the agent of mediation is language.
>
> —James Berlin 1987

> Advanced literacy requires learners to adopt a stance that will allow them to see and to change their relationship to language, including the language of the academy; but the language of the academy itself will have to be redefined as multiple and changeable if we and our students are to have a hand in "inventing" it.
>
> —Susan Wall and Nicholas Cage 1991

> The university stands—or should stand—behind enquiry in schools as the curator of that uncertainty without which the transmission of knowledge becomes a virtuoso performance in gentling the masses.
>
> —Lawrence Stenhouse 1985

The purpose of graduate studies in composition is at least threefold: to introduce students to the existing knowledge of the field; to offer theoretical perspectives for interpreting this knowledge and for generating more knowledge; and to make available approaches for knowledge making at the personal, local, and global levels. As a field, we need to do a better job of meeting these goals, especially in terms of teaching graduate students how to construct and integrate levels of knowledge. Teacher research, especially that which is informed by the lessons of feminist studies, offers a principled way to do this within the experience of each practitioner. And it is just this kind of integration, beginning with the individual, which the field most needs: "What we need . . . are programmatic changes that provide occasions for graduate students themselves to relate their theoretical desires to the needs they anticipate, and particularly the kind of teaching responsibilities they will have" (Slevin 1989, 34). The need for better integration underlies a recent proposal from the Carnegie Foundation for the Advancement of Teaching calling for a redefinition of *scholarship* to acknowledge the value of personal, local, and practical knowledge, as represented in creative teaching, curriculum development, and textbook writing (Mooney 1990).

Such broadened definitions of scholarship must also form the basis of graduate education. Currently, the move toward theory and away from practice directs our training of scholars to such an extent that "promising graduate students are usually encouraged to seek jobs that require little teaching. And those who express a strong desire to teach—who *want* positions in two- and four-year colleges—may well hear what a friend of mine heard: 'Why would you want to do that? You're bright; you could do much better than that'" (Peterson 1991, 28; emphasis hers). This statement, undoubtedly voiced by a graduate faculty member with the best of intentions, illustrates not only the separation of teaching and research, but also the perpetuation of a negating hierarchy which privileges scholarship and trivializes teaching. At my own university, I am continually confronted with this attitude. Recently, an associate professor gave the following advice to a group of new teaching assistants during an orientation session: "Your teaching can take over your life. Be careful or it will interfere with your work." The message to these young academicians, who had not yet walked through the door of their first classroom, was that research is their "real work," and teaching is merely a distraction from it. Ironically, the messenger is a well-regarded professor who has won a university award for outstanding teaching. When speaking in an official capacity, this professor apparently felt it necessary to evoke the traditional hierarchy, even though doing so negated some of her own best work.

A second example from my institution illustrates how the devaluing of teaching is played out at the level of curriculum development. When asked by the provost to comment on a proposal for a new Ph.D. program in rhetoric at a competing university, an administrator in my department responded in terms of the old hierarchy. Specifically, he took issue with an emphasis in the proposal on "applied theoretical research on the contexts in which communications are generated and used." My colleague responded: "Does this sound like pedagogy? Too much, too much. And too much pedagogy means too little theory." He went on to define theory as "a body or bodies of knowledge that will be used to found the study of rhetoric and communication" and cited poststructuralism-postmodernism as an example of a theory that "would seem necessary to their enterprise and should be included." Although the proposal had referred to feminist, linguistic, and contemporary rhetorical theory, these were dismissed as "vague" perspectives by my colleague. I see in this response not only the unquestioned privileging of theory at the expense of practice, but also the unexamined assumption that theory is de facto a valued body of knowledge rather than one perspective on knowledge making which *ascribes* value, and that poststructuralism is the only body of knowledge worth promoting. This is the kind of limited thinking which drives most graduate programs in English departments and which forms the basis of graduate students' initiation into the field.

There is evidence other than anecdotal to support my claim that graduate programs in composition, too, perpetuate hierarchical thinking about theory and pedagogy. Carol Berkenkotter, Thomas Huckin, and John Ackerman's 1988 study of a student in a Ph.D. program in rhetoric serves as a case in point. In these final pages, I offer my own critical reading of that study, as well as the comments of graduate students in my teacher-research seminar, to illustrate that our graduate courses and our responses to graduate students' writing firmly negate the value of personal knowledge and teaching. I propose that the field needs to broaden its definition of scholarship and develop graduate programs that allow for alternative perspectives.

The Berkenkotter et al. study is an important one in composition, for it is the first to trace the intellectual and rhetorical development of a graduate student. As such, it makes a genuine contribution to our understanding of the influences on advanced students' learning. Further, it is a well-documented, carefully drawn case study and a good example of what Linda Brodkey calls "analytic" ethnography, as opposed to "interpretive" ethnography, where "analysis is to demonstration as interpretation is to dialectics" (1987, 27). Analytic ethnography deals with proof and certainty, while interpretive ethnography deals with doubt and uncertainty: "[A]nalysis and interpretation can also be understood as the difference between discovery and construction. Whereas analysis presumes that researchers discover information in data, interpretation presumes that researchers construct information from data" (31). Brodkey's distinction between analytic and interpretive is essentially the same distinction I point out in Chapter 1 between scientific and humanist approaches to composition scholarship and in Chapter 3 between paradigmatic and narrative thinking.

Whatever terminology we choose, we must acknowledge that these methodological approaches represent distinct epistemologies. Analytic researchers believe that truths can be found and reported; interpretive researchers believe that truths are variable because they are rhetorically and socially constructed. Graduate programs reflect these different epistemological orientations. Programs which are primarily influenced by the analytic perspective tend to be heavily product oriented; they focus on finding meaning through rigorous research and on *reporting* it via formal discourse strategies. Theory, from this perspective, is a *body of knowledge* that must be mastered and displayed for admittance to the field. In contrast, programs influenced by the interpretive perspective (such as the one my colleague was responding to) tend to be more process oriented; they focus on *constructing* meaning within different contexts through a variety of discourse strategies. Theory, from this perspective, is a *process of knowledge making,* and admittance to the field depends on one's ability and willingness to think through and challenge existing knowledge. The analytic, product-oriented perspective of Berkenkotter, Huckin, and Ackerman underlies teaching in most graduate programs in composition. This approach has its benefits, but it also limits intellectual and rhetorical diversity in the field. I suggest that English departments need to acknowledge the legitimacy of a more interpretive, process-oriented perspective and that one way to promote this perspective is by teaching graduate students to be teacher-researchers.

The Graduate Experience: An Analytic Perspective

The purpose of the Berkenkotter et al. study is to determine "how graduate students attain advanced academic literacy in the context of graduate school" by tracing the development of Nate, a student in his first year of the Ph.D. rhetoric program at Carnegie Mellon University (CMU). Data for the study consist of transcribed interviews with Nate, papers and personal memos written for professors, and Nate's weekly self-reports written specifically for the researchers. Berkenkotter et al. see these texts as constituting "*the visible index of his initiation into an academic discourse community*" (1988, 11; emphasis theirs). Although they acknowledge that the academic discourse community reflected in Nate's writing is specifically that of the CMU rhetoric program, which consists of classical and contemporary rhetoricians as well as cognitive psychologists, their analysis repeatedly suggests that the rhetoric program, in turn, represents the larger discourse community of composition studies. They claim, for example, that the CMU program is "aimed at producing an intellectual hybrid: a scholar familiar with historical and contemporary rhetorical theory, who can communicate through such journals as *College English* and *College Composition and Communication,* yet also a competent researcher who can write social science expository prose for educational research publications such as *Research in the Teaching of English* and *Written Communication*" (13). They determine that Nate is learning how "to communicate in the language of his discipline" (15), and they document his frustration "that he had not cracked the code of academic writing" (21). Further, when they evaluate Nate's progress toward contributing to the discourse community, they compare his writing to that of published composition scholars, only one of whom is part of the CMU community; the rest—Patricia Bizzell, Maxine Hairston, George Hillocks, Kenneth Kantor, James Kinneavy, Barry Kroll, Lee Odell, and J. C. Schafer—clearly represent the larger composition community.

Thus the claims that CMU produces a "hybrid" scholar capable of writing for all the major journals in the field and that Nate is learning to use "the language of his discipline" and "the code of academic writing" suggest that Berkenkotter et al. consider their analysis a reflection of the larger discourse community of composition. One gets the impression that they are "speaking for the discipline" and not just for the CMU community, despite their disclaimer that Nate's writing specifically reflects CMU's expectations for "social science research writing." I think they are right, for the most part, in assuming that they are speaking for the field. What I want to examine here is how the analytic, product-oriented thinking reflected in this study causes composition faculty to ignore or dismiss alternative forms of knowledge making in their teaching and evaluation of graduate students.

Many of the conclusions Berkenkotter et al. draw about Nate's growth as a scholar reflect hierarchical thinking which privileges disciplinary knowledge over personal knowledge, theory over practice, and written product over the writing process. In describing Nate's background, for example, they clearly distinguish between the expressive writing he has producd throughout his humanities-based education and the expository writing he is now learning in the social science-based CMU program. Specifically, in their analysis of one of his papers—"'Voice' in Reading and Writing: A Working Definition, Applications and Implication"—which Nate wrote before entering CMU, they found "a number of linguistic and rhetorical features that are discrepant with the discourse conventions of social science expository prose," including "heavy use of sentential parallelism, so heavy in fact that, except for its syntactic complexity, it resembles that used by gospel preachers"; too much variation in vocabulary; mixed metaphors; and a loosely organized style that does not focus hierarchically on a single point (1988, 17–18). Berkenkotter et al. equate Nate's expository writing with that which is informal, intellectually

uncomplicated, and academically inappropriate, while they characterize expository writing as that which is formal, intellectually
complex, and academically appropriate:

> One might best describe the shift that Nate was forced to make in
> graduate school as the transition from using a register for written
> discourse based on an informal repertoire to using a more formal
> register appropriate to academic discourse within a disciplinary
> community. The product of a dominant "expressive" movement
> in recent American writing pedagogy . . . Nate was an articulate
> writer of informal prose . . . who could control his text production
> processes *when not burdened by such cognitively complex tasks*
> *as adopting an appropriate register* (which included using rhe-
> torical and stylistic conventions with which he was unfamiliar)
> and instantiating abstract concepts into prose. (19; emphasis
> mine)

The authors consider Nate's expressive writing too "writer-based" in
its reliance on first-person pronouns to achieve cohesion, rather than
logical connectives and discourse demonstratives, and in its "dense,
passive" style, which suggests that he "is still wrestling with the ideas
himself instead of trying to explain them to a reader" (20). That
Berkenkotter et al. see expressive writing as inferior to expository
writing is apparent in their assertion that, for one assignment, Nate
"had found it difficult to express himself in an academic style of
writing and had *reverted* to his more accustomed, informal style" (29;
emphasis mine).

From this analytic perspective, a graduate student must write at all
times as a researcher reporting formal knowledge, and not as a teacher
or student in the midst of constructing that knowledge. This expectation is apparent in the ways Berkenkotter et al. describe the CMU
program: they emphasize that students receive training in empirical
research methodology, which is "quite rigorous" and involves "carrying out research projects, giving oral presentations, and writing
'publishable' or 'national conference' quality papers" (1988, 13). In
this community, the rite of initiation is "to publish and be cited" as
a researcher (12). Thus, when Nate writes as a teacher and a graduate
student rather than as a researcher, Berkenkotter et al. find his work
unacademic and inappropriate. They use Nate's critique of Eliot
Mishler's article "Meaning in Context: Is There Any Other Kind?"
(1979) to exemplify what happens when, "faced with formal writing
assignments such as critiques and research proposals and reports,
Nate frequently 'choked' when he tried to write" (Berkenkotter et al.
1988, 21). In this critique, Nate does not write from the stance of the
confident, all-knowing researcher, but begins by admitting that "I am

not a social scientist nor a historian or philosopher of science, so I cannot assail [Mishler's] criticisms of these disciplines" (22). Berkenkotter et al. conclude that "the focus of the piece is not on the Mishler essay, as one might expect in a critique, but rather on Nate's personal response. These problems suggest that the writer was neither able to reframe the abstract propositional information in the Mishler essay to fit a situationally appropriate rhetorical purpose, nor able to marshal the necessary strategic knowledge of genre and register to meet the requirements of the assignment" (22). Thus the fact that Nate does not display expected discourse conventions in this writing suggests to Berkenkotter et al. that he is intellectually as well as rhetorically deficient.

A memo Nate wrote to his professor a few days after submitting the Mishler critique, however, suggests other explanations:

> I read the article carefully, slowly, thoughtfully. Over the weekend before the critique was due I took his [Mishler's] criticisms of empirical research and ran with them. I thought about my history of teaching and writing and the "truth" that I held so dear. So I tried to point out in my critique, I should be in Mishler's camp. For example, I have believed in the power of voice long before I began to wonder just what the phenomenon means. Like many teachers I trust what I tacitly understand. My curiosity and initiative brought me to this campus. . . . What I've found is another way of seeing (with) the very empirical tools that Mishler disdains. . . . All of this is exciting for me. And troublesome. Mishler made me confront my re-tooling, my new orientation. I don't have the language to accurately capture what is going on. . . . Maybe it is too soon for me to critique Mishler. . . . I'm just beginning to understand the issues.
>   This brings me to my writing in your course. Maybe I choke at the chance to critique Mishler because I try to say too much. You and Hayes are profound. My thoughts and the writing I've used to capture them are shallow. . . . I lost, if you will, my voice—or never had it from the start. . . . I think it is more a question of trying to say too much too soon. The same grievous error plagues my writing as when my students write to please only the teacher. They write to become someone they really know nothing about.
> (23)

From the analytic perspective of Berkenkotter et al., Nate's memo is of interest primarily because of its form; it is an expressive approach to an expository task. From an interpretive perspective, however, the memo is important for what it reveals about Nate's learning process. It illustrates, for instance, his epistemological and ideological struggles with the two perspectives on knowledge making—the interpretive, humanistic view, which he brought with him to CMU and which the

Mishler article represents, and the analytical, social science view which his professor and the Ph.D. program at CMU represent. Nate realizes that it is "too soon" (both intellectually and politically) for him to critique successfully the epistemological assumptions of his professor and the institution he has just entered as a graduate student. He acknowledges that he is intimidated by the professor (she is profound, while he is shallow) and indicates that he sees himself as a student, not as the accomplished scholar and intellectual peer who would critique Mishler. His professor, in asking him to critique Mishler from the perspective of a researcher, is in fact asking him to be someone he "really know[s] nothing about."

Issues for Graduate Programs and the Field

The case study of Nate raises questions that Berkenkotter, Huckin, and Ackerman and all graduate faculty in composition must address openly in terms of their own programs:

1. What purposes does writing serve in graduate school?
2. How does graduate student writing reflect the epistemological and ideological assumptions of the graduate program and, by extension, the field?
3. What is the stance of the graduate faculty and, by extension, the field of composition on diversity and resistance as reflected in graduate student writing?

What Purposes Does Writing Serve in Graduate School?

The conventional responses to this question are "to learn how to contribute to the field as scholars" and "to display knowledge for purposes of evaluation." From the analytic perspective, the ability to "contribute to the field," as the study by Berkenkotter et al. indicates, is measured solely in terms of the quality of graduate students' texts and the conventions displayed therein. If a text is deemed appropriate for a national conference or a refereed journal, it is an acceptable contribution. Graduate students display knowledge of the field by showing in their writing that they can frame ideas in terms of established theory and can say how their own thinking supports, refutes, or extends this theory. How students learn to write papers of this type is not of particular interest. This point is illustrated in the experience of most faculty who read graduate student writing in the form of applications for M.A. and Ph.D. programs, essays accompanying grant and fellowship submissions, seminar papers, Ph.D. qualifying exams, and master's essays and dissertations. When asked to describe their method of evaluation, faculty members in these situations often say they know what good graduate writing is when they see it but cannot name its specific features; they express even less interest in speculating about how it was produced.

Two examples from my own department illustrate this reluctance of English faculty members to think substantively about graduate student writing. Last year a student was denied admittance to the Ph.D. program on the basis of his writing sample, a paper he had written for a graduate seminar as an M.A. student, presumably one on which he had received an "A." In the paper, the student began by discussing his doubts and reservations about poststructuralist theory and then used a sports metaphor as a framing device to talk about his reading of texts. Faculty response to this rhetorical approach was overwhelmingly negative: one member of the graduate committee said he "didn't like the student's writing" and found the extended metaphor "weird"; another said the student should be "more sophisticated in his approach to texts" and that reliance on the sports metaphor demonstrated a lack of intellectual and political savvy. No one on the committee voiced a position suggesting that the *purpose* of a Ph.D. program is to teach the student exactly what we were faulting him for not having. It was as if the graduate committee were looking for a colleague, not a student; they seemed more interested in identifying someone who had already joined the academic club than in teaching him how to acquire and sustain a membership.

A second example comes from the discussions (and evasions) in my department about the nature and purpose of the Ph.D. qualifying exams. In the past, faculty members have read, responded to, and evaluated students' exams without deliberating much among themselves or fully articulating their expectations for students. Evaluations have been based, for the most part, on tacit, unexamined assumptions (often derived from faculty members' own experiences of taking qualifying exams) about what constitutes "general knowledge" of the field and how a student demonstrates this knowledge. The graduate committee has never described explicitly in writing just what constitutes a passing or failing exam, even though students could benefit enormously from such attempts at articulation. It goes without saying, then, that the faculty has not begun to consider the intellectual or rhetorical processes required of students to produce this kind of writing.

Even composition specialists such as Berkenkotter et al., despite their stated goal of determining "how graduate students attain advanced academic literacy in the context of graduate school," focus exclusively on the "what" rather than the "how" of Nate's writing. This emphasis was immediately clear to the graduate students who read the study for my English 702 seminar on researching teaching (see Chapter 5). Andrea, for example, points out that the case study "contributes virtually nothing to [the readers'] understanding of how the subject, Nate, learns and appropriates CMU's discourse conventions. It only displays—in a very reductive manner—the ways in which Nate has *not* mastered the discourse." Indeed, the study illustrates that the "paradigm shift" experienced in the undergraduate classroom from a focus on product to a focus on process has not found its way into the graduate curriculum.

A more interpretive, process-oriented graduate program would focus on additional purposes for writing: to generate and sustain a conversation with established scholars; to connect personal knowledge with theoretical knowledge; to reflect on experience; to test the consequences of following various theoretical perspectives; to articulate hypotheses, beliefs, assumptions, and personal theories; and to express doubts, anxieties, hopes, and fears about entering the scholarly community. From an interpretive perspective, graduate students write in order *to construct* the field *for themselves* and to consider the personal possibilities of researching and teaching within it. A more interpretive approach to the Berkenkotter et al. case study would focus on Nate's reasons for writing and his motivation for entering the CMU community. For example, why would Nate, an ardent believer in expressionist epistemology who says he has "moved dramatically away from academic writing and certainly away from any traces of the scientific habit" (1988, 18), choose to attend a Ph.D. program which stakes its reputation on empirical research in the social science tradition? Why did Nate select a graduate program that would challenge all his previous beliefs about writing, teaching, and composition scholarship? Was he fully aware of the intellectual, political, and practical implications of this choice? If not, when and how did he develop this awareness and what were his reactions to it? What else besides class readings and interactions with the CMU faculty influenced Nate's writing?

The Berkenkotter et al. study suggests that texts and teachers are the primary (if not the only) influence in graduate school, but these are only two components of an educational experience. Surely Nate's interactions with others, both in and out of the rhetoric program, influenced his writing. How, for example, did he fit in with the other graduate students? Was he a teaching assistant? Did he perceive any hierarchies between graduate students in the rhetoric program and those in the literature program? If Nate was a research assistant or a fellow who was "relieved" of teaching responsibilities, how did this role affect his thinking about teaching? about composition theory and its relationship to teaching? How did Nate perceive and respond to the politics of the CMU English department? Did he ever have doubts about his chosen field? If so, where and how did he express them? From an interpretive perspective, student texts are the tip of the iceberg; real understanding of how a student learns requires understanding of the experiences and thoughts that surround the production of those texts. In order to get access to this information, we would have to hear more from Nate himself, especially since he is, as we find out later, the third coauthor of the study (Berkenkotter 1991a). Given their product orientation, however, Berkenkotter et al. do not reveal that Nate is both subject and author of the study, nor do they say how their collaborative efforts may have affected development of the study or interpretation of the findings.

How Does the Writing We Assign to Graduate Students Reflect Our Epistemological Assumptions?

If the samples of Nate's writing are representative of what graduate students in composition are typically asked to write, and I think they are, we can conclude that faculty members consider the writing of analyses and critiques to be the best orientation to the field. This is a traditional analytic approach to graduate studies which is in many ways successful. However, it is not the only approach, and it is not necessarily the best one for all students at all stages in their learning. In assigning certain types of writing, faculty members need to keep in mind that they are also assigning value; an exclusive emphasis on analysis and critique implicitly says to students that only these forms of writing are essential to their development as scholars. Consider, for example, the claim of Berkenkotter et al. that, in submitting expressive, self-reflective writing to his professor, Nate was "reverting" to a less valued form.

When viewed from the analytic perspective, expressive writing is highly inappropriate, for the coherent display of established knowledge rather than the messy process of knowledge making is what is taught and promoted. This product orientation is clear in the conclusions Berkenkotter et al. draw about Nate's development as a writer. They see evidence of growth in the fact that later papers show "perhaps most importantly, he has stopped overusing the first-person singular pronoun" and that "instead of foregrounding himself and his feelings and beliefs, he now seems to be concentrating primarily on the subject matter, employing conventions that communicate (semiotically) distance and objectivity" (1988, 34). Further, they find that, while Nate's use of informal, personal writing enabled him to learn the subject matter of the field (what they refer to as declarative knowledge), it "may have slowed his progress as an academic writer" because it interfered with "the development of the procedural knowledge needed to construct text structures appropriate to formal expository discourse" (38). Because Nate sometimes chose to write in the expressive rather than the expository mode, Berkenkotter et al. assume that this meant he "had difficulty" switching modes: "Ideally, a writer like Nate would adroitly shift between informal and formal registers depending upon the goals for a piece of writing and the reader's linguistic expectations. For Nate, however, the acquisition of this multi-register fluency was impeded by his political and practical preferences for expressive discourse" (38).

These conclusions suggest a view that personal knowledge and expressive writing are a hindrance to one's growth and, therefore, to one's acceptance in the discourse community. In this view, graduate students must always write as researchers informing an audience about established knowledge. They are expected to adopt this stance in their first graduate paper and maintain it through the completion and defense of their dissertations. The assumption underlying this expectation is that students can simply *choose* to "write like a researcher," even though, as in Nate's case, they may know little about how, why, and to whom a researcher writes. Gay, one of the students in English 702, exemplifies the effect of this expectation on some graduate students' attitudes and self-confidence. A returning student in her early forties, Gay had completed a master's degree and a good portion of a Ph.D. in literature at another university before leaving school to pursue other interests, including raising two young children and teaching composition part-time. When she entered the Ph.D. program in composition at Wayne State University, Gay had been teaching as an adjunct faculty member in the English department for nearly ten years and had established a reputation as a competent, dedicated teacher. Yet much to her surprise, she was denied a teaching assistantship her first year in the graduate program because, as a faculty member later informed her, her application was written from the perspective of a teacher, rather than a theoretical scholar. Gay expressed both anger and defensiveness at the faculty assumption that, in choosing to take a pedagogical stance, she was *therefore* incapable of choosing a theoretical one. During our class discussion of the Berkenkotter et al. article, Gay identified with Nate's need to write from the perspective of a student and a teacher, saying, "I've been knocked down myself for being too pedagogical in my writing." She also revealed her negative feelings about the hierarchy she perceives between theory and practice in the English department: "I resist the idea that theory is the be all and end all. Are we supposed to parade a theory and genuflect before it?" Her first experiences at Wayne State have suggested to her that "genuflecting" is indeed what most faculty members want from graduate students.

Several colleagues in my department do not "allow" their graduate students to do personal writing (that which foregrounds the writer's experience over the content of a text) because they do not consider it intellectually rigorous enough. They argue that the academy does not value personal knowledge, as evident in what gets published in journals and supported by grants, and therefore that graduate students should not be writing expressively. In fact, some faculty members believe they would actually be doing students a *disservice* by allowing them to write in a form they cannot use for master's essays, qualifying exams, or dissertation prospectuses. This totalizing approach to the teaching of graduate writing, albeit well intentioned, merely perpetuates the dichotomies between personal and public knowledge, theory and practice that seriously inhibit enlightened, broad-based, multimodal, multidisciplinary inquiry in English studies.

When graduate students are asked to write only critically and analytically about readings just partially understood, they are placed forever in a position of inferiority to professors, who will inevitably know the texts better. Savvy students realize that the professor is saying, in assigning such writing, "Show me that you value what I value by writing as I do." Yet the same argument for personal writing in undergraduate composition classes can be made for personal writing in graduate courses: when writing is based on students' experiences and personal theories, the professor can be a real reader; when writing is based exclusively on canonical texts that the professor "owns" in terms of prior knowledge and expertise, the professor will always be evaluator and judge. Sometimes, graduate students do need a good, strong critic; at other times, though, they need a supportive, receptive reader. They are no different from established writers and scholars in this regard.

Another argument for personal writing in graduate studies is that it can facilitate learning and understanding. From the interpretive perspective, the most significant finding of Berkenkotter et al. is that, during the course of his graduate studies, Nate continued to write expressively, despite strong programmatic influences to the contrary. In doing so, he created an environment more conducive to his own learning. Berkenkotter et al. acknowledge that

> the informal, expressive pieces Nate wrote provided him the opportunity to give free rein to his intellect. It appears that by ignoring many of the constraints imposed by the genre and register of academic writing expected of him, he could more easily explore new ideas. In his first semester, as exemplified in the two Mishler pieces, he would do this by writing a "companion document" that embodied a complete switching of modes, e.g. the informal epistolary genre instead of the formal academic one. In the second semester, however, he performed the same kind of switch within the same document, relaxing some constraints and adhering to others. (1988, 27)

What Nate was writing is what our English 702 class, following John Van Maanen, called "confessionals"—reflective pieces that reveal one's hopes and doubts about the thinking and research one is engaged in. The scholar who writes confessionals sees research as an art more than a science, and "the reader who wonders why the confessional writers don't do their perverse, self-centered, anxiety work in private and simply come forward with [a] . . . fact or two are, quite frankly, missing the point" (Van Maanen 1988, 93). The point is that research is a hermeneutic process, an act which "begins with the explicit examination of one's own preconceptions, biases, and motives, moving forward in a dialectic fashion toward understanding by way of a continuous dialogue between interpreter and interpreted" (93). In such research, when done well, "the personal voice can be a gift to readers and the confessional becomes a self-reflective meditation on the nature of . . . understanding; the reader comes away with a deeper sense of the problems posed and the enterprise itself" (92).

An interpretive approach to graduate studies would allow, even encourage, students to write expressively throughout their course work. Students would work on integrating personal, local, and global knowledge and gradually develop the ability and confidence to adopt the researcher's rhetorical stance. As Jill, another English 702 student, noted in her written comments on the case study, Berkenkotter et al. prematurely compare Nate's writing to that of established researchers in composition:

> In spite of [Nate's] obvious comprehension difficulties, the authors (and, again, by extension the program) continue their close analysis of [his] writing style, citing lack of continuity and lack of clear rhetorical pattern. . . . Doesn't the wisdom and even common

> sense of taking such a course of action come into question? Has not
> a very important factor been overlooked? How would you or I, or
> the authors of this study, do when asked to comprehend the
> concepts, theories, ideas, and practices in, for instance, computer
> science texts when we had very little previous knowledge?
> Compound that with the requirement that we must write much the
> way that experts in the field do. Then evaluate us immediately and
> throughout our struggle and rate our growth and worth in relation
> to samples from our work. . . . Wouldn't most of us be like Nate?

Jill is describing what Clifford Geertz (1973) calls the tension between
a need to grasp and a need to analyze. When entering into a field,
graduate students need time to grasp information as students before
being asked to analyze and critique it as researchers.

The "grasping" period for graduate students in composition could
include writing of many kinds—personal essays, reflective pieces,
descriptions of teaching and learning experiences past and present,
summaries of and responses to readings, and evaluations of their own
and others' pedagogy. Such variety would allow students the kind of
learning experience that Nate had to generate for himself, one which
validates the relevance of personal and practical knowledge to the
construction of theoretical knowledge.

As already noted, faculty typically reject these forms of writing in
graduate school, considering them "nonacademic" and therefore
inappropriate. I myself struggled with this assumption when teaching
the English 702 seminar. As a faculty member in a graduate program
which privileges analytic writing, I found myself conflicted in that
class between my own desire to teach an interpretive inquiry which
mediates inner and outer worlds and my responsibility to teach
students how to write in ways that my colleagues would value. This
conflict is apparent in the issues I raised in my notebook after our
midterm discussion on audience for the final paper:

> Is it OK to encourage students to write for an audience of teachers?
> Is it OK to emphasize pedagogical findings over theoretical ones?
> If I'm not training traditional research scholars, does that mean
> I'm not doing my job, that I'm guilty of some kind of educational
> malpractice? At what point in a graduate program do we encour-
> age students to be *nontraditional* scholars who *challenge* prevail-
> ing views and behaviors? Am I most responsible for expanding the
> experience and perspective of my students or for perpetuating the
> field as we know it? (And must there always be conflict between
> these two responsibilities?)

As I saw it then, if my responsibilities lay with the field of composition as currently constituted, rather than with the development of
individual thinkers and writers, that meant I had to teach and

evaluate students' writing analytically. But did I really want to teach that way? Wouldn't I be discouraging students from exploring alternatives, from challenging and resisting the very assumptions that keep the field from moving forward?

What Is Our Response to Resistance in Graduate Student Writing?

That Berkenkotter et al. see Nate's "political and practical preferences" as an impediment, rather than an asset, to his development as a scholar suggests that we as a field have not yet considered either the purpose or potential of resistance in graduate students' learning. Indeed, Berkenkotter et al. gloss over both the evidence of resistance in Nate's writing and its possible significance. Consider, for example, Nate's statement in a self-report that "I feel like I'm butting heads finally with ACADEMIC WRITING—and it is monstrous and unfathomable. Young, Waller, and Flower write differently from me. . . . I feel that they have access to the code and I do not" (1988, 21). For Berkenkotter et al., this is an example of Nate's growing awareness of his "stylistic short-comings." From an interpretive perspective, however, this statement shows Nate confronting the expectations of a discourse community he is not entirely sure he wants to join. Andrea, for example, sees it as the only instance in the article in which Nate's "obvious resistance to academic writing [is] even acknowledged." For her, in not investigating the effect of Nate's self-reflection on his learning, Berkenkotter et al. have illustrated that "personal insight is, unfortunately, frowned upon by social-science model researchers, yet it highlights the important issue of how resistace influences a so-called 'novice' writer's appropriation of a new discourse. . . . In a sense, the study has left out a crucial ingredient: the subject."

Other students in the English 702 seminar suggested reasons why Nate might resist joining the CMU discourse community. Mary, for example, considers the "standard social science terminology" that Berkenkotter et al. look for in Nate's writing to be "imprecise jargon" and believes that "when Nate learned the academic language required of him, he appears to have lost some of the poetry of his earlier more informal writing, such as the excerpt on inner voice." Bill writes that the Berkenkotter et al. study creates for him "some questions as to the underlying assumptions concerning linguistic competence and some uneasiness about the egocentrism and club-like nature of various academic communities." These graduate students see evidence that, although Nate felt strong pressure to "join the club" at CMU, his initial reponse was to resist. Nate himself admits in a self-report that, during his first months in the program, he listened more "to the words in my head than studying the words on the page I was expected to emulate" (1988, 19).

Probable sources for the words in his head are Nate's previous teaching and learning experiences. Nate came to the CMU program after having taught composition at an open-admissions university in Missouri. He also had delivered several conference papers. His formal education included a bachelor's degree in English and an M.Ed. in curriculum and instruction, as well as participation in a National Endowment for the Humanities summer seminar on the writing process with John Warnock at the University of Wyoming. Yet Berkenkotter et al. consider Nate essentially untutored in the field of composition studies, referring to his "relative ignorance of a complex and far-reaching corpus of scholarship and research that defines the interdisciplinary Rhetoric program at Carnegie Mellon" (1988, 38). One wonders how Nate was accepted into the prestigious CMU program, given this "ignorance." It is more likely that Nate was not ignorant, but resistant. He may have known about the "corpus of scholarship and research" and, rather than modeling his own writing after it, may have chosen instead to follow the words in his head. There is some evidence, too, that these words were in conflict with those he was reading at CMU. Berkenkotter et al., for example, note that the "experience of writing in the Laramie community affected Nate deeply and gave him a firmly ingrained sense of himself as a writer" (17). They also note that he received considerable support for his writing from fellow seminar participants, as well as colleagues in Missouri (21). Nate may have felt pulled between the Wyoming and the CMU communities and perhaps worked these frustrations out in his academic writing. Thus his "political and practical preferences" could be seen as a source of conflict which *initiated* intellectual growth, rather than limited it.

An interpretive approach to graduate studies in composition, then, would openly address student resistance and make it an object of study. Nate's case suggests many forms of resistance—epistemological, political, rhetorical, and pedagogical—which could be explored in light of other graduate students' experiences in constructing a place for themselves in the field.

Conclusions: Interpretive Pedagogy, Feminist Pedagogy, and Teacher Research

Graduate programs in composition need to envision a field that overcomes limiting dichotomies and damaging hierarchies which privilege theory over practice, research over teaching, and public over personal knowledge. They need to develop an interpretive perspective which not only allows for but encourages diversity in knowledge making. Both teacher research and feminist pedagogy provide models for this kind of inquiry.

In answer to the question, "Why write?" the teacher-research response is, "To come to a personal understanding of the field through reflection on and analysis of one's own experiences as a teacher and researcher." To the question, "How does writing reflect epistemology?" teacher-researchers respond that writing reflects one's willingness to question and challenge the status quo and to act on the new knowledge created in this process; teacher-researchers write in order to articulate for themselves and others what changes need to be made to improve teaching and learning. Finally, to the question, "How do we respond to resistance in students' writing?" teacher-researchers would openly acknowledge it, study it, and reflect on it collaboratively with other teachers and students, trying to understand more fully the role it might play in both learning and teaching. Teacher-researchers would want to determine what classroom conditions seem to encourage students to problematize their knowledge and what conditions limit or mitigate against this process.

Both teacher research and feminist pedagogy are, in the main, emancipatory and change oriented. They seek to empower through reflective practice by encouraging teachers and learners to "analy[ze] ideas about the causes of powerlessness, recognizing systematic oppressive forces, and acting both individually and collectively to change the conditions of [their] lives" (Lather 1991, 4). Both, too, acknowledge the methodological implications of such research: the need to focus on difference and diversity in knowledge making, eschewing totalizing tendencies; the importance of establishing reciprocity between researcher and researched, constructing rather than imposing meaning through negotiation with others; the importance of dialectical theory building, where theory both informs and grows out of context-embedded data and personal experience; and the importance of addressing issues of validity (what constitutes good research and practice) through a vigorous self-reflexivity and critique of the beliefs that inform our work. In *Getting Smart: Feminist Research and Pedagogy with/in the Postmodern,* Patti Lather provides a working list of questions for the self-reflexive researcher who is influenced by feminist-emancipatory ideology. Such a researcher is willing to observe herself observing and to acknowledge the political nature of those observations, realizing that no inquiry is ever value-free and that every perspective is necessarily limited and limiting.

The following questions are the kind we need to inform an interpretive pedagogy in graduate composition programs: What have we investigated? What have we repressed and denied? In our research, did we consider the limits of our observations and conceptualizations? What binaries and hierarchies structure our arguments? Did we acknowledge and encourage ambivalence, ambiguity, and multiplicity, or did we prematurely impose order and structure on our thinking? How, in short, have we "policed the boundaries of what can be imagined" (Lather 1991, 84) in our own intellectual lives and in the life of the field?

I hope that such honest questions will underlie the next great paradigm shift in composition toward an emancipatory pedagogy in graduate studies—one which trains students, in Lawrence Stenhouse's words, "in a mastery of seeking rather than knowing."

Epilogue

In this book I have used teacher research to address the theory-practice dilemma in composition studies. My intent was to extend existing arguments in the field, engaging and provoking others to pursue them. As I see it, the book is an initial effort to open up the conversation about what constitutes knowledge in composition to more participants, including K–12 teachers and graduate students.

There are many directions I could have taken in arguing for the importance of teacher research. I could have talked about students' role in the making of classroom-based knowledge, but this has been addressed in others' research, most notably Marian Mohr and Marion Maclean's *Working Together* (1987) and selections in Jay Robinson's *Conversations on the Written Word* (1990), Don Daiker and Max Morenberg's *The Writing Teacher as Researcher* (1990), and Dixie Goswami and Peter Stillman's *Reclaiming the Classroom* (1987). I also could have examined the role of the institution, be it school, district, college, or university, in facilitating and limiting teacher research. Although this is a much-needed area of inquiry, it was beyond the scope of this study and my current interests. Teachers and researchers wishing to pursue it, however, will find relevant the political-historical insights of James Berlin and Gerald Graff, the neo-Marxist perspectives of Henry Giroux and Antonio Gramsci, and the poststructuralist views of Susan Miller. Meriting further study is James Berlin's astute observation that his "real fear about the attenuated politics of the U.S. version of 'action research' is finally that its democratic, egalitarian, and contestatory qualities will be lost through appropriation by the very forces it opposes" (1990, 14). One approach to such inquiry would be a long-term study of National Writing Project participants, because the primary purpose of the project is to create teacher-consultants who will *change schools from within.* As yet, there has been no critical research to determine whether and to what extent this grass-roots approach really works in transforming pedagogy.

I could also have described the step-by-step process of creating, conducting, interpreting, and writing about classroom inquiry, but that, too, has already been done, at least from the perspective of analytical inquiry. I invite the interested reader to examine the work of Lee Odell and Miles Myers for this information. Composition studies still needs a good description of the teacher-research process from an interpretive perspective, but the work-in-progress of Susan Lytle and Marilyn Cochran-Smith promises to address this need, at least in part.

Finally, I could have produced a more collaborative work in which teachers and graduate students contributed chapters, thus better reflecting the dialectic nature of the teacher-research enterprise. This is the approach taken by Sondra Perl and Nancy Wilson in *Through Teachers' Eyes* (1986) and Glenda Bissex and Richard Bullock in *Seeing for Ourselves* (1987). I chose another direction, however, given the motivations for this book: my own need to come to terms—personally, intellectually, politically—with composition as a field and my particular place in it. In writing about K–12 teachers and graduate students, I do not mean to leave the impression that they need a scholar-theorist-university researcher to speak for them. This has never been my belief or my intention. Rather, in writing the book from my perspective alone, I am attempting to work out my own thinking on a few key issues in composition studies. In other words, this book is as much for me as it is for my readers. As Gloria Steinem notes in her autobiographical book, *Revolution from Within* (1992), people teach what they need to learn and write what they need to know.

The field of composition needs guidance in developing graduate curricula around teacher research, as well as long-term case studies and ethnographies which chronicle students' personal, theoretical, and pedagogical development within these programs. We need more research in other contexts, too, such as elementary and secondary schools, community colleges, adult education programs, and community literacy projects to find out how classroom-based research affects teaching and learning.

It is my hope that this book will encourage others to pursue these various lines of inquiry and, in so doing, contribute to the classroom-based knowledge that the field so desperately needs in order to bridge the widening gap between theory and practice.

Appendix A
Interview of National Writing Project Teacher-Researchers

1. What did you know about teacher research before you became part of the National Writing Project seminar?
2. When you were first introduced to the concept of teacher research, what were your impressions?
3. Tell me a little about what you learned as a result of conducting your own teacher research during the past year.
4. Tell me a little about some of the problems you experienced as a teacher-researcher, if any.
5. Who do you think benefits from teacher research, if anyone?
6. When I say the word "theory," what do you think of? Do you see any relationship between theory and teacher research?
7. Teacher research has been called a "movement" and a "quiet revolution" (Bullock, Britton) in education. Do you agree with these characterizations?
8. Do you intend to pursue teacher research further? Why or why not?
9. If you were involved in training other teachers to become researchers, what would you do? Do you see any place for this type of training in colleges of education?
10. Before we conclude the interview, do you have any further comments or questions for me?

Consent to Participate in Study of Teacher-Researchers

I am writing a book on teacher research and am interested in documenting the experiences of practicing teacher-researchers. If you consent to participate in an interview and allow me to quote from you and your work in my study, please sign below.

Do you prefer that I use a pseudonym when reporting your interview responses?

Yes_____   No_____   No preference_____

Signature_____

Date_____

Appendix B
English 702—Studies
in Composition Theory:
Researching Teaching, Winter 1991

Ruth Ray

Class meets: 5:30-8:15 Wednesdays

Office hours: M, W, F 11-12:00 and by appt. , 577-7696 (Room 103 at 51 W. Warren)

Required Texts:
> John Van Maanen, *Tales of the Field*
> Shirley Brice Heath, *Ways with Words*
> Donald Daiker and Max Morenberg, *The Writing Teacher as Researcher*
> Glenda Bissex, *GNYS AT WRK*
> Coursepack at Kinko's

Overview:
> This is a course in research methodology. We will focus exclusively on inquiry conducted by teachers in their own composition classrooms. You will first gain a broad overview of the theoretical, epistemological, and political premises of this form of inquiry by reading about the teacher-research movement in education. We will then study in depth the two primary methodologies used by classroom researchers: ethnography and case study. You will experience firsthand the strengths and the limitations of these methodologies in the process of conducting your own research projects for the course.

The goals of the course are for you to
> 1. Learn about the research other teachers have conducted, the methodologies relied on in this body of research, and how to determine its value and relevance;
> 2. Become a reflective, analytical teacher who sees the composition classroom as a place of inquiry and change—for yourself as well as your students;
> 3. Challenge, through research, your own and others' beliefs and assumptions about some aspect of writing or the teaching of writing that arises in your own interactions with students;
> 4. Conduct an original study which allows you to test the methodological issues raised in class against your own research experiences.

The course will progress along these lines:
> - We will read all assigned texts and discuss our reactions in class.
> - Each student will conduct an extended research project over the semester and will present drafts of this work in progress for class critique (Weeks 13–15).

- Each student will keep a log in which he/she collects data for the research project and *draws connections between the issues raised in the readings and the issues raised in the ongoing research.*
- Each student will meet in conference with me at least once during the semester (Week 11).

Final grades will be based on the following criteria:*

    Class participation—10%
    Research log—25%
    In-class reports from research log—15%
    Final draft of research project—50%

* The grades given in a graduate class are A, B, and C. An "A" represents outstanding work and marked improvement over the semester in a student's thinking and writing; a "B" represents good work and adequate effort over the semester; and a "C" represents poor work and an overall inability to meet the expectations of the instructor. Please understand that I make full use of this grading scale. The course is structured so that you receive considerable feedback on your reading and writing (from me *and* your classmates) through-out the semester. I expect you to be prepared for every class and to meet the deadlines. During our class meetings, I will act as facilitator and coach, rather than authority and critic. Since I am not lecturing or presenting a body of material for you to "master," what you learn will be directly related to the effort you put into it—the seriousness with which you attend to the readings, the questions you raise in class discussions, the connections you draw between the readings and your own research project, and the time and attention you devote to conducting and reporting your research.

Research Log

You will need to purchase an 8 1/2 x 11-inch 3-ring binder for the research log—something with which you can insert and remove pages. You wil use the log to record all thoughts, questions, data, hypotheses, and conclusions related to your research project. (Please do not keep class notes in the log.) Log entries are the first pieces of writing you will bring to class for commentary and discussion, so be prepared to duplicate pages for distribution, to read aloud from your log, or to summarize your entries for the rest of us. You should be writing 1–2 pages per week in your log at the beginning of the semester and many more as your research progresses. We will do the initial entry in class together on the first night.

Logs should contain some or all of the following:*

1. Descriptions of events and interactions that occur in or around the class-room or tutoring lab
2. Miscellaneous interruptions, behavior and management problems, teaching plans, fleeting thoughts, and stray details that contribute to an understanding of the learning environment
3. Bits of conversation, phrases overheard from students or other teachers and jotted down quickly at the time or immediately afterwards
4. Surprise findings or happenings, puzzling things that seem unexplainable or unexpected

5. Character sketches of students or other teachers

6. "Thick descriptions" of the learning environment

7. Notes and transcriptions of interviews and conferences with students, parents, other teachers, administrators, etc.

8. Full texts or excerpts from students' writing

9. Sample survey questions and survey results

10. Reflections on what is happening in the study—speculative writings full of questions and tentative hypotheses about certain findings

11. Reflections after rereading log entries—attempts to see connections and patterns in the research, attempts at shaping the focus of the research question, and attempts at analyzing findings in terms of theories and readings discussed in class

12. Responses to the class readings

13. Thoughts on and reactions to the research process itself—to what you are noticing in yourself, your thinking, your own and your classmates' reactions to your findings

* Adapted from Marian M. Mohr and Marion S. Maclean, *Working Together: A Guide for Teacher-Researchers,* Urbana, Ill. : National Council of Teachers of English, 1987.

Each log entry should be dated and titled.

Logs will be given an overall grade at the end of the semester on the basis of the number, focus, content, extensiveness, and thought-provoking quality of the entries.

Class Schedule

Week 1—January 9

Introduction to Classroom-Based Inquiry:
Begin research logs (handout)
Research questions

Week 2—January 16

The Teacher-Research Movement:
R. Ray, Introduction and Chapter 3, "The Argument for Teacher Research," coursepack
Berlin, "The Teacher as Researcher," 3–14 (Daiker and Morenberg)
Hollingsworth, "Teachers as Researchers," coursepack
Lunsford, "The Case for Collaboration," 52–60 (Daiker and Morenberg)
Kantor, "Learning from Teachers," 61–69 (Daiker and Morenberg)

Week 3—January 23

Doing Teacher Research:
Jackson, "The Mimetic and the Transformative," coursepack
Preface to *Reclaiming the Classroom,* coursepack
Berthoff, "The Teacher as REsearcher," coursepack
Heath, "A Lot of Talk," coursepack

Macrorie, "Research as Odyssey," coursepack
Odell, "Planning Classroom Research," coursepack

Week 4—January 30

Introduction to Ethnography:
Van Maanen, Tales of the Field, including preface
*Research logs: commentary on a reading

Week 5—February 6

Issues in Ethnography:
Geertz, "Thick Description," coursepack
Clifford, "Partial Truths," coursepack
North, "The Ethnographers," coursepack

Week 6—February 13

Ethnography in Education:
Heath, *Ways with Words:* Prologue (1–14), Chapter 2 (30–72), Chapter
5 (149–189), and Chapter 6 (190–235)

Week 7—February 20

Doing Ethnography in Schools:
Heath, *Ways with Words:* Chapter 8 (265–314), Chapter 9
(315–342), and Epilogue (343–369)
*Research logs: some thick description from your study

Week 8—February 27

Case-Study Research:
Newkirk, "Narrative Roots" handout
Bissex, "Small Is Beautiful," 70–75 (Daiker and Morenberg)
Bissex, "Why Case Studies?" coursepack
Merriam, "The Case Study Approach to Research Problems,"
coursepack

Week 9—March 6

Case Studies in Education:
Bissex, *GNYS AT WRK*

Week 10—March 13

Spring break

Week 11—March 18 and 19

Individual conferences as scheduled (No class on March 20)

Week 12—March 27

Case Studies in Education:
R. Ray, "Language and Literacy from the Student Perspective," 321–335
(Daiker and Morenberg)
Grimm, "Tutoring Dyslexic College Students," 336–342 (Daiker and
Morenberg)
Emig, "Lynn: Profile of a Twelfth-Grade Writer," coursepack
*Research logs: a problem with case-study research

Week 13—April 3

How Research Changes Teachers and Teaching:
L. Ray, "Reflections on Classroom Research," coursepack
Kroll, "Observing Students' Reflective Thinking," 237–246 (Daiker and Morenberg)
Reither, "Writing Student as Researcher," 247–255 (Daiker and Morenberg)
Writing workshop: review drafts of final papers

Week 14—April 10

Writing Workshop:
Review drafts of final papers

Week 15—April 17

Writing Workshop:
Review drafts of final papers

Week 16—April 24

Final Exam Week:
Final papers and research logs due

Course Bibliography

Berlin, James. 1990. "The Teacher as Researcher." In Daiker and Morenberg, 3–14.

Berthoff, Ann E. 1987. "The Teacher as REsearcher." Goswami and Stillman, 28–39.

Bissex, Glenda L. 1980. *GNYS AT WRK: A Child Learns to Write and Read.* Cambridge: Harvard University Press.

———. 1987. "Why Case Studies?" *Seeing for Ourselves: Case-Study Research by Teachers of Writing.* Eds. Glenda L. Bissex and Richard H. Bullock, 7–19. Portsmouth, N.H. : Heinemann.

———. 1990. "Small Is Beautiful." In Daiker and Morenberg, 70–75.

Britton, James. 1987. "A Quiet Form of Research." In Goswami and Stillman, 13–19.

Clifford, James. 1986. "Introduction: Partial Truths." *Writing Culture: The Poetics and Politics of Ethnography.* Eds. James Clifford and George E. Marcus, 1–26. Berkeley: University of California Press.

Daiker, Donald, and Max Morenberg, eds. 1990. *The Writing Teacher as Researcher: Essays in the Theory and Practice of Class-Based Research.* Portsmouth, N.H. : Boynton/Cook Heinemann.

Emig, Janet. 1971. *The Composing Processes of Twelfth Graders.* Urbana, Ill.: National Council of Teachers of English.

Geertz, Clifford. 1973. "Thick Description: Toward an Interpretive Theory of Culture." *The Interpretation of Cultures,* 3–30. New York: Basic.

Goswami, Dixie and Peter R. Stillman, eds. 1987. *Reclaiming the Classroom: Teacher Research as an Agency for Change.* Upper Montclair, N.J. : Boynton/Cook.

Grimm, Nancy. 1990. "Tutoring Dyslexic College Students: What These Students Teach Us about Literacy Development." In Daiker and Morenberg, 336–342.

Heath, Shirley Brice. 1987. "A Lot of Talk about Nothing." Goswami and Stillman, 39–48.

———. 1983. *Ways with Words: Language, Life and Work in Communities and Classrooms.* Cambridge: Cambridge University Press.

Hollingsworth, Sandra. 1990. "Teachers as Researchers: Writing to Learn about Ourselves—and Others." *The Quarterly of the National Writing Project and the Center for the Study of Writing,* Fall: 10–18.

Jackson, Philip W. 1986. "The Mimetic and the Transformative: Alternative Outlooks on Teaching," *The Practice of Teaching.* 115–145. New York: Teachers College Press.

Kroll, Barry M. 1990. "Observing Student's Reflective Thinking: A Teacher Research Project." In Daiker and Morenberg, 23–246.

Lunsford, Andrea. 1990. "The Case for Collaboration." In Daiker and Morenberg, 52–60.

Macrorie, Ken. 1987. "Research as Odyssey." Goswami and Stillman, 49–58.

Merriam, Sharan B. 1988. *Case Study Research in Education: A Qualitative Approach.* San Francisco: Jossey-Bass.

Newkirk, Thomas. 1992. "Narrative Roots of Case Study." *Methods and Methodology: Issues in Composition Research.* Eds. Gesa Kirsch and Patricia Sullivan, 139–152. Carbondale: Southern Illinois University Press.

North, Stephen M. 1987. "The Ethnographers." *The Making of Knowledge in Composition: Portrait of an Emerging Field,* 272–313. Upper Montclair, N.J. : Boynton/Cook.

Odell, Lee. 1987. "Planning Classroom Research." Goswami and Stillman, 128–16.

Pratt, Mary Louise. 1986. "Fieldwork in Common Places." *Writing Culture: The Poetics and Politics of Ethnography.* Eds. James Clifford and George E. Marcus, 27–50. Berkeley: University of California Press.

Ray, Lucinda. 1987. "Reflections on Classroom Research." Goswami and Stillman, 219–242.

Ray, Ruth. 1990. "Language and Literacy from the Student Perspective: What Can We Learn from the Long-Term Case Study?" In Daiker and Morenberg, 321–335.

———. 1993. *The Practice of Theory: Teacher Research in Composition.* Urbana, Ill. : National Council of Teachers of English.

Reither, James A. 1990. "Writing Student as Researcher: Learning from Our Students." In Daiker and Morenberg, 247–255.

Van Maanen, John. 1988. *Tales of the Field: On Writing Ethnography.* Chicago: University of Chicago Press.

English 702: End-of-Term Review Questions

Research Issues

1. What is teacher research and how does it differ from other forms of inquiry in education and composition studies? Would you say that it is a new form of inquiry?

2. What are the epistemological, methodological, and political assumptions underlying the teacher research movement?

3. What research questions can and cannot be appropriately addressed through teacher research?

4. What does it mean to "politicize" one's research and teaching? Or would you say that research and teaching are always already "politicized"?

5. What "counts" as new research knowledge in a field and why? On the basis of your observations and reading experience in the field of composition studies, who would you say gets to make knowledge and for whom is it made?

6. Do the findings of teacher-researchers constitute new knowledge in composition studies? If so, how does the knowledge created by teachers differ from the knowledge created by traditional university researchers?

Teaching/Research Connections

1. How, according to teacher-researchers, do theory, practice, and research inform one another? How does classroom-based research change teaching, for example? (Or doesn't it?)

2. Why do traditional researchers typically privilege theory over practice?

3. Why do most teachers typically privilege practice over theory?

4. How likely is it that theory and practice will be equally valued within the American research university? Within the public school system?

5. How does one's philosophy of learning and teaching affect the kind of classroom inquiry one conducts? (Think, for example, of Philip Jackson's two intellectual traditions and what they suggest about differing approaches to seeing, knowing, learning, and teaching.)

Methodological Issues: Ethnography and Case Studies

1. What are the various forms of ethnography, according to Van Maanen, and how do they differ in terms of assumptions about the observer and the phenomena being observed?

2. What are some of the different issues that arise in writing ethnographies and case studies? (Consider: locus of authority, presence of the ethnographer in the account, how and whether generalizations are made and justified, the social science perspective vs. the literary/interpretive perspective on reporting data, audience, and purpose of the study.)

3. How might the presence of the teacher-researcher affect an ethnographic study in terms of design and interpretation of findings? (Consider Newkirk's claim that, in accounting for "context," the researcher must also reflexively look at the discourse community s/he is a member of and explore the ways its beliefs, expectations and conventions predispose him/her to collect and account for data in certain ways.)

4. How might a classroom ethnography differ from the kinds of ethnographies that anthropologists write?

5. What is the place of personal narrative, if any, in the construction of knowledge in the field of composition?

6. How are ethnographies and case studies verified? How can you tell a good account from a poor one?

7. What is the place of theory, if any, in constructing and interpreting ethnography and case study?

Appendix C
Permission to Participate in a
Study of Teacher-Researchers

As part of my book on teacher research in composition, I am writing a chapter on training graduate students to conduct classroom-based research. In this chapter, I want to illustrate what teachers come to know about theory and practice through analysis of their own classrooms.

I would like your permission to quote from you and your work from English 702, Researching Teaching, Winter 1991. Specifically, I would like to tape the final three class sessions and, if appropriate, quote, summarize, or paraphrase from selected parts of your research log and/or final paper.

I will not use your real name in my writing; a pseudonym will be used to identify you and your work. My analysis of your talk and writing for the book will take place well after English 702 is over and will have no effect on my assessment of your abilities as a graduate student or your grade for the course. Further, please feel free to decline to participate in the study if you do not feel comfortable doing so; your abstention will in no way affect my opinion of you or my assessment of your work in this class.

If you assent to participating in this study, please sign below.

_____ (signature)

_____ (date)

As researcher, I acknowledge your permission to use the material identified above in my work and agree to present it accurately in publication. I further agree not to identify you by name unless you specifically authorize me to do so. I will provide you a copy of this agreement for your personal records.

_____ (signature)

_____ (date)

Works Cited

Aisenberg, Nadya, and Mona Harrington. 1988. *Women of Academe: Outsiders in the Sacred Grove.* Amherst: University of Massachusetts Press.

Atwell, Nancie. 1987a. "Class-Based Writing Research: Teachers Learning from Students." In *Reclaiming the Classroom,* edited by Dixie Goswami and Peter Stillman, 87–94. Upper Montclair, N.J.: Boynton/Cook.

———. 1987b. *In the Middle: Writing, Reading, and Learning with Adolescents.* Portsmouth, N.H.: Boynton/Cook.

Bartholomae, David. 1985. "Inventing the University." In *When a Writer Can't Write: Studies in Writer's Block and Other Composing-Process Problems,* edited by Mike Rose. New York: Guilford.

Bateson, Mary Catherine. 1989. *Composing a Life.* New York: Penguin.

Baym, Nina. 1987. "The Madwoman and Her Languages: Why I Don't Do Feminist Literary Theory." In *Feminist Issues in Literary Scholarship,* edited by Shari Benstock, 45–61. Bloomington: Indiana University Press.

Belenky, Mary Field, Blythe McVicker Clinchy, Nancy Rule Goldberger, and Jill Mattuck Tarule. 1986. *Women's Ways of Knowing: The Development of Self, Voice, and Mind.* New York: Basic Books.

Berkenkotter, Carol. 1991a. "Paradigm Debates, Turf Wars, and the Conduct of Sociocognitive Inquiry in Composition." *College Composition and Communication* 42 (May): 151–69.

———. 1991b. "Representing Knowledgeable Subjects' Perspectives in 'Polyphonic Texts'." Conference on College Composition and Communication, Boston, March 22.

Berkenkotter, Carol, Thomas Huckin, and John Ackerman. 1988. "Conventions, Conversations, and the Writer: Case Study of a Student in a Rhetoric Ph.D. Program." *Research in the Teaching of English* 22: 9–41.

Berlin, James. 1987. *Rhetoric and Reality: Writing Instruction in American Colleges, 1900-1985.* Carbondale: Southern Illinois University Press.

———. 1988. "Rhetoric and Ideology in the Writing Class." *College English* 5: 477–94.

———. 1990. "The Teacher as Researcher: Democracy, Dialogue, and Power." In *The Writing Teacher as Researcher,* edited by Donald Daiker and Max Morenberg, 3–14. Portsmouth, N.H.: Boynton/Cook Heinemann.

Berthoff, Ann E. 1987a. "From Dialogue to Dialectic to Dialogue." In *Reclaiming the Classroom,* edited by Dixie Goswami and Peter Stillman, 75–86. Upper Montclair, N.J.: Boynton/Cook.

————. 1987b. "The Teacher as REsearcher." In *Reclaiming the Classroom,* edited by Dixie Goswami and Peter Stillman, 28–39. Upper Montclair, N.J.: Boynton/Cook.

————. 1990. "Killer Dichotomies: Reading In/Reading Out." In *Farther Along: Transforming Dichotomies in Rhetoric and Composition,* edited by Kate Ronald and Hephzibah Roskelly, 12–24. Portsmouth, N.H. Boynton/Cook Heinemann.

Bissex, Glenda L. 1980. *GNYS AT WRK: A Child Learns to Write and Read.* Cambridge, Mass.: Harvard United Press.

————. 1987. "Why Case Studies?" In *Seeing for Ourselves: Case-Study Research by Teachers of Writing,* edited by Glenda L. Bissex and Richard H. Bullock, 7–19. Portsmouth, N.H.: Heinemann.

————. 1990. "Small Is Beautiful: Case Study as Appropriate Methodology for Teacher Research." In *The Writing Teacher as Researcher,* edited by Donald Daiker and Max Morenberg, 70–75. Portsmouth, N.H.: Boynton/Cook Heinemann.

Bissex, Glenda L., and Richard H. Bullock. 1987. *Seeing for Ourselves: Case-Study Research by Teachers of Writing.* Portsmouth, N.H.: Heinemann.

Bizzell, Patricia. 1982. "Cognition, Convention, and Certainty: What We Need to Know about Writing." *PRE/TEXT* 3: 213–43.

Braddock, Richard, Richard Lloyd-Jones, and Lowell Schoer. 1963. *Research in Written Composition.* Urbana, Ill.: National Council of Teachers of English.

Brandt, Deborah. 1988. "Toward an Understanding of Context in Composition." *Written Communication* 3: 139–57.

Brannon, Lil. 1985. "Toward a Theory of Composition." *Perspectives on Research and Scholarship in Composition,* edited by Ben W. McClelland and Timothy R. Donovan. New York: Modern Language Association.

Britton, James, Tony Burgess, Nancy Martin, Alex McLeod, and Harold Rosen. 1975. *The Development of Writing Abilities,* 11–18. School Council Research Series. London: Macmillan Education.

Brodkey, Linda. 1987. *Academic Writing as Social Practice.* Philadelphia: Temple University Press.

Bruffee, Kenneth A. 1972. "The Way Out." *College English* 33: 457–70.

————. 1984. "Collaborative Learning and the 'Conversation of Mankind'." *College English* 46: 635–52.

Bruner, Jerome. 1986. *Actual Minds, Possible Worlds.* Cambridge, Mass.: Harvard University Press.

Bullock, Richard H. 1987. "A Quiet Revolution: The Power of Teacher Research." In *Seeing for Ourselves,* edited by Glenda L. Bissex and Richard H. Bullock, 21–27. Portsmouth, N.H.: Heinemann.

Bullock, Richard, and John Trimbur, eds. 1991. *The Politics of Writing Instruction: Postsecondary.* Portsmouth, N.H.: Boynton/Cook Heinemann.

Calkins, Lucy McCormick. 1985. "Forming Research Communities among Naturalistic Researchers." *Perspectives on Research and Scholarship in*

Composition, edited by Ben W. McClelland and Timothy R. Donovan, 125–44. New York: Modern Language Association.

Campioni, Mia, and Elizabeth Gross. 1983. "Love's Labours Lost: Marxism and Feminism." In *Beyond Marxism: Interventions after Marx*, edited by S. Allan and P. Patton, 113–41. Leichardt: Intervention Pub.

Carr, Wilfred, and Stephen Kemmis. 1986. *Becoming Critical: Education, Knowledge, and Action Research*. London: Falmer Press.

Caywood, Cynthia L., and Gillian R. Overing. 1987. *Teaching Writing: Pedagogy, Gender, and Equity*. Albany, N.Y.: SUNY Press.

Chodorow, Nancy. 1978. *The Reproduction of Mothering*. Berkeley: University of California Press.

Christian, Barbara. 1989. "The Race for Theory." In *Gender & Theory: Dialogues on Feminist Criticism*, edited by Linda Kauffman, 225–37. Oxford: Basil Blackwell.

Clifford, James. 1986. "Introduction: Partial Truths." In *Writing Culture: The Poetics and Politics of Ethnography*, edited by James Clifford and George E. Marcus, 1–26. Berkeley: University of California Press.

Clifford, James, and George E. Marcus, eds. 1988. *Writing Culture: The Poetics and Politics of Ethnography*. Berkeley: University of California Press.

Cochran-Smith, Marilyn, and Susan L. Lytle. 1990. "Research on Teaching and Teacher Research: The Issues That Divide." *Educational Researcher* 19(2): 2–11.

Coles, Robert. 1989. *The Call of Stories: Teaching and the Moral Imagination*. Boston: Houghton.

Connors, Robert J. 1983. "Composition Studies and Science." *College English* 45: 1–20.

Cooper, Charles R., and Lee Odell, eds. 1978. *Research on Composing: Points of Departure*. Urbana, Ill.: National Council of Teachers of English.

Cooper, Marilyn M., and Michael Holzman. 1989. *Writing as Social Action*. Portsmouth, N.H.: Boynton/Cook.

Cross, K. Patricia, and Thomas A. Angelo. 1988. *Classroom Assessment Techniques: A Handbook for Faculty*. Ann Arbor, Mich.: National Center for Research to Improve Postsecondary Teaching and Learning.

Daiker, Donald A., Andrew Kerek, and Max Morenberg. 1978. "Sentence-combining and Syntactic Maturity in Freshman English." *College Composition and Communication* 29: 36–41.

Daiker, Donald A., and Max Morenberg, eds. 1990. *The Writing Teacher as Researcher: Essays in the Theory and Practice of Class-Based Research*. Portsmouth, N.H.: Boynton/Cook Heinemann.

Dewey, John. 1929. *Experience and Nature*, 2nd ed. Reprinted 1971, La Salle, Ill.: Open Court.

Doheny-Farina, Stephen. 1986. "Writing in an Emerging Organization: An Ethnographic Study." *Written Communication* 3: 158–85.

Doheny-Farina, Stephen, and Lee Odell. 1985. "Ethnographic Research on Writing: Assumptions and Methodology." In *Writing in Nonacademic*

Settings, edited by Lee Odell and Dixie Goswami, 503–35. New York: Guilford Press.

Duckworth, Eleanor. 1986. "Teaching as Research." *Harvard Educational Review* 56: 481–95.

Dyson, Anne Haas. 1984. "Learning to Write/Learning to Do School: Emergent Writers' Interpretations of School Literacy Tasks." *Research in the Teaching of English* 18: 233–64.

Eagleton, Terry. 1983. *Literary Theory: An Introduction.* London: Basil Blackwell.

Ebert, Teresa L. 1991. "The 'Difference' of Postmodern Feminism." *College English* 8: 886–904.

Ede, Lisa, and Andrea Lunsford. 1990. *Singular Texts/Plural Authors: Perspectives on Collaborative Writing.* Carbondale, Ill.: Southern Illinois University Press.

Elbow, Peter. 1973a. *Embracing Contraries: Explorations in Learning and Teaching.* New York: Oxford University Press.

———. 1973b. *Writing without Teachers.* New York: Oxford University Press.

———. 1990. *What Is English?* New York: Modern Language Assocation.

Emig, Janet. 1971. *The Composing Processes of Twelfth Graders.* Urbana, Ill.: National Council of Teachers of English.

Felski, Rita. 1989. *Beyond Feminist Aesthetics: Feminist Literature and Social Change.* Cambridge, Mass.: Harvard University Press.

Fetterley, Judith. 1978. *The Resisting Reader: A Feminist Approach to American Fiction.* Bloomington: Indiana University Press.

———. 1986. "Reading about Reading: 'A Jury of Her Peers,' 'The Murders in the Rue Morgue,' and 'The Yellow Wallpaper'." In *Gender and Reading: Essays on Readers, Texts, and Contexts,* edited by Elizabeth A. Flynn and Patrocinio P. Schweickart, 147–64. Baltimore: Johns Hopkins University Press.

Fish, Stanley. 1980. *Is There a Text in This Class? The Authority of Interpretive Communities.* Cambridge, Mass.: Harvard University Press.

———. 1989. *Doing What Comes Naturally: Change, Rhetoric, and the Practice of Theory in Literary and Legal Studies.* Durham, N.C.: Duke University Press.

Flower, Linda S., and John Hayes. 1981. "A Cognitive Process Theory of Writing." *College Composition and Communication* 32: 365–87.

Flynn, Elizabeth A. 1988. "Composing as a Woman." *College Composition and Communication* 39: 423–35.

———. 1991. "Composition Studies from a Feminist Perspective." In *The Politics of Writing Instruction: Postsecondary,* edited by Richard Bullock and John Trimbur, 137–54. Portsmouth, N.H.: Boynton/Cook Heinemann.

Flynn, Elizabeth A., and Patrocinio P. Schweickart, eds. 1986. *Gender and Reading: Essays on Readers, Texts, and Contexts.* Baltimore: Johns Hopkins University Press.

Fox Keller, Evelyn. 1985. *Reflections on Gender and Science.* New Haven, Conn.: Yale University Press.

Freire, Paulo. 1968. *Pedagogy of the Oppressed.* New York: Seabury.

Fulkerson, Richard. 1990. "Composition Theory in the Eighties: Axiological Consensus and Paradigmatic Diversity." *College Composition and Communication* 41: 409–29.

Gabriel, Susan L., and Isaiah Smithson. 1990. *Gender in the Classroom: Power and Pedagogy,* Urbana: University of Illinois Press.

Gadamer, Hans-Georg. 1976. *Philosophical Hermeneutics,* translated by David E. Linge. Los Angeles: University of California Press.

Geertz, Clifford. 1973. *The Interpretation of Cultures.* New York: Basic.

———. 1983. *Local Knowledge: Further Essays in Interpretive Anthropology.* New York: Basic.

Gere, Anne Ruggles. 1985. "Empirical Research in Composition." In *Perspectives on Research and Scholarship in Composition,* edited by Ben W. McClelland and Timothy R. Donovan. New York: Modern Language Association.

Gilbert, Sandra M. 1985. "What Do Feminist Critics Want? A Postcard from the Volcano." In *The New Feminist Criticism: Essays on Women, Literature, and Theory,* edited by Elaine Showalter, 29–45. New York: Pantheon Books.

Gilbert, Sandra M., and Susan Gubar. 1989. "The Mirror and the Vamp: Reflections on Feminist Criticism." In *The Future of Literary Theory,* edited by Ralph Cohen, 144–66. New York: Routledge.

Gilligan, Carol. 1982. *In a Different Voice: Psychological Theory and Women's Development.* Cambridge, Mass.: Harvard University Press.

Giroux, Henry A. 1988. *Teachers as Intellectuals: Toward a Critical Pedagogy of Learning.* Granby, Mass.: Bergin & Garvey.

Goswami, Dixie, and Lee Odell. 1981. *Writing in a Social Service Agency.* Washington, D.C.: Report to the National Institute of Education.

Goswami, Dixie, and Peter R. Stillman, eds. 1987. *Reclaiming the Classroom: Teacher Research as an Agency for Change.* Upper Montclair, N.J.: Boynton/Cook.

Graff, Gerald. 1987. *Professing Literature: An Institutional History.* Chicago: University of Chicago Press.

———. 1989. "The Fture of Theory in the Teaching of Literature." In *The Future of Literary Theory,* edited by Ralph Cohen, 250–67. New York: Routledge.

Gramsci, Antonio. 1971. *Selections from Prison Notebooks,* edited and translated by Quinten Hoare and Geoffrey Smith. New York: International Publishers.

Graves, Donald H. 1975. "An Examination of the Writing Processes of Seven Year Old Children." *Research in the Teaching of English* 9: 227–41.

———. 1983. *Writing: Teachers and Children at Work.* Exeter, N.H.: Heinemann.

Grossman, Pamela L. 1990. *The Making of a Teacher: Teacher Knowledge and Teacher Education.* New York: Teachers College Press.

Hairston, Maxine. 1985. "Breaking Our Bonds and Reaffirming Our Connections." *College Composition and Communication* 36: 272–82.

Harding, Sandra. 1987. "Introduction: Is There a Feminist Method?" In *Feminism and Methodology,* edited by Sandra Harding, 1–14. Bloomington: Indiana University Press.

Harkin, Patricia. 1991. "The Postdisciplinary Politics of Lore." In *Contending with Words: Composition and Rhetoric in a Postmodern Age,* edited by Patricia Harkin and John Schilb, 124–38. New York: Modern Language Association.

Harste, Jerome, Virginia Woodward, and Carolyn Burke. 1984. *Language Stories and Literacy Lessons.* Portsmouth, N.H.: Heinemann.

Heath, Shirley Brice. 1983. *Ways with Words: Language, Life and Work in Communities and Classrooms.* Cambridge: Cambridge University Press.

Heidegger, Martin. 1971. *Poetry, Language, Thought,* translated by Albert Hofstadter. New York: Harper and Row.

Hillocks, George, Jr. 1986. *Research on Written Composition: New Directions for Teaching.* Urbana, Ill.: ERIC/RCS and NCRE.

Hollingsworth, Sandra. 1990a. "Learning to Teach the Culturally-Diverse through Collaborative Conversation: A Feminist Pedagogy." Annual meeting of the American Educational Research Association, Boston, April.

———. 1990b. "Teachers as Researchers: Writing to Learn about Ourselves— and Others." *The Quarterly of the National Writing Project and the Center for the Study of Writing* Fall: 10–18.

Hustler, D., A. Cassidy, and E. C. Cuff. 1986. *Action Research in Classrooms and Schools.* London: Allen & Unwin.

Irmscher, William F. 1987. "Finding a Comfortable Identity." *College Composition and Communication* 38: 81–87.

Jackson, Philip W. 1986. *The Practice of Teaching.* New York: Teachers College Press.

Jardine, Alice. 1985. *Gynesis: Configurations of Woman and Modernity.* Ithaca, N.Y., and London: Cornell University Press.

Jensen, Julie, ed. 1989. *Stories to Grow On: Demonstrations of Language Learning in K8 Classrooms.* Portsmouth, N.H.: Heinemann.

Kantor, Kenneth. 1984. "Classroom Contexts and the Development of Writing Intuitions: An Ethnographic Case Study." In *New Directions in Composition Research,* edited by Richard Beach and Lillian S. Bridwell, 72–94. New York: Guilford Press.

———. 1990. "Learning from Teachers." In *The Writing Teacher as Researcher,* edited by Donald Daiker and Max Morenberg, 61–69. Portsmouth, N.H.: Boynton/Cook Heinemann.

Kantor, Kenneth J., Dan R. Kirby, and Judith P. Goetz. 1981. "Research in Context: Ethnographic Studies in English Education." *Research in the Teaching of English* 15: 293–309.

Kemmis, Stephen. 1982. *The Action Research Reader.* Waurn Ponds, Victoria: Deakin University Press.

Kidder, Tracy. 1989. *Among School Children.* Boston: Houghton Mifflin.

Knoblauch, C. H. 1985. "Modern Rhetorical Theory and Its Future Directions." In *Perspectives on Research and Scholarship in Composition,* edited by Ben W. McClelland and Timothy R. Donovan, 26–44. New York: Modern Language Association.

Knoblauch, C. H., and Lil Brannon. 1988. "Knowing Our Knowledge: A Phenomenological Basis for Teacher Research." In *Audits of Meaning: A Festschrift in Honor of Anne E. Berthoff,* edited by Louise Z. Smith, 17–28. Portsmouth, N.H.: Heinemann.

Komarovsky, Mirra. 1985. *Women in College: Shaping New Feminine Identities.* New York: Basic Books.

Kotlowitz, Alex. 1991. *There Are No Children Here.* New York: Doubleday.

Kuhn, Thomas. 1970. *The Structure of Scientific Revolutions.* 2nd ed. Chicago: University of Chicago Press.

Lacey, Paul A. 1990. "Let's Not Perpetuate Our Mistakes of the Past as We Prepare a New Professorial Generation." *The Chronicle of Higher Education* April 18: B1, B3.

Lamb, Catherine W. 1991. "Beyond Argument in Feminist Composition." *College Composition and Communication* 42: 11–24.

Lather, Patti. 1991. *Getting Smart: Feminist Research and Pedagogy with/in the Postmodern.* New York: Routledge.

LeFevre, Karen Burke. 1987. *Invention as a Social Act.* Carbondale: Southern Illinois University Press.

Lytle, Susan L., and Marilyn Cochran-Smith. 1989. "Teacher Research: Toward Clarifying the Concept." *The Quarterly of the National Writing Project and the Center for the Study of Writing* April: 1–3, 22–26.

Maimon, Elaine P. 1983. "Maps and Genres: Exploring Connections in the Arts and Sciences." In *Composition and Literature: Bridging the Gap,* edited by Winifred Bryan Horner, 110–25. Chicago: University of Chicago Press.

———. 1986. "Knowledge, Acknowledgment, and Writing across the Curriculum: Toward an Educated Community." In *The Territory of Language: Linguistics, Stylistics, and the Teaching of Writing,* edited by Donald McQuade, 89–100. Carbondale: Southern Illinois University Press.

Malson, Micheline R., Jean F. O'Barr, Sarah Westphal-Wihl, and Mary Wyer, eds. 1986. *Feminist Theory in Practice and Process.* Chicago: University of Chicago Press.

Manicas, Peter T., and Paul F. Secord. 1983. "Implications for Psychology of the New Philosophy of Science." *American Psychologist* 38: 399–413.

Marks, Elaine, and Isabelle de Courtivron, eds. 1980. *New French Feminisms.* Brighton, England: Harvester.

McCarthy, Lucille. 1991. "Researcher and Teacher Sharing Authority: Equal Risk, Equal Voice." Conference on College Composition and Communication, Boston, March 22.

McCormick, Kathleen. 1987. "Literary Theory in the Undergraduate Curriculum." Paper presented at the English Coalition Conference, Wye Woods, Maryland.

McKeachie, Wilbert J., and Kenneth E. Eble. 1985. *Improving Undergraduate Education through Faculty Development.* San Francisco: Jossey-Bass.

Miller, Susan. 1991a. "The Feminization of Composition." In *The Politics of Writing Instruction: Postsecondary,* edited by Richard Bullock and John Trimbur, 39–53. Portsmouth, N.H.: Boynton/Cook Heinemann.

———. 1991b. *Textual Carnivals: The Politics of Composition.* Carbondale: Southern Illinois University Press.

Mishler, Eliot G. 1979. "Meaning in Context: Is There Any Other Kind?" *Harvard Educational Review* 39: 1–19.

Moffett, James. 1968. *Teaching the Universe of Discourse.* Boston: Houghton Mifflin.

Mohr, Marian, and Marion S. Maclean. 1987. *Working Together: A Guide for Teacher-Researchers.* Urbana, Ill.: National Council of Teachers of English.

Moi, Toril. 1985. *Sexual/Textual Politics: Feminist Literary Theory.* London: Methuen.

Mooney, Carolyn J. 1990. "Higher-Education Conferees Applaud Carnegie Plan to Broaden the Definition of Faculty Scholarship." *Chronicle of Higher Education* April 11: 1A, 16A.

Murray, Donald M. 1991. "All Writing Is Autobiography." *College Composition and Communication* 42: 66–74.

Myers, Miles. 1985. *The Teacher-Researcher: How to Study Writing in the Classroom.* Urbana, Ill.: National Council of Teachers of English.

Newkirk, Thomas. 1983. "Anatomy of a Breakthrough: A Case Study of a College Freshman Writer." In *New Directions in Composition Research,* edited by Richard Beach and Lillian S. Bridwell, 131–47. New York: Guilford Press.

———. 1991. "The Politics of Composition Research: The Conspiracy against Experience." In *The Politics of Writing Instruction: Postsecondary,* edited by Richard Bullock and John Trimbur, 119–35. Portsmouth, N.H.: Boynton/Cook Heinemann.

———. 1992. "Narrative Roots of Case Study." In *Methods and Methodology: Issues in Composition Research,* edited by Gesa Kirsch and Patricia Sullivan, 130–52. Carbondale: Southern Illinois University Press.

North, Stephen M. 1987. *The Making of Knowledge in Composition: Portrait of an Emerging Field.* Upper Montclair, N.J.: Boynton/Cook.

———. 1991. "Exploring Relationships between Teaching and Research." Conference on College Composition and Communication, Boston, March 20.

Odell, Lee. 1987. "Planning Classroom Research." In *Reclaiming the Classroom,* edited by Dixie Goswami and Peter Stillman, 128–60. Upper Montclair, N.J.: Boynton/Cook.

Works Cited

Olson, Gary A. 1991. "The Politics of Publishing Composition Scholarship." Conference on College Composition and Communication, Boston, March 20.

Paglia, Camille. 1990. *Sexual Personae*. New Haven, Conn.: Yale University Press.

Perl, Sondra, and Nancy Wilson. 1986. *Through Teachers' Eyes: Portraits of Writing Teachers at Work*. Portsmouth, N.H.: Heinemann.

Perry, William. 1970. *Forms of Intellectual and Ethical Development in the College Years: A Scheme*. New York: Holt.

Peterson, Jane E. 1991. "Valuing Teaching: Assumptions, Problems, and Possibilities." *College Composition and Communication* 42: 25–35.

Phelps, Louise Wetherbee. 1988. *Composition as a Human Science: Contributions to the Self-Understanding of a Discipline*. New York: Oxford University Press.

———. 1991. "Practical Wisdom and the Geography of Knowledge in Composition." *College English* 8: 863–85.

Piaget, Jean. 1965. *Language and Thought of a Child*, translated by Marjorie Bagain. New York: Free.

Polanyi, Michael. 1962. *Personal Knowledge: Towards a Post-Critical Philosophy*. Chicago: University of Chicago Press.

Pratt, Mary Louise. 1986. "Fieldwork in Common Places." In *Writing Culture: The Poetics and Politics of Ethnography*, edited by James Clifford and George E. Marcus, 27–50. Berkeley: University of California Press.

Ray, Lucinda C. 1987. "Reflections on Classroom Research." In *Reclaiming the Classroom*, edited by Dixie Goswami and Peter Stillman, 219–42. Upper Montclair, N.J.: Boynton/Cook.

Rich, Adrienne. 1979. *On Lies, Secrets, and Silence: Selected Prose—1966–78*. New York: Norton.

Robinson, Jay. 1990. *Conversations on the Written Word: Essays on Language and Literacy*. Portsmouth, N.H.: Boynton/Cook Heinemann.

Rorty, Richard. 1979. *Philosophy and the Mirror of Nature*. Princeton, N.J.: Princeton University Press.

Ruddick, Sara. 1977. *Working It Out: 23 Women Writers, Artists, Scientists, and Scholars Talk about Their Lives and Work*, edited by Sara Ruddick and Pamela Daniels. New York: Pantheon.

Schaafsma, David W. In press. *Eating on the Street: Teaching Literacy in a Multi-cultural Society*. New York: Teachers College Press.

Scholes, Robert. 1985. *Textual Power: Literary Theory and the Teaching of English*. New Haven, Conn.: Yale University Press.

Schon, Donald. 1983. *The Reflective Practitioner*. San Francisco: Jossey-Bass.

———. 1987. *Educating the Reflective Practitioner*. San Francisco: Jossey-Bass.

Schwartz, Jeffrey. 1990. "On the Move in Pittsburgh: When Students and Teacher Share Research." In *The Writing Teacher as Researcher*, edited by Donald Daiker and Max Morenberg, 153–66. Portsmouth, N.H.: Boynton/Cook Heinemann.

Schweickart, Patrocinio P. 1986. "Reading Ourselves: Toward a Feminist Theory of Reading." In *Gender and Reading: Essays on Readers, Texts, and Contexts,* edited by Elizabeth A. Flynn and Patrocinio P. Schweickart, 31–62. Baltimore: Johns Hopkins University Press.

Shor, Ira. 1987. *Freire for the Classroom: A Sourcebook for Liberatory Teaching.* Portsmouth, N.H.: Heinemann.

Showalter, Elaine. 1985a. "Feminist Criticism in the Wilderness." In *The New Feminist Criticism: Essays on Women, Literature, and Theory,* edited by Elaine Showalter, 243–70. New York: Pantheon Books.

———. 1985b. "Introduction: The Feminist Critical Revolution." In *The New Feminist Criticism: Essays on Women, Literature, and Theory,* edited by Elaine Showalter, 3–17. New York: Pantheon Books.

———. 1987. "Women's Time, Women's Space: Writing the History of Feminist Criticism." In *Feminist Issues in Literary Scholarship,* edited by Shari Benstock, 30–43. Bloomington: Indiana University Press.

Simeone, Angela. 1987. *Academic Women: Working towards Equality.* South Hadley, Mass.: Bergin & Garvey.

Slevin, James F. 1989. "Conceptual Frameworks and Curricular Arrangements: A Response." In *The Future of Doctoral Studies in English,* edited by Andrea Lunsford, Helene Moglen, and James Slevin 30–39. New York: Modern Language Association.

Sommers, Nancy I. 1979. "The Need for Theory in Composition Research." *College Composition and Communication* 30: 46–49.

Steinem, Gloria. 1992. *Revolution from Within: A Book of Self-Esteem.* Boston: Little, Brown.

Stenhouse, Lawrence. 1985. *Research as a Basis for Teaching: Readings from the Work of Lawrence Stenhouse,* edited by Jean Rudduck and David Hopkins. London: Heinemann Educational Books.

Stotsky, Sandra. 1989. "How to Restore the Professional Status of Teachers: Three Useful but Troubling Perspectives." *College English* 51: 750–58.

Threatt, Susan. 1990. "When Teachers Do Research . . . What Do They Do and Where Do They Belong?" Wyoming Conference on English, University of Wyoming, Laramie, June 26.

Tinberg, Howard B. 1991. "'An Enlargement of Observation': More on Theory Building in the Composition Classroom." *College Composition and Communication* 42: 36–44.

Todd, Janet. 1988. *Feminist Literary History.* New York: Routledge.

Tompkins, Jane. 1989. "Me and My Shadow." In *Gender and Theory: Dialogues on Feminist Criticism,* edited by Linda Kauffman, 121–39. Oxford: Basil Blackwell.

Van Maanen, John. 1988. *Tales of the Field: On Writing Ethnography.* Chicago: University of Chicago Press.

Vygotsky, Lev. 1978. *Thought and Language.* Cambridge, Mass.: MIT Press.

Walizer, Marue English. 1986. "The Professor and the Practitioner Think about Teaching." *Harvard Educational Review* 56: 520–26.

Wall, Susan, and Nicholas Cage. 1991. "Reading Basic Writing: Alternatives to a Pedagogy of Accommodation." In *The Politics of Writing Instruction: Postsecondary*, edited by Richard Bullock and John Trimbur, 227–46. Portsmouth, N.H.: Boynton/Cook Heinemann.

Warnock, John. 1976. "Who's Afraid of Theory?" *College Composition and Communication* 27: 16–20.

Wittgenstein, Ludwig. 1953. *Philosophical Investigations*. Oxford: Basil Blackwell.

Young, Art. 1990. "Storytelling in a Technical Writing Class: Classroom-Based Research and Community." In *The Writing Teacher as Researcher*, edited by Donald Daiker and Max Morenberg, 168–87. Portsmouth, N.H.: Boynton/Cook Heinemann.

Young-Bruehl, Elisabeth. 1986. "The Education of Women as Philosophers." In *Feminist Theory in Practice and Process,* edited by Micheline R. Malson, Jean F. O'Barr, Sarah Westphal-Wihl, and Mary Wyer, 35–49. Chicago: University of Chicago Press.

———. 1991. "Pride and Prejudice: Feminist Scholars Reclaim the First Person." *Lingua franca* February: 15–18.

Index

Author

Ruth Ray is assistant professor of English at Wayne State University in Detroit, where she directs the composition program. She has published articles and chapters on case-study research, computers and writing, and cross-cultural rhetoric, as well as teacher research. As an administrator, she is working to promote curriculum development as a form of inquiry, collaborating with graduate students and faculty members on a freshman composition course that explores gender, class, and cultural differences. She has received the Wayne State University President's Award for Excellence in Teaching and has also been honored by the Michigan Association of Governing Boards for her outstanding teaching.